HISTORICAL
ATLAS
OF
THE
NAPOLEONIC
ERA

HISTORICAL
ATLAS
OF
THE
NAPOLEONIC
ERA

Angus Konstam

THE LYONS PRESS
Guilford, Connecticut
An imprint of The Globe Pequot Press

Historical Atlas of the Napoleonic Era

First Lyons Press Edition 2003

The Lyons Press is an imprint of The Globe Pequot Press

Text and design © 2003 Thalamus Publishing

For Thalamus Publishing

Project editor: Warren Lapworth
Mapping and design: Roger Kean
Portrait illustrations: Oliver Frey

10 9 8 7 6 5 4 3 2 1

ISBN 1-58574-867-6

Library Of Congress Cataloging-in-Publication data is available on file

Printed in Spain

Picture acknowledgments
Archivo Iconografica, S.A./CORBIS: 17 (top), 19, 33, 39, 40, 47, 71 (left), 76, 77, 95, 100, 101, 102, 103, 107, 114, 130, 142, 150–151, 67;
Yann Arthus-Bertrand/CORBIS: 184–185;
Austrian Archives/CORBIS: 84; Bettman/CORBIS: 17 (bottom), 32, 35, 42, 55, 56, 61 (top), 65, 82, 92–93, 94, 120, 121, 124, 129, 135 (bottom), 155, 158, 161, 166, 171, 174; Stefano Bianchetti/CORBIS: 88, 178–179;
Burstein Collection/CORBIS: 44, 112, 113 (top); Christie's Images/CORBIS: 38, 111, 126–127, 145, 169 (bottom); Gianni Dagli Orti/CORBIS: 9, 14, 22, 23, 28, 41, 75, 80, 83, 91, 141, 143, 148, 149, 164, 165;
Leonard de Selva/CORBIS: 53, 110, 157; Oliver Frey/Thalamus Studios: 15 (top and center), 17 (inset), 18, 22 (right), 29, 31, 45, 49 (bottom), 58 (top), 63, 71 (right), 72 (top), 73 (right), 74 (bottom), 77, 78, 89 (both), 93 (top), 95 (top), 96, 106 (top), 108 (inset), 115 (right), 121 (center and bottom), 124 (top), 127, 128, 138, 140, 141 (bottom), 144 (bottom), 147, 149 (top), 151, 154 (both bottom), 184, 188–189; Christel Gerstenberg/CORBIS: 15 (bottom), 25, 26, 27, 68, 69, 122, 180–181;
Todd A. Gipstein/CORBIS: 2–3, 7, 183;
Peter Harholdt/CORBIS: 185; Historical Picture Archive/CORBIS: 30–31, 34, 43, 49, 54–55, 58, 62–63, 72, 73, 74, 78, 96–97, 137, 144;
Hulton-Deutsch Collection/CORBIS: 8, 57, 67, 106–107;
Massimo Listri/CORBIS: 125; Lawrence Manning/CORBIS: 182;
Francis G. Mayer/CORBIS: 113 (bottom), 156;
National Gallery Collection/CORBIS: 12, 105, 146, 186;
Michael Nicholson/CORBIS: 135 (top); Paul A. Souders/CORBIS: 159;
Stapleton Collection/CORBIS: 52, 60 (bottom), 109, 115, 117, 138, 169 (top), 170, 172–173, 175; The State Russian Museum/CORBIS: 85, 123;
WildCountry/CORBIS: 180; CORBIS: 1, 7

Contents

6   Introduction—The Corsican Colossus

8   Chapter One—A Whiff of Grapeshot
The Young Bonaparte, 1789–95

10   The French Revolution
12   Enemies On All Sides
14   Citizen Soldiers
16   Taking Toulon
18   Paris—A City Divided

20   Chapter Two—General of the Republic
Italy, 1796–1798

22   The Army of Italy, 1796
24   Bonaparte's First Campaign
26   The Austrian Army, 1796–1815
28   The Bridge at Lodi
30   Castiglione: On the Defensive
32   Arcola: Sidestep and Thrust
34   Rivoli: The Battle for Italy

36   Chapter Three—The New Alexander
Egypt, 1798–1800

38   Nelson and the British Navy
40   Battle of the Pyramids
42   Battle of the Nile
44   Death and Failure at Acre
46   Bonaparte as First Consul
48   Battle of Marengo

50   Chapter Four—War of the Three Emperors
The Austerlitz Campaign, 1805

52   Emperor Napoleon
54   The Grande Armée
56   Invasion of England
58   Expecting Every Man to do His Duty
60   The Strategic Situation in 1805
62   Maneuver at Ulm
64   Battle of Austerlitz

66   Chapter Five—Master of Europe
The Campaigns of 1806–7

68   The Prussian Army
70   Campaigning in Prussia
72   Jena-Auerstadt
74   The Winter Campaign
76   Battle of Eylau
78   Battle of Friedland
80   The Treaty of Tilsit
82   The Code Napoleon
84   The Changing Face of Warfare

86   Chapter Six—Crisis on the Danube
The Wagram Campaign of 1809

88   Campaigning on the Danube
90   The Drive on Vienna
92   Aspern-Essling
94   Battle of Deutsch-Wagram
96   Affairs at Home

98   Chapter Seven—The Spanish Ulcer
War in the Peninsula, 1807–14

100   Spain in 1807
102   The French Invasion
104   Britain's Iron Duke
106   The British Army
108   Roliça to Talavera
110   Defending Portugal
112   The Guerrilla War
114   Salamanca to Vitoria
116   Over the Pyrenees

118   Chapter Eight—Disaster in the Snow
The Russian Campaign, 1812

120   Invasion of Russia
122   The Russian Army
124   Battle of Borodino
126   Napoleon in Moscow
128   The Retreat from Moscow
130   Over the Berezina

132   Chapter Nine—Napoleon at Bay
The Campaigns of National Liberation, 1813–14

134   Notions of National Unity
136   Battles of Lützen and Bautzen
138   Armistice
140   Battle for Dresden
142   Routed at Leipzig
144   On the Brink of Disaster
146   The 1814 Campaign
148   A Gamble Outside Paris
150   Abdication of an Emperor

152   Chapter Ten—The Eagle and the Lion
The War of 1812

154   American War in Canada
156   The War at Sea
158   Sacking Washington and Baltimore
160   Battle of New Orleans

162   Chapter Eleven—One Hundred Days
The Waterloo Campaign, 1815

164   Return from Elba
166   The Struggle Renewed
168   Skirmish at Quatre Bras
170   Battles of Ligny and Wavre
172   Waterloo
174   End of the Napoleonic Era

176   Chapter Twelve—Aftermath
The Napoleonic Legacy

178   Exile to St. Helena
180   The Congress of Vienna
182   The Death of Napoleon
184   French Napoleonic Heritage

186   Appendix 1—Napoleon's Art of War
187   Appendix 2—The Rating System of Ships-of-War
188   Appendix 3—The Marshals of France
190   Index

INTRODUCTION

The Corsican Colossus

A symbol of the era named after him, Napoleon Bonaparte was hated and feared by much of Europe, but remains a popular and honored hero of the French, who generously remember him for his liberal legal code as much as for his generalship.

*F*rom humble Corsican origins, Napoleon Bonaparte came to stand alongside the most recognizable figures of history. His achievements place him among the greatest captains in history—military geniuses such as Alexander the Great, Julius Caesar, Gustavus Adolphus, and the Duke of Marlborough. He became the embodiment of French glory, imperial grandeur, and ultimately, of a self-destructive lust for power. He has also been described as the enemy of mankind, a despot who ruled Europe as a dictator, who ruthlessly crushed those who stood in his path.

This range of feelings continues to the present day. To most French people, he is a great hero, a leader who saved the legacy of the French Revolution and steered France toward greatness. He was also the leader who betrayed the revolution, turning his back on the ideals of liberty, equality, and fraternity in exchange for the imperial mantle. A consummate politician and showman, he did much to nullify this about-face by portraying himself as a liberal conqueror, spreading the ideals of the Revolution throughout a Europe ruled by absolutist monarchs.

His significance is not in question. Napoleon Bonaparte dominated the period from the French Revolution until 1815 so completely that the era has become known as the Napoleonic Age. For much of this time he remained the Master of Europe, controlling the destiny of millions of people, from the Baltic Sea to the Mediterranean, and from the English Channel to the Russian steppes.

Apart from his military achievements, Napoleon gave France stability, a centralized government, and a legal system. Napoleonic France was a meritocracy, where every soldier purportedly carried a marshal's baton in his knapsack, and a career was open to all citizens of talent, regardless of birth. He promoted the development of the modern state through his administrative and legal reforms, yet also developed a repressive secret police system.

He unified Europe with his Grande Armée, an army which repeatedly defeated all of the major European powers. Although Napoleon never ruled the seas, his troops remained the unchallenged masters of the battlefield in most of Europe until 1813. The exception was in Spain, where an unwise French invasion in support of Bonaparte's dynastic ambitions in the peninsula triggered a long and bloody war. A popular nationalist rising led to a draining guerrilla war that cost thousands of lives.

The same antipathy to French domination erupted in the rest of Europe after Napoleon's retreat from Moscow in 1812. European powers such as Prussia and Austria were able to throw off the Napoleonic shackles, tapping into German patriotic fervor to launch a war of liberation that would finally end in Bonaparte's defeat.

One of his great gifts was his ability to present himself in a good light. With the support of writers, artists, news editors, playwrights, and architects, the majority of French citizens were willing to support this seemingly benevolent dictator. Following his defeat in Russia, it became increasingly difficult to convince the population of Europe that the future lay in Napoleon's imperial realm. Increasingly, military defeats, the defection of former allies, and the steady loss of French resources and manpower brought the Napoleonic world crashing down, forcing Bonaparte's abdication in 1814.

He still remained a popular leader to many Frenchmen, and a hero to his former soldiers. It was to the latter that he addressed his plea for support when he returned from exile in 1815: "Soldiers! In my exile I have heard your voice!" His renewed bid for power cost the lives of thousands more men and women before the Napoleonic dream finally ended on the battlefield of Waterloo.

Following his death in 1821, subsequent generations have viewed Napoleon Bonaparte and his legacy in many ways, from the pale mimicry of imperial grandeur in France during the mid-19th century to the abiding fascination in his military and civil achievements. Tyrant or hero, genius or madman, there is no escaping the ramifications of his life, or the subsequent effect he had in the creation of modern Europe. This book examines this crucial period in world history, and looks into the career of the man who still captivates our imagination.

CHAPTER ONE

A Whiff of Grapeshot

The Young Bonaparte, 1789–95

The Napoleonic era arose imperially like a phoenix from the ashes of the French Revolution. For Captain Napoleone di Buonaparte, the heady events of 1789 presented an opportunity for advancement. Although the young di Buonaparte played a relatively minor part in events before 1796, he was a staunch advocate of revolutionary ideals; in particular, at first he saw the revolution as a means of furthering the political independence of his native Corsica which had passed form the Genoese sphere of influence to France in the year of his birth, 1769.

Torn between his military training and the struggle for control of Corsica, di Buonaparte became increasingly involved in this minor conflict, his first taste of action. He kept abreast of the latest military developments and spent much of the period studying military theory and developing his own skills as an artillery officer, against the backdrop of the French Revolution and the wars that followed it.

As a serving army officer, this was an opportune

time for the young Corsican. While his military duties kept him away from the turmoil in Paris, he used the instability to further his career. Still an artillery officer, he became a major in a Corsican battalion in September 1791, and a colonel in April 1792. However, his activities in Corsica led to the loss of his regular army commission, prompting a trip to Paris in 1792, where he lobbied for reinstatement. He arrived in time to witness the boiling over of tensions between the Paris mob, the National Assembly, and the imprisoned king. Mob violence and the inability of revolutionary troops to maintain order had a profound effect on the 22-year-old.

When an internal revolt by French Royalists (the Vendéan Revolt) occurred and an amphibious attack by Britain took place at Toulon, Napoleone di Buonaparte found himself in the right place at the crucial time. What followed would become the stuff of legend.

Europe in 1772, at the height of the *Ancien Régime* (1715–83)

This was the Europe that Napoleon Bonaparte would soon overthrow, a Europe of great but tottering powers lording it over a host of smaller states, some already subsumed, others fiercely independent. A patchwork of uneasy alliances and ruling family feuds meant that often far-flung territories kept switching hands between the greater powers. In the north, a coalition of German-Baltic states was conglomerating to become the new great force of Prussia.

Europe in 1772

- France
- Austrian Habsburg empire
- Brandenburg-Prussia
- Spanish Bourbon territory
- United Kingdom and Hanover (union from 1714)
- Ottoman empire
- Russia
- Savoyard Sardinia-Piedmont
- —— borders
- boundary of the Holy Roman Empire

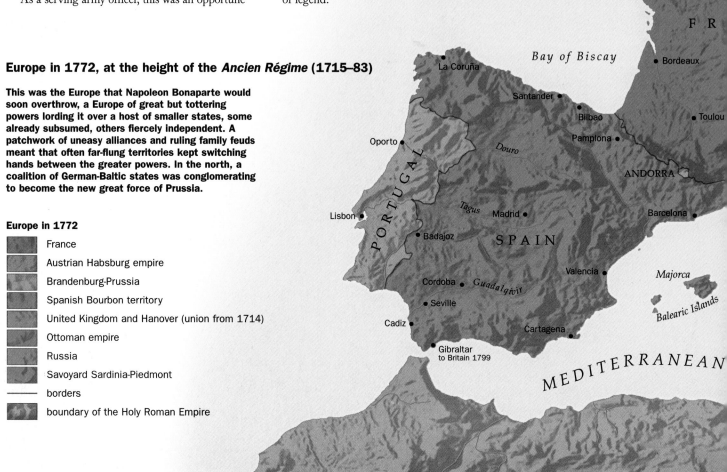

NORTH SEA

Gulf of Bothnia

• Christiania

SWEDEN

Uppsala •

• Helsingfors (Helsinki)

Gulf of Finland

Karelia
to Russia 1721

• St. Petersburg

Ingria
to Russia 1721

Lake Vänern

Stockholm •

Reval
(Talinn)

• Novgorod

Estonia
to Russia 1721

Lake
Peipus

RUSSIA

Göteborg •

DENMARK-NORWAY

Lake
Vättern

BALTIC SEA

Livonia
to Russia 1721

Courland

• Riga

Polish Livonia
to Russia 1772

• Moscow

Copenhagen •

Western Dvina

• Smolensk

Königsberg •

PRUSSIA

Lithuania

White
Russia
to Russia
1772

East Friesland
to Brandeburg-Prussia 1744

Danzig •

West
Prussia
to Brandenburg-
Prussia 1772

POLAND

nd

HANOVER

BRANDENBURG

Amsterdam •

NETHERLANDS

Berlin •

Warsaw •

Great Poland

Volhynia

Austrian
Netherlands

• Brussels

Cologne •

SAXONY

Elbe

• Leipzig

Silesia
from Austria to
Brandenburg-
Prussia 1742

Oder

• Lublin

• Kiev

Reims •

Frankfurt •

Dresden •

Vistula

Ukraine

Paris •

Rhine

Main

Prague •

Bohemia

Krakow •

Podolia

Nancy •

Nuremberg •

Moravia

C E

Lorraine
to France 1766

Rhine

Danube

BAVARIA

Austria

to Russia
1774

Munich •

Vienna

AUSTRIAN EMPIRE

Styria

• Buda

Jedisan

Bern •

SWISS
CONFEDERATION

Tyrol

Carinthia

Hungary

MOLDAVIA

Geneva •

Carniola

Lyon •

Rhône

Milan •

MILAN

• Venice

V
E
N
I
C
E

Banat
to Austria
1718

Turin •

Lesser
Wallachia
to Austria
1718-39

WALLACHIA

GENOA

Avignon •

*Ligurian
Sea*

Florence •

PARMA
to Spain 1731
to Austria 1733
to Spain 1748

Bosnia

Serbia
to Austria
1718-39

• Bucharest

Danube

Marseilles •

TUSCANY
to Austria 1737

SARDINIA-PIEDMONT

PAPAL STATES

ADRIATIC SEA

MONTENEGRO

OTTOMAN

Bulgaria

BLACK SEA

Corsica
to France
1768/9

Rome •

Minorca
to Spain 1782

NAPLES
to Spain 1735

Adrianople •

BENEVENTO

Naples •

*Tyrrhenian
Sea*

Albania

Thessalonica •

• Constantinople

SARDINIA
to Sardinia-
Piedmont 1720

Taranto •

*Ionian
Sea*

AEGEAN SEA

EMPIRE

S E A

• Caligari

Morea

Palermo •

• Athens

SICILY
to Austria 1720
to Spain 1735

Syracuse •

Sea of Crete

Rhodes

Crete

The French Revolution

In the summer of 1789, France exploded in bloody revolution. After decades of scandal, courtly excess, and social unrest, the people had reached breaking point. A decade of political and military instability, terror, regicide, and war began.

*D*uring the late 18th century, enlightened thinkers wrote of social equality, the will of the majority, and the end of the feudal system that still bound most of Europe's rural population to its aristocratic masters. Power, these writers claimed, should not be restricted to an aristocratic elite, the Church, or a mercantile class, but be vested in the population of a country as a whole.

In France, the influence of the First Estate (the Church) was matched only by the Second Estate, comprising the aristocracy. A series of bad harvests led to starvation and widespread poverty. Increased taxation to pay for military expansionism and courtly excesses was applied unevenly, and the exception of many of the notables of the First and Second Estates meant that the burden of payment lay with the poor and the mercantile classes. Demands for reform were ignored, and resentment increased among the Third Estate—the bulk of the French population, who felt denied any political voice.

In the summer of 1789, an insurrection by representatives of the Third Estate came at the same time as an agrarian revolt and mob insurrection in Paris. In June, the Third Estate declared itself a National Assembly, effectively taking political power from the hands of the king and his nobles. For the first time, liberty and equality were attainable by the French citizenry, and while the Paris mob stormed the Bastille in July, the National Assembly laid down the framework for a new revolutionary government.

In October, Louis XVI and his family were forcibly removed from the royal palace at Versailles to Paris. Church possessions were seized in the name of the people, and the peasantry seized the landed estates. When the king attempted to flee in June 1791, he was caught and returned to Paris, a prisoner of his own

The Fortress of the Bastille, built between 1369 and 1382, became the center of focus for the French Revolution when a mob of Parisians, led by the National Guard, stormed it on July 14, 1789 to free "political" prisoners.

people. Three months later he approved the new French Revolutionary constitution, based on the notions espoused by Thomas Paine in his *Declaration of the Rights of Man*: the abolition of privilege, the liberty of the individual, and the equality of man.

Escaping the Terror

The National Assembly evolved into the Legislative Assembly in October 1791, and its floor became a battleground for a series of political factions and revolutionary figures: Feuillant, Girondin, Danton, Barras, Hébert, and Robespierre the most famous, or notorious. While the revolutionary leaders were engaged in factional in-fighting, mob rule became a tool of power. When Napoleon Bonaparte visited Paris in 1792, he witnessed the storming of Tuileries Palace and the massacring of aristocratic prisoners.

Royalist and Federalist uprisings broke out in the French countryside, and the army was rent by political upheavals. Worse still, this instability led to what became known as the Terror. It was a period when political opponents of the revolutionary faction were ousted from power and many were executed one after another by a new means of production-line killing—the guillotine (*see panel*)—while pressure from the mob led to the execution of fallen aristocrats. One after another, factional leaders were ousted from power or executed, while pressure from the mob led to the mass execution of former aristocrats.

Ironically, Doctor Joseph Ignace Guillotin (1738–1814) belonged to a small reform movement that wanted to banish the death penalty completely. Worse, the killing device that came to bear his name was intended to remove public execution to a more private—and humane—method. Guillotin worked with German engineer and harpsichord maker, Tobias Schmidt, to build a prototype machine. With the French Revolution came a new penal code that stated "Every person condemned to death shall have his head severed," which was very egalitarian, since all classes of people were now executed equally. The first guillotining took place on April 25, 1792, when Nicolas Jacques Pelletie was executed at Place de Grève on the Right Bank of the Seine. The last execution by guillotine took place in Marseilles, France on September 10, 1977.

The killings included King Louis XVI on January 21, 1793, an act which enraged the crowned heads of Europe and plunged France into war. War was welcomed by the Legislative Assembly as a means of unifying the French citizenry against a common enemy. It did not always go well, and unsuccessful generals were also sent to the guillotine, and a string of military reverses only further destabilized the political situation in France.

By June 1794 the Terror was in full flow, an orgy of bloodletting that deprived the revolution of effective leadership at a time when political stability was of paramount importance. The Terror ended on July 28, 1794, with the execution of its architect, Maximilien Robespierre. Following his feared regime, there came a period of relative stability, during which the French government could concentrate on defense of the state against its enemies without.

Above: A Danish painting gruesomely depicts the execution by guillotine of the French queen, Marie-Antionette, in Paris on October 16, 1793.

11

Enemies On All Sides

The monarchs of Europe dispatched armies to crush the rogue state. Although the revolutionaries were victorious at first, enemies multiplied following the execution of Louis XVI. France was fighting for her very survival.

"The Battle of Valmy" by Horace Vernet, 1826. During the fighting of 1792, a determined French cannonade kept the Austro-Prussian army at bay and saved Paris from capture.

*L*ess than three weeks after the storming of the Bastille, Frederick-Wilhelm II of Prussia and Leopold II of Austria signed the Declaration of Pillnitz, stating their intention to restore Louis XVI to the throne by force of arms. This anti-revolution coalition was ratified by formal alliance in February 1792, and allied troops began gathering on the French borders.

Despite the military build-up, the kings of Europe seemed reluctant to act. In some respects, the revolution needed a war to divert the attention of the French citizenry from the shortcomings of the National Assembly. Consequently, the French government declared war on Austria on April 20, 1792, extending the conflict to include the Piedmontese island of Sardinia a month later.

The French army was woefully ill-prepared for war. Since the revolution began, officers had fled. The remaining rank-and-file were weakened by desertion or political ostracism, and by April 1792, only 50,000 soldiers remained under arms. Revolutionary volunteers, who lacked the training of the regular army, augmented this force during the spring of 1792. It was hoped that their revolutionary zeal would overcome their military shortcomings.

Unfortunately, the citizen army's first campaign ended in disaster. A three-pronged invasion of the Austrian Netherlands (now Belgium) in late April 1792 came to naught when two French columns were intimidated into an untimely retreat.

The routed troops shot their generals in the process.

By summer, the allies were ready. An 80,000-strong army commanded by the Prussian Duke Ferdinand of Brunswick massed on the Rhine, while a second force of 40,000 men gathered in the Austrian Netherlands. Brunswick's force was the bulk of the Prussian army, plus an Austrian division, French Royalist volunteers, and contingents from many of the smaller German states. This polyglot force advanced on a broad front, laying siege to border fortresses in an effort to secure lines of communication back across the Rhine.

No conclusion

The allied advance ground to a temporary halt on the banks of the Aisne, some 100 miles from Paris. This allowed the French armies of General François Kellerman and General Charles Dumouriez to combine into a force of some 36,000 men. By the time the allies resumed their advance, the French were waiting for them. Due to the dispersion of the allied force, the two sides were well matched, and at the Battle of Valmy (September 20, 1792) a French cannonade deterred any serious Prussian attack. Deeming the French position to be impregnable, Brunswick retreated. Paris had been saved, French morale soared, but the war would continue.

General Dumouriez led a French army into the Austrian Netherlands and clashed with the Austrians at the Battle of Jemappes (November 6, 1792). A French victory encouraged the National Assembly to declare that France would "offer fraternity and aid to all nations who wished to regain their freedom." Armed with this justification for invasion, Dumouriez captured Brussels and drove the Austrians from Belgium. Rather than encourage the freedom of the local population, the French annexed the region.

The execution of Louis XVI in January 1793 led to an escalation of the war. On February 1, France declared war on Britain and Holland, adding Spain to the list of enemies five weeks later. In a seesaw campaign for control of the Netherlands, a French invasion was defeated at the Battle of Neerwinden (March 18), but French victories at Hondschoote (September 8) and Fleurus (October 15–16, 1793) restored the situation.

Political intrigue in Paris led to the defection of the gifted Dumouriez to the allies and the execution of less successful French generals such as Adam-Philippe Custine and Jean Houchard. Lazare Carnot, Minister of War, masterminded French strategy during this crucial period and imparted a degree of stability to the volatile military situation. While the end of the Terror improved the morale of France's principal commanders, the enemies of the revolution had not been defeated.

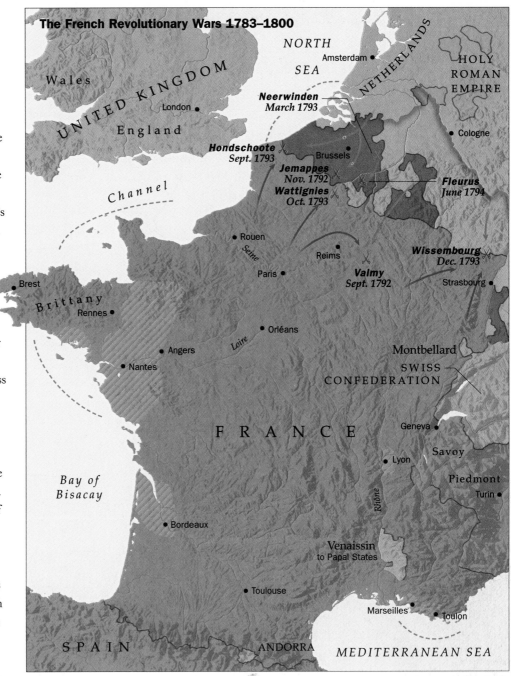

The French Revolutionary Wars 1783–1800

NORTH SEA

Wales

UNITED KINGDOM

England

Amsterdam •

NETHERLANDS

HOLY ROMAN EMPIRE

London •

• Cologne

Neerwinden March 1793

Hondschoote Sept. 1793

Brussels •

Jemappes Nov. 1792

Wattignies Oct. 1793

Fleurus June 1794

Channel

• Rouen

Reims ×

Wissembourg Dec. 1793

Seine

Paris •

Valmy Sept. 1792

Strasbourg •

Brest •

Brittany

Rennes •

• Orléans

Loire

Montbellard

SWISS CONFEDERATION

• Angers

• Nantes

F R A N C E

Geneva •

Savoy

• Lyon

Piedmont

Bay of Biscay

Rhône

Turin •

• Bordeaux

Venaissin to Papal States

• Toulouse

Marseilles •

• Toulon

S P A I N

ANDORRA

MEDITERRANEAN SEA

Europe in 1783

- France
- Brandenburg-Prussia
- Austrian Netherlands
- Spain
- Sardinia-Piedmont
- French Royalist revolution, 1783
- French gains by 1800
- ✗ French victory
- ✗ Allied victory
- —— border
- ----- British blockade

Citizen Soldiers

During the first years of the French Revolution, the old Royal Army was paralyzed by mutiny, desertion, and suspicion. The French citizen army prevented its collapse in the face of foreign invasion, and slowly evolved into the force that rule Europe.

A French gouache of 1792 shows the 10th Batallion of Soldiers of Paris during the Battle of Jemappes, 1792.

*D*uring the decades before the French Revolution, the Royal Army underwent a series of reforms. A divisional structure was developed, while new tactical doctrines emphasized the deployment of lines and columns, creating flexibility on the battlefield denied to other armies and their traditional linear deployment. A new range

late-18th century reformers such as de Bourcet, Gribauval, and de Guibert. Many revolutionaries viewed the army with suspicion and recommended its replacement with a new citizen army whose loyalty would be unquestionable. The National Guard was a step in this direction, but the real impetus for a citizen army came in April 1792, when France was plunged into war with Austria and Prussia.

Following the fall of the Bastille, the majority of French officers left the army; the navy Louis XV had developed was similarly affected by revolutionary turmoil. By the time the war began, neither force was ready for battle. The shout of "La patrie en danger!" (the homeland in danger) served as a rallying cry,

of mobile artillery pieces was introduced, while logistical detachments improved the supply chain. While many historians have credited Napoleon with these innovations, recognition should be given to

and thousands flocked to the colors to defend France against foreign invasion.

When the initial wave of volunteers dried up, the National Assembly resorted to conscription. A *levée en masse* was called, forcing all levels of the French population to take an active part in their country's defense, through conscription or the allocation of virtually all national resources to the prosecution of the war. The need for manpower and resources became imperative in early 1793, when Britain and Spain joined the anti-French coalition.

Mixed forces and formations

By the spring of 1794, over 750,000 men were under arms, a feat largely due to the efforts of Lazare-Nicolas-Marguerite Carnot (1753–1823), who served as Minister for War. He overcame the restrictions imposed by the Terror to create a well-organized citizen army that could stand against the best professional armies in Europe. In the hands of commanders such as Barthélemy Joubert, Jean-Victor Moreau, and Napoleon Bonaparte, his remodeled French army would bring victory to the republic.

Since the citizen army usually relied on superiority in numbers, it could risk heavy casualties in order to ensure victory. The face of warfare was changing, and the French built on reforms introduced before the revolution to create a battle-winning doctrine that made the best possible use of its citizen army. From early 1794, the use of untrained infantry in dense columns, supported by clouds of skirmish troops, became a standard form of deployment. A refinement was the adoption of *l'ordre mixte* (mixed order), where lines and columns formed into a mutually supporting formation.

Initially, old pre-revolution units were used to provide the line element of these formations, because the training of the regulars was crucial to encourage the poorly trained citizen levies. Political suspicion of the old army led to the amalgamation of old and new units during 1794, a move that improved the overall level of training in the army, with veterans passing on their skills to new comrades-in-arms.

By the end of the year, the French Revolutionary Army had developed into a flexible military machine, whose troops retained the best tactics of the pre-revolutionary era with the new doctrines imposed by the *levée en masse*, such as the use of skirmishers and mass columns. The resulting army was easily able to counter the antiquated rigid-line formations employed by the Prussians and Austrians.

Lazare-Nicolas-Marguerite Carnot, a military engineer by training, became the military genius of the revolution and played a major administrative part in French successes during the Napoleonic Wars. After Robespierre's fall, Carnot avoided punishment for his own part in the Terror and became a member of the Directory of Seven (*see page 18*).

Left: Engraving of soldiers of the French Revolutionary Army fighting "Imperialists." Captain Claude Joseph Rouget de Lisle (1760–1836), **above,** unwittingly provided the army with a rousing anthem when, at an evening gathering of officers in April 1792, he improvised the song which would become famous as the *Marseillaise*—now the French national anthem.

Taking Toulon

In 1793, internal rivalries flared into small pro-Royalist uprisings. At Toulon a Royalist coup led to the capture of the Mediterranean port by the British. The siege that followed gave the young Bonaparte an opportunity to demonstrate his martial abilities.

Although Napoleon Bonaparte later dubbed himself a "child of the Revolution," he played a minimal part in the great upheavals of the period. Born the son of a minor Corsican nobleman in 1769, Napoleone di Buonaparte was educated at the Royal School of Brienne before becoming an artillery cadet at L'École Militaire in Paris, arriving in the capital in October 1784. A year later he joined La Fère artillery regiment at Vallence, and by January 1786 he had become a commissioned officer in the Royal Artillery.

By the beginning of the French Revolution in 1789, di Buonaparte was stationed in Auxonne, although a succession of illnesses led to much recuperative leave in Corsica. He was a fervent Corsican nationalist and spent the next two years embroiled in his native island's revolutionary movement. Having spent too long away from his regiment, his commission was withdrawn by the National Assembly. In Paris he lobbied for his reinstatement, and left the city with a fresh commission as a Captain of Artillery.

His first official experience of action came in early 1793, when he participated in a failed amphibious attack on the Sardinian anchorage of La Maddalena. The debacle not only led to di Buonaparte's split with the Corsican revolutionaries, it also imbued a distrust of amphibious operations that may explain his later reluctance to invade England.

Di Buonaparte left Corsica with his family and returned to his old artillery unit. To emphasize the rejection of his Corsican roots, he changed the Italian spelling of Buonaparte to the French Bonaparte.

By this stage, France was threatened by powerful Prussian and Austrian armies, a Spanish force was probing north across the Pyrenees, and the British Royal Navy had established a blockade of the French coast. A Royalist insurrection in the Vendée region south of Nantes served as the focal point for anti-revolutionary activity in France, while other insurrections in Brittany, at Sancerre on the Loire, and Lyon on the Rhône raised the specter of civil war.

Focussing the assault

While Captain Bonaparte was demonstrating his loyalty to the revolution by countering this insurrection, a more serious Royalist upheaval took place in Toulon. On August 27, 1793 the city declared support for the royalist Bourbon cause, and solicited the protection of Britain and Spain. While the British fleet captured the French Toulon fleet, British and Spanish troops landed to support Royalists in the city.

A French army of 17,000 men under General Carteaux was sent south to besiege Toulon, but despite outnumbering the allied garrison, no attempt was made to recapture the port. By the time Bonaparte arrived on September 16, Carteaux's artillery commander had been wounded. The young Corsican captain was nominated as his replacement.

Bonaparte noted that the British had built a series of forts around the perimeter of the inner harbor (known as La Petit Rade), while others protected the outer roads (La Grande Rade). French forts to the west prevented further expansion of the allied

French and Allied positions at Toulon, December 1793

FRANCE

Ollioules •
Ft. des Pomets
Ft. Croix
Mount Faron
Ft. Rouge
Ft. Blanc
Ft. Faron
La Valette •
Ft. de la Convention
Camp de Ste. Anne
Ft. de la Farinière
Ft. L'Artiques
Ft. de la Poudrière
Toulon
Ft. Ste. Catherine
Ft. Malbousquet
Ft. de la Petit Rade
position of British fleet
Ft. de la Montagne
La Petit Rade
Ft. La Malgue
Ft. des Sans Culottes
Ft. des Jacobins
Ft. St. Louis
La Seine •
Grosse Tour
L'Eguilette
La Grande Rade
Ft. des Quatre Moulins
Tour de la Balaquier
Ft. de la Grande Rade
Ft. Mulgrave
Ft. des Hommes-sans-Peur
Ft. des Chasse-Coquins
Ft. des Sablettes
Ft. du Brégnant

0		1		2		3 m
0	1	2	3	4	5 km	

✚ forts constructed by the French force
✚ forts occupied by the Allies

MEDITERRANEAN SEA

In the days before the turmoil of the French Revolution, the Mediterannean port of Toulon was a thriving and propserous city. Detail of a painting of 1756 by Joseph Vernet.

Below: General Jean-François Carteaux (1751–1813), seen in an engraving in the thick of the fighting for the capture of Toulon, was considered by Bonaparte a man of "inconceivable ignorance."

bridgehead. Bonaparte realized that the promontory known as Point de l'Eguilette was key to the defense, but Carteaux favored an attack on the heights of Mount Faron, to the north. Undeterred, while Carteaux launched a series of unsuccessful assaults, Bonaparte encircled the British defenses on Point de l'Eguilette. Carteaux's failure led to his replacement by General Jacques Dugommier, who promptly agreed to Bonaparte's plans to attack Point de l'Eguilette. The assault was launched on December 17, supported by a heavy artillery bombardment. Despite being wounded in the attack, Bonaparte captured the position, and within hours his guns were in place on the point.

Admiral Lord Hood commanding the British fleet had little option but to abandon Toulon, taking most of the captured French fleet with him and destroying whatever was left behind. French troops marched into the port on December 19; a victory largely the result of Bonaparte's initiative.

Paris—A City Divided

Thrust into the limelight at a time when the Terror was reaching its height, Napoleon Bonaparte was lucky to escape with his life. Never a supporter of mob rule, he demonstrated his loyalty to the French Revolution by firing on the Paris mob.

Maximilien François de Robespierre, architect of the Terror. A means of ridding France of the Ancien Régime, the Terror swept out of control. It is believed that as many as 40,000 went to the guillotine before it ended.

In the confusion that followed the end of Robespierre's reign of terror, the young Napoleon Bonaparte rose rapidly into favor with France's new government. Detail from a painting of General Bonaparte in council by François Bouchot.

Officially, during the Siege of Toulon, Napoleon Bonaparte served as artillery adviser to the successive commanders of the besieging force. Unofficially it was recognized that he devised the stratagem that ended the siege. He was promoted to the rank of General de Brigade (Brigadier), a decision ratified by the Committee of Public Safety in February 1794.

The leaders of the revolution were well aware of the abilities of the 23-year-old commander, but fame came at a price. Hundreds of senior officers had fallen from political favor since the start of the revolution, several of them executed. Military rank brought involvement in politics, and promotion came at a dangerous time.

In Paris, Maximilien François de Robespierre (1758–94) dominated the political stage. A staunch left-wing Jacobin, Robespierre led the opposition to the center-left Girodin faction in the National Assembly. After voting for the execution of King Louis XVI, he was appointed to the Committee of National Security, responsible for the arrest and execution of enemies of the revolution.

In the summer of 1793 Robespierre masterminded a Jacobin coup that ousted the Girodin faction, and consequently he became the dominant figure in the new revolutionary government. From July 1793 he was the most important member of the Committee of Public Safety, the inner circle that effectively ran the government. Robespierre was also a firm believer in the Terror as a means to maintain power and unite the country behind the revolutionary government through fear and intimidation.

His younger brother Augustin met the young Captain Bonaparte in mid-1793 and became a committed patron of the Corsican officer, a political patronage partly responsible for Bonaparte's appointment as the artillery adviser at Toulon. It also linked Bonaparte to Robespierre, whose heavy-handed and bloodthirsty policies were earning him enemies in Paris.

On Thermidor 9 of Year II (July 27, 1794) a *coup d'état* by the moderate Paul Barras (1755–1829) overthrew the effective dictator Robespierre. The man who had sent over 40,000 people to the guillotine in less than a year was himself guillotined the following day, along with his brother and other leading Jacobins.

Terror follows terror

During the "white terror" that followed, Robespierre's supporters were arrested and executed. Bonaparte was imprisoned in August 1794 on a charge of treason, but his complicity with the Robespierre faction was too tenuous to prove and his life was spared. He came to the attention of Paul Barras, who had replaced Robespierre as de-facto head of the French government, the so-called Directory of Seven (*Directoire*, effective between 1795–99). On his release Bonaparte was appointed to the Bureau Topographique, where he spent the next year developing strategic plans for the Minister of War, Lazare-Nicolas-Marguerite Carnot, also a member of the Directory.

Until September Bonaparte remained vulnerable to political changes. Dismissed from his post that month, he remained in Paris, where Barras saw him as a potential supporter who could help ensure the loyalty of the army in any future coup. By the end of the month, Paris was in turmoil. The mob rose in revolt against attempts to solidify power into the hands of the Directory. With Paris and the National Guard in revolt against the revolutionary government, Barras ordered Bonaparte to restore order in the city. Sending his supporter Captain Murat to seize the artillery park outside the city, Bonaparte moved the guns into Paris and ringed the seat of power at Tuileries Palace.

On Vendémiaire 13 (October 5) the mob advanced on Tuileries, where Bonaparte ordered his gunners to fire grapeshot into the crowd. Over 200 rioters were mown down and hundreds more wounded in a calculated act of brutality. The mob dispersed, the government was saved, and Bonaparte's "whiff of grapeshot" ensured his position in the army as a ruthless supporter of the directorate. His reward was to be be a military command in Italy and a position of prominence within the French Revolutionary Army.

CHAPTER TWO

General of the Republic

Italy, 1796–1798

*I*n February 1796, the relatively obscure and inexperienced General Napoleon Bonaparte was made commander of the French Army of Italy. To many veterans it was a strange choice, and explained away as a political appointment. The Army of Italy was near to starvation, poorly equipped, and lacked even the most basic supplies, such as shoes or coats. Despite these limitations, the 27-year-old commander inspired the hard-bitten men, turning them from a dispirited force into a victorious army in a matter of weeks. What followed was a campaign that many historians consider to be a classic of military history, since it introduced the doctrines with that Napoleon Bonaparte would later use.

He faced two armies in Italy. The small Sardinian (or Piedmontese) army lacked the motivation and leadership to do more than defend its mountain province. The second force was that of the Austrian Empire, a professional and highly trained army, albeit conservative in deployment and tactics.

A small and highly motivated citizen army was pitted against an enemy who fought in the style of the 18th century. The greatest advantages the French possessed were their élan in battle and their ability to move quickly while living off the land. Bonaparte made full use of these abilities.

The French first drove a wedge between the Sardinians and the Austrians in northwestern Italy, then defeated each in turn, in a series of small but hard-fought actions. After crossing the River Po, Bonaparte's army besieged the main Austrian army in Mantua and forced the remainder to retreat to the Quadrilateral, a region of four major fortresses that secured Austria's hold on northeastern Italy. The campaign now became a series of battles as the Austrians tried to relieve the city while the French tried to stop them. Finally, in January 1797, the French won a decisive battle at Rivoli. Mantua fell soon afterward, and with it came control of the whole of Northern Italy. General Bonaparte was no longer an unknown commander, but was fast becoming the arbiter of victory in Europe.

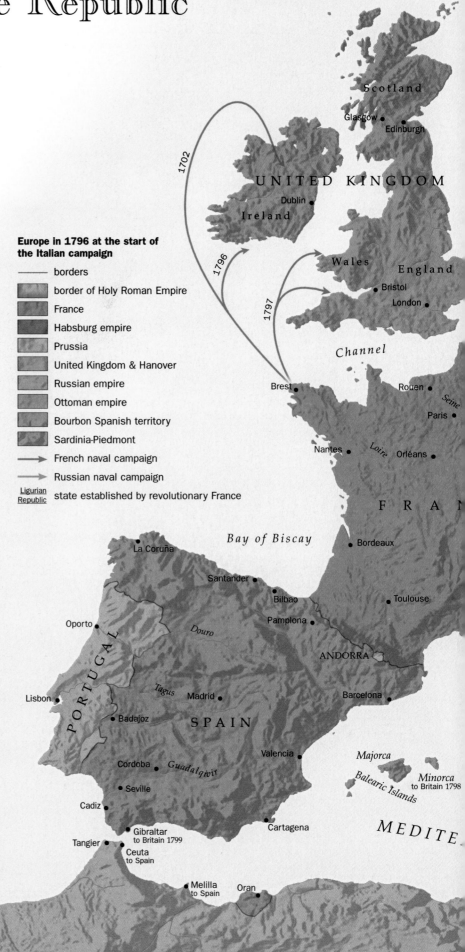

Europe in 1796 at the start of the Italian campaign

- —— borders
- border of Holy Roman Empire
- France
- Habsburg empire
- Prussia
- United Kingdom & Hanover
- Russian empire
- Ottoman empire
- Bourbon Spanish territory
- Sardinia-Piedmont
- → French naval campaign
- → Russian naval campaign
- Ligurian Republic state established by revolutionary France

NORTH
SEA

Gulf of Bothnia

Christiania •

SWEDEN

Uppsala •

• Stockholm

Lake Vänern

Lake Vättern

• Göteborg

Helsingfors
(Helsinki) •

Reval
(Talinn) •

Gulf of Finland

• St. Petersburg

Estonia

Lake Peipus

• Novgorod

BALTIC SEA

• Riga

Samogitia

• Moscow

• Copenhagen

Swedish
Pomerania

Königsberg •

• Danzig

Pomerania

West
Prussia

P R U S S I A

New East Prussia

Lithuania
and
Black Russia

Western Dvina

• Smolensk

RUSSIAN
EMPIRE

Batavian Republic
1795–1806

Amsterdam •

NETHERLANDS

HANOVER

Brandenburg

Berlin •

South Prussia
from 1793

Warsaw •

Podlesia

Austrian Netherlands

• Brussels

Cologne •

SAXONY

Leipzig •

Elbe

• Dresden

Silesia

Oder

West Galicia
to Prussia 1795
to Austria 1797

• Lublin

Volhynia

• Kiev

Ukraine

Reims •

Rhine

Frankfurt •

Main

Nuremberg •

Prague •

Bohemia

Vistula

Red Russia

Galicia and Lodomeria

Podolia

Nancy •

Rhine

Moravia

Krakow •

BAVARIA

Danube

Munich •

Austria

Vienna •

H A B S B U R G   E M P I R E

to Russia
1774

• Bern

SWISS
CONFEDERATION

Tyrol

Styria

Buda •

Bessarabia

Jedisan

Geneva •

Carinthia

Carniola

Hungary

• Moldavia

Lyon •

SARDINIA-
PIEDMONT

Milan •

MILAN

Mantua •

V E N I C E

Venice •

Slovenia

Banat

• Sebastopol

vignon •

Genoa •

GENOA
Ligurian Republic
1797–1805

• Florence

Fano

Adriatic Sea

Bosnia

Serbia

Wallachia

• Bucharest

Danube

BLACK SEA

Marseilles •

• Toulon

TUSCANY

Herzegovina

Russian Black Sea fleet, 1798–1800

*Corsica
to Britain
1794–96*

Elba

PAPAL
STATES

Roman
Republic
1798–99

Rome •

Parthenopean Republic 1798–99

RAGUSA

MONTENEGRO

O T T O M A N

Bulgaria

Adrianople •

• Constantinople

Ajaccio •

Naples

Naples •

Taranto •

Albania

Rumelia

Thessalonica •

E M P I R E

SARDINIA-
PIEDMONT

Sardinia

Tyrrhenian Sea

Bonaparte 1798

Desaix 1798

KINGDOM OF
NAPLES AND
SICILY

A E G E A N   S E A

• Caligari

Palermo •

• Messina

*Ionian islands
from Venice
to France 1797
to Russia 1799*

• Athens

Morea

—RANEAN SEA

Syracuse •

Sicily
Independent of
Naples 1799

Sea of Crete

Rhodes

Bonaparte to Egypt 1798

Malta
from the Knights of St. John
to France 1798
to Britain 1800

Kythera
from Venice
to France 1797
to Russia 1799

Crete

21

The Army of Italy, 1796

On March 27, 1796, Citizen General Napoleon Bonaparte assumed command of the French Republic's Army of Italy. This mutinous, disaffected body of 37,000 men was ill-equipped, unpaid, and under-nourished.

"Depart du Citoyen." A French print of the 1790s shows youthful villagers dressed in the finery of their citizen army uniforms, preparing to leave for war. The reality of war quickly ended any idealistic or romantic notions.

The Army of Italy was a miniature version of the Revolutionary French Army, complete with the same mixture of political fervor, egalitarianism, and revolutionary zeal. However, an abysmal lack of logistical support obliged the troops to fight with little more than their ideals for weapons. Bonaparte and Berthier changed all that.

Louis Alexandre Berthier (1753–1815) had fought a useful campaign against the British in America before returning to Paris in 1789 as something of a hero. He was made Major-General of the National Guard at Versailles, where he protected the royal family and helped two of the king's aunts to flee to safety. His reputation saved him from the worst effects of the Terror and, in August 1792, he was appointed Chief of Staff to the French Revolutionary Army general François Kellerman. Bonaparte was well aware of Berthier's capabilities, and had him assigned as his Chief of Staff for the Italian campaign.

On paper, the Army of Italy was supposed to have over 63,100 men, but desertion and illness had cost the army dear. Lack of provisions meant that it was in a wretched condition. As Bonaparte reported in a letter to the Directory in Paris, "I found this army not only destitute of everything, but without discipline. Their insubordination and discontent were such that the malcontents had formed a party for the Dauphin, and were singing songs opposed to the tenets of the Revolution. You may, however, rest

glory. I am come to lead you to the most fertile plains that the sun beholds! Rich provinces, opulent, all shall be at our disposal, and there you shall acquire riches, honor and glory! Soldiers of Italy! With such a prospect before you, can you fail in courage and constancy?" Bonaparte was certainly a charismatic leader, despite his small stature and lack of experience, and his soldiers responded with enthusiasm.

The Citizen General's attempts to raise morale were only part of the solution. The army needed complete re-organization. While Bonaparte weeded out officers and men whose loyalties or abilities were considered suspect, he discovered that his senior staff was comprised of some exceptional men, responding enthusiastically to Bonaparte's call for reform. *Generals-de-Division* André Massena, Jean Mathieu Sérurier, and Pierre François Augereau became some of Bonaparte's most trusted subordinates. When the relatively unknown Corsican general first arrived in Italy, it was assumed that he was little more than a political appointment and lacking in military ability. He soon proved their assumptions wrong with his strategical and tactical skills in the campaign that followed.

As Chief of Staff, Berthier had less than two weeks to solve the supply problems, while helping Bonaparte to plan for the campaign. He excelled himself. Subsequently, Napoleon Bonaparte rarely fought without relying on Berthier to organize and supply his army. Somehow Berthier found mules to transport supplies. Within a matter of days the soldiers began to receive shoes, clothing, food, wine, ammunition, and even some pay.

By early April 1796, Bonaparte was ready to lead this army into battle. This, his first campaign, would lay the foundations for the Napoleonic myth. The ragged soldiers of the Army of Italy would transform the political map of Europe forever.

assured that peace and order will be re-established; by the time you receive this letter, we shall have come to an engagement."

Bonaparte eased the army's supply problems as best as he could, then planned to throw it into action against the Austrians and Sardinians. As he saw it, victory would unite his army into a fighting force. Conversely, he must have been aware that defeat would mean the disintegration of the Army of Italy, an outcome that would almost certainly lead to the invasion of southern France by the Austrians, supported by the hovering British fleet.

A spirited leader

In his later life, Bonaparte recalled the speech he gave to his soldiers on the day he assumed command. Although the words were probably written later, the general spirit of the exhortation is probably accurate. "Soldiers! You are hungry and naked: the Republic owes you much, but she has not the means to pay her debts. Your patience and courage amid these rocks are deserving of admiration, but it procures you no

"Ramplon Taking an Oath to the Country on the Canon." The new war-like spirit motivating the French is well captured in this picture by French Canadian artist Jacques Grasset de Saint-Saveur (1757–1810). De Saint-Saveur, who became popular in Paris after he moved to Europe, was better known for his illustrations of costumes.

Bonaparte's Chief of Staff in Italy, Louis Alexandre Berthier, would become one of his most trusted officers, and a Marshal of France in 1804.

Bonaparte's First Campaign

In theory, the spring offensive against the Sardinian and Austrian armies was part of a bigger offensive by the French Republic, albeit one of limited scope. Bonaparte had different plans; he used the campaign as a springboard into the fertile plains of Italy.

*M*aster strategist Lazare Carnot had decreed that the Army of Italy's role should be diversionary. If it was only reasonably successful, it would divert troops from the primary campaigning front in Germany. In the event that the Austrians and Sardinians were comprehensively defeated, Carnot planned to unite Bonaparte's Army of Italy and General Moreau's Army of the Tyrol to create a force capable of threatening Austria's capital, Vienna.

The Army of Italy was strung out along the coastal fringe of Italy, from Nice on the French border to the port of Genoa, some 75 miles to the northeast. To the north, a force under Kellerman guarded the French alpine passes to prevent an attack on southern France. Two armies confronted them from strong defensive positions in the Ligurian Alps, which

formed the southern border of Piedmont. First, the 25,000 man strong Sardinian-Piedmontese army commanded by Austrian Baron Michael von Colli held the western end of the Ligurian Massif. The terms Piedmontese, Savoyard, and Sardinian were interchangeable, reflecting the complex political situation facing the Savoyard king. To the east, 35,000 Austrians commanded by General Johann Beaulieu threatened Genoa.

Bonaparte's plan was simple but risky. He intended to drive a wedge between the two opposing forces and seize the central position. With the two allied armies unable to support each other, he would be free to defeat them in turn, using half of his army to screen one enemy while the other half concentrated on attacking the other. Bonaparte, not tied down by a baggage train, could march 20 miles a day compared to his opponents' 12. Once the initiative was seized, he could dictate where and when any battle was fought. Although outnumbered in general, Bonaparte reasoned that by splitting the enemy forces he gained numerical superiority on each of his

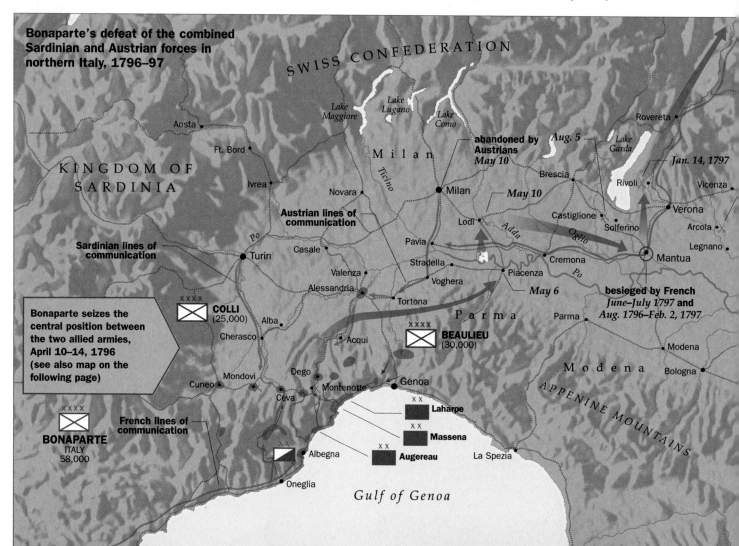

Bonaparte's defeat of the combined Sardinian and Austrian forces in northern Italy, 1796–97

SWISS CONFEDERATION

Lake Maggiore
Lake Lugano
Lake Como
Lake Garda

Aosta
Rovereta
Ft. Bord
Milan
Ivrea
Novara
Brescia
Rivoli
Vicenza
Verona
Lodi
Castiglione
Solferino
Arcola
Legnano
Mantua
Pavia
Cremona
Piacenza
Stradella
Voghera
Tortona
Acqui
Alessandria
Valenza
Casale
Turin
Cherasco
Alba
Cuneo
Mondovi
Ceva
Dego
Montenotte
Genoa
Albegna
Oneglia
La Spezia
Parma
Modena
Bologna

KINGDOM OF SARDINIA

Milan

Ticino
Adda
Oglio
Po

abandoned by Austrians May 10
Aug. 5
Jan. 14, 1797
May 10
May 6

besieged by French June–July 1797 and Aug. 1796–Feb. 2, 1797

Austrian lines of communication

Sardinian lines of communication

Bonaparte seizes the central position between the two allied armies, April 10–14, 1796 (see also map on the following page)

XXXX
COLLI (25,000)

XXXX
BEAULIEU (30,000)

XXXX
BONAPARTE ITALY 58,000

French lines of communication

XX **Laharpe**
XX **Massena**
XX **Augereau**

Parma
Modena

APPENINE MOUNTAINS

Gulf of Genoa

two battle fronts.

The allies had planned a spring campaign, and Beaulieu had already begun his advance on Genoa; but it was the French who struck first. On April 10, 1796 Bonaparte marched his army north from the coast, heading for the gap between the two allied armies. Two days later he fought his first battle.

Dividing the enemies

An Austrian force of some 6,000 blocked the French advance, occupying a line of hills just south of the village of Montenotte. Bonaparte launched a two-pronged frontal attack, with La Harpe's command of Augereau's division launching a direct attack against the Austrian left, while Massena attacked the enemy's right flank. General Argenteau and his Austrians retreated in disorder before the ferocity of the 9,000-strong French army. Bonaparte had secured his position between the allied armies.

Leaving Massena to hold off Beaulieu's Austrians, Bonaparte marched the rest of his army west toward Colli's Sardinians. On April 14 Massena improved his position by seizing Dego, but the following day he was caught unawares by General Wukassovitch's Austrian attack and the French were ignominiously ejected from the town. Bonaparte was forced to retrace his

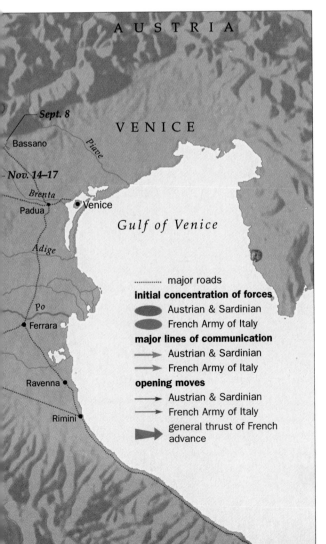

steps to restore the situation, and Dego was recaptured later the same day (*see map on following page*).

With his eastern flank secured, Bonaparte turned on Colli. The Sardinians repulsed an initial French attack launched by Augereau on their position at Ceva on April 16. The reappearance of Bonaparte forced the Sardinians to withdraw or risk being outflanked. Bonaparte caught up with Colli on April 21. The Battle of Mondovi was another triumph for the French, largely through the efforts of General Sérurier, who personally spearheaded the assault on the well-defended Sardinian position. Their morale broken, Sardinian King Victor Amadeus was forced to sue for peace. Under the terms of the Armistice Treaty of Cherasco (April 28), Savoy withdrew from the anti-French alliance, its capital Turin was ceded to the French, and the royal family went into exile.

Within ten days, Bonaparte had ensured the safety of southern France and forced the isolated Austrian army to withdraw toward its bases in the Po valley. He had fulfilled his promise to the troops and brought them to the edge of the rich and fertile heart of Italy.

Austrian cavalrymen of the 18th century. Pictured are an ulhan, a cuirassier, and a hussar. Despite the strength of the Austrian Imperial Army, poor leadership and outdated methods were to hinder success during the Italian campaigns.

The Austrian Army, 1796–1815

Often defeated and sometimes bowed into submission, Austria's army always seemed willing to renew the fight. Each time, they were a little more experienced. From the time of Bonaparte's first campaign in Italy until his surrender at Fontainebleu nearly two decades later, Austria remained the greatest threat to his aspirations.

Facing: A corporal and a soldier from the Austrian Border (Grenze) Artillery, c.1813.

Below: Austrian infantry dressed in the uniform of the pre-1798 German line.

In 1792 the Austrian Empire of Francis I (1768–1835) included territories as far apart as the Spanish Netherlands and Italy, but its heart lay in central and eastern Europe. His subjects included Germanic Austrians, Czechs, Hungarians, Walloons, Poles, Serbo-Croats, and a range of smaller national or ethnic groups. The polyglot nature of the Imperial and Royal Army made national identity and patriotism difficult to maintain. Consequently, the Austrians relied on a combination of volunteers and a partial conscription system to fill the ranks.

The Austrian army of 1792 was well prepared for a war, at least of the kind it had fought against Frederick the Great of Prussia a half-century earlier. It favored defensive tactics and lacked the logistical support to wage war far from its network of depots and fortresses. It used the same linear tactics that were the standard throughout Europe. By deploying in long, cumbersome firing lines, the Austrians were ill-prepared to fight a French army that emphasized the use of assault columns and skirmishers. Linguistic problems and the amateurish approach of the Austrian officer corps were a further hindrance.

According to returns published in 1796, the army consisted of 180,000 infantry, 48,000 cavalry, and 15,000 gunners. The majority were native Austrians (or Germans), but this encompassed troops from all over the empire, apart from Hungary, which itself was a cover-all grouping encompassing most Slavic regions. The line infantry predominated, with 45 of the 57 regiments being Austrian, the remainder classified as Hungarian. Each contained two active battalions of six companies, and a reserve (depot) battalion of four companies, giving a total theoretical strength of 3,000 men. Hungarian regiments were larger, having three field battalions and a depot formation.

While each regiment contained two grenadier companies, they rarely fought alongside their parent formation, and were instead grouped into grenadier battalions. When war broke out with France, Austria's army lacked light infantry but contained a number of "light units"—the Grenzer and Frei Korps. The 17 Grenze (or Border) regiments were raised on the empire's eastern frontier, where they guarded against a Turkish invasion, but joined the main army in time of war. Frei Korps were ad-hoc formations, usually raised from volunteers, and were not considered part of the regular army.

Learning from mistakes

The cavalry consisted of regiments of eight heavy *cuirassier*, 12 medium dragoon or *cheveau-léger*, 12 light hussar, and a regiment of *ulhans* (lancers). Although the number of regiments increased during the Napoleonic period, the basic ration of light, medium, and heavy cavalrymen remained the same. On paper, regimental strength was 1,200–1,500 men.

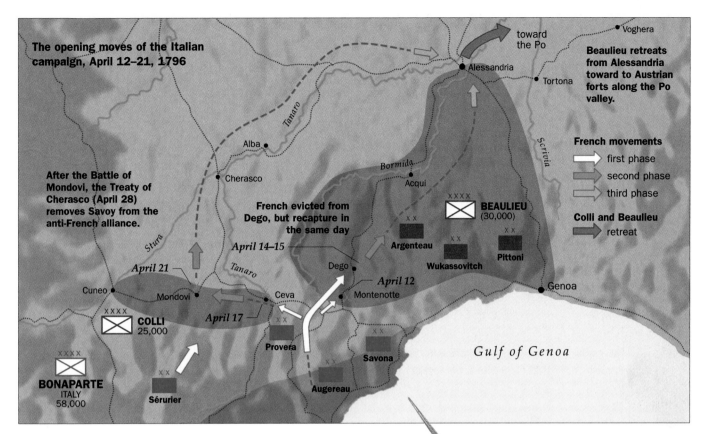

The opening moves of the Italian campaign, April 12–21, 1796

toward the Po

Beaulieu retreats from Alessandria toward to Austrian forts along the Po valley.

After the Battle of Mondovi, the Treaty of Cherasco (April 28) removes Savoy from the anti-French alliance.

French evicted from Dego, but recapture in the same day

April 14–15

April 21

April 17

April 12

French movements
→ first phase
→ second phase
→ third phase

Colli and Beaulieu
→ retreat

BEAULIEU (30,000)

Argenteau

Wukassovitch

Pittoni

Dego

Montenotte

Genoa

COLLI 25,000

BONAPARTE ITALY 58,000

Sérurier

Provera

Savona

Augereau

Cuneo

Mondovi

Ceva

Gulf of Genoa

Alba

Cherasco

Acqui

Alessandria

Tortona

Voghera

Tanaro

Stura

Tanaro

Bormida

Scrivia

Austrian artillery was considered well-trained, although their doctrine of parceling out guns to infantry regiments meant that it was several years before Austrian gunners could match the battlefield presence of the French.

The Austrian army that fought Bonaparte's in 1796 was a relic of the previous century. Its troops paid dearly for their officers' lack of ability and the hidebound conservatism of their commanders. After the defeat of Austria in 1796–7, Archduke Charles reformed the army, reducing the emphasis on linear tactics and making battlefield formations more manageable. The army was defeated again in 1800 and 1805, largely because these reforms had not taken full effect.

The case was very different in 1809, when a reorganized and rejuvenated Austrian army inflicted a humiliating defeat on Napoleon Bonaparte at Aspern-Essling, before succumbing to the French juggernaut at Wagram. Emboldened by its partial success, the army introduced further reforms, such as the creation of army corps in the French style. While it participated in the French invasion of Russia in 1812, the troops lacked much will to fight for the former enemy. The French defeat meant that a new campaign was virtually inevitable, so the emperor ordered the mobilization of the *landwehr* (or militia formations) to augment the main field army. In mid-1813 the Austrians declared war, and this time Austrian commitment was never in question. The Austrian army harried the French all the way back to Paris and were instrumental in Bonaparte's final defeat.

The Bridge at Lodi

With the Austrian army retreated to Milan, Bonaparte launched a masterly campaign of maneuver, aimed at forcing them to abandon the city without a fight. The climax came at Lodi, where all that lay between the French and victory was a long wooden bridge.

"Bataille du Pont de Lodi" by Fyain, painted shortly after the battle at Lodi Bridge shows the Austrians drawn up on the far side of the Adda, almost hidden behind the smoke from their guns, as the French prepare to assault the bridge.

W hile the ink was still wet on the Armistice of Cherasco, Bonaparte ordered his troops to march toward the Po. The Austrians expected a frontal assault and deployed accordingly, covering the main crossing points in the upper Po Valley, between Turin and Milan. Instead, Bonaparte ordered Sérurier's division to occupy the southern bank of the river and creating a "curtain of maneuver" to prevent his real intentions from being discovered.

Safe from the eyes of enemy scouts, he marched the rest of his army east toward Piacenza, which was only lightly held by the Austrians, who expected the brunt of Bonaparte's attack to fall further to the east. General D'Allemagne's advanced guard was a *corps*

d'elite composed mainly of grenadiers. This spearhead fought its way across the Po at Piacenza on May 6, 1796 and held the bridgehead while the rest of the French army came up behind them. The dashing Colonel Lannes who led the crossing would become one of Bonaparte's most spirited marshals.

Under cover of the Piacenza crossing, General Augereau managed to cross further to the east, while Massena reinforced D'Allemagne. Faced with the bulk of the French army threatening his line of communications, Austrian General Beaulieu had little option but to order a retreat to the east, before the French cut off his army completely. Milan was abandoned on May 10; a week later, Bonaparte would enter the city in triumph.

In the meantime, both armies were now north of the Po, the Austrians retreating toward the River Adda to the east, the French concentrating their forces north of Piacenza. Beaulieu planned to form a new defensive line along the Adda, but Bonaparte had little intention of giving his enemy a chance to

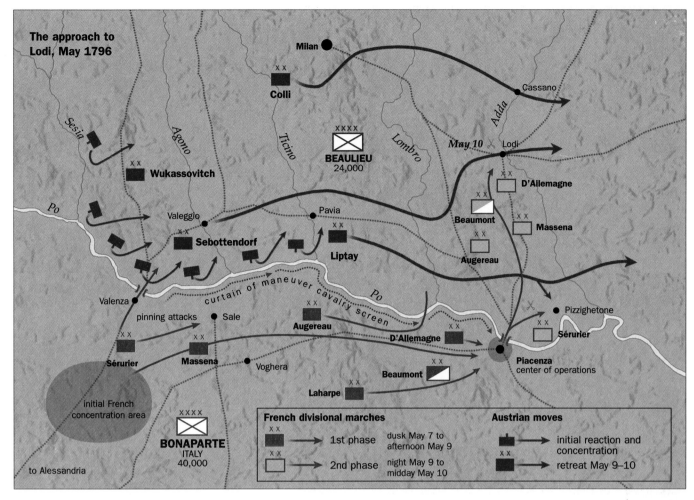

The approach to Lodi, May 1796

Milan
Colli
Cassano
Adda
Wukassovitch
Sesia
Agono
Ticino
Lombro
BEAULIEU 24,000
May 10 Lodi
D'Allemagne
Po
Valeggio
Pavia
Beaumont
Sebottendorf
Massena
Liptay
Augereau
Valenza
curtain of maneuver cavalry screen
Po
pinning attacks
Sale
Augereau
D'Allemagne
Pizzighetone
Sérurier
Sérurier
Massena
Voghera
Beaumont
Piacenza center of operations
initial French concentration area
Laharpe
to Alessandria
BONAPARTE ITALY 40,000

French divisional marches			Austrian moves	
x x	→ 1st phase	dusk May 7 to afternoon May 9	→	initial reaction and concentration
x x	→ 2nd phase	night May 9 to midday May 10	→	retreat May 9–10

regroup. D'Allemagne was ordered to advance to the northeast and seize the crossing over the Adda at Lodi. The capture of the bridge at Lodi would give the French a chance to trap the retreating Austrian army. At the very least, the enemy would be denied the opportunity to form a defensive line on the Adda.

Becoming the Little Corporal

Beaulieu had placed a divisional-sized garrison at Lodi—10,000 men, commanded by General Sebottendorf. The French advance guard reached Lodi early on May 10 and drove the Austrian skirmishers back over the river to the east. When Bonaparte arrived he found the defenders formed up on the far bank, with a clear line of fire. The bridge was being swept by fusilades of grapeshot and musket fire.

While he waited for the main body of the army to reach Lodi, Bonaparte gathered his artillery of 24 guns and sited them on the western bank, ranging in each gun himself. Under his direction, they pounded the Austrian positions. This was a mundane task for a general and earned Bonaparte the nickname "Little Corporal" and the admiration of his men. When the assault troops were ready, Bonaparte exhorted the men with a speech, then led them onto the bridge.

The first assault was beaten back by a withering fire. Massena led the next charge, and this time the assault was a success. The French established a

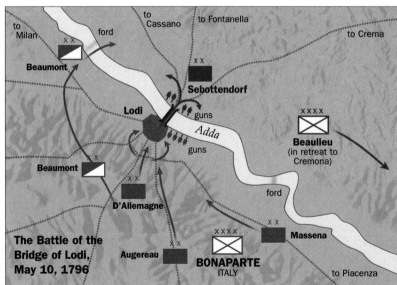

to Milan
to Cassano
to Fontanella
to Crema
ford
Beaumont
Sebottendorf
Lodi
guns
Adda
Beaulieu (in retreat to Cremona)
Beaumont
guns
D'Allemagne
ford
Massena
The Battle of the Bridge of Lodi, May 10, 1796
Augereau
BONAPARTE ITALY
to Piacenza

bridgehead on the far bank. While reinforcements raced across the bridge, other French groups crossed the river by boat and by ford further upstream. The line of the Adda had been breached.

Bonaparte was denied a complete victory, since Beaulieu's army escaped to the east, but the French had maintained the initiative, forcing the Austrians to continue their retreat to the fortress stronghold of Mantua. It also gave Bonaparte his conviction that he was *un homme supérieur*, destined for great things. This realization could only be enhanced a few days later, when he entered Milan as a conqueror.

General Johann Peter Freiherr von Beaulieu (1725–1819).

Castiglione: On the Defensive

The Austrian Army in Lombardy had been outmaneuvered and outfought by the French. Besieged in the fortress city of Mantua, the relief of the army became the focal point for the rest of the Italian campaign.

*F*ollowing his retreat from Milan, General Beaulieu tried to establish a defensive line along the River Mincio, then the Adige, but both times the French gained a bridgehead on the eastern bank and the Austrians were forced to continue their retreat. By early June 1796, Bonaparte had split the Austrian army in two. While one part retreated north toward the Tyrol, the remainder sought refuge behind the near-impregnable walls of Mantua. Bonaparte sent Sérurier to screen the fortress with 9,000 men, while the rest of the French army took up blocking positions to the north and east.

Under the command of General Dagobert Würmster, one of Austria's most experienced generals, a force of 24,000 men was gathered to relieve Mantua. His plan was to approach Mantua by marching alongside the Adige, to the east of Lake Garda. He was supported by a second force of 18,000 men under General Peter Quasdanovitch, who was ordered to march down the western shore of the lake, in an attempt to cut French communications. A further force of 5,000 moved on Mantua from the east, the plan being that after Mantua's relief the 12,700-strong garrison would join the fight.

This overly complex plan failed to take into account that the French army was faster and therefore responded to threats with greater alacrity. Bonaparte's army used interior lines of troop movements, so groups of men were able to move quickly from one threatened section of the front to the next. This ability was denied Würmster, since the three elements of his force—divided by a lake and a major river—were unable to support each other.

Würmster's plan was to unite with Quasdanovitch on the southern tip of Lake Garda, giving him 42,000 men to face Bonaparte's 46,000. The Mantua garrison would tip the balance. While Würmster approached Verona, forcing Massena to abandon the

Sited on the western bank of the Mincio, the city of Mantua became a focus for continual siege and battle during 1796.

town, Quasdanovitch captured Brescia, severing French communications with Milan. The problem, however, was the Austrians' slow advance and the distance between their two main columns.

A proud achievement

The western Austrian column posed the most serious threat. Bonaparte concentrated his army to meet it and reluctantly raised the siege of Mantua on July 31. Sérurier marched to join Bonaparte, abandoning his siege train of 179 guns in the process. This left Würmster free to relieve Mantua.

On August 3 Bonaparte fought Quasdanovitch at Lonato, a running fight that sent the eastern Austrian column retreating for the safety of the Tyrol. In a classic example of Napoleonic strategy, Bonaparte fought a battle from a central position: while Massena and Bonaparte fought Quasdanovitch, Augereau blocked the advance of Würmster, who was moving west toward Castiglione, south of Lonato. Augereau performed brilliantly. In later years, when the mediocre Augereau was criticized in front of Napoleon, he would reply, "Ah, but remember what he [Augereau] did for us at Castiglione." Augereau bought time for Bonaparte to defeat each enemy column in turn.

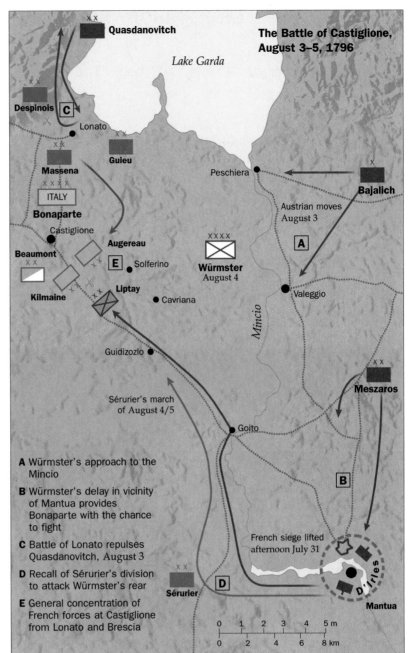

The Battle of Castiglione, August 3–5, 1796

A Würmster's approach to the Mincio

B Würmster's delay in vicinity of Mantua provides Bonaparte with the chance to fight

C Battle of Lonato repulses Quasdanovitch, August 3

D Recall of Sérurier's division to attack Würmster's rear

E General concentration of French forces at Castiglione from Lonato and Brescia

On August 5 the Army of Italy attacked Würmster south of Castiglione. The Austrians were drawn up in a line anchored on the heights of Solferino. While Massena and Augereau launched frontal attacks on the Austrian line, a group of two demi-brigades commanded by General Despinois worked their way along the heights toward the tower that dominated Solferino. Würmster's line held, but it was pinned all along its front.

At that crucial moment, Sérurier's division (temporarily commanded by General Fiorella) appeared from the southeast, behind the Austrian left flank. This coincided with the capture of Solferino's tower by Despinois. Würmster ordered a retreat, but the French were exhausted and the Austrians escaped. Within days the Austrians had withdrawn to the north of Lake Garda and Mantua was once again ringed by French troops. Bonaparte had won a notable victory, but the Austrians were far from beaten.

General Pierre François Charles Augereau's (1757–1816) delaying tactics were crucial to the French victory.

Arcola: Sidestep and Thrust

The Castiglione campaign had brought a temporary respite to the Austrian garrison of Mantua, but the siege was resumed. Würmster immediately began to organize a second relief attempt. Bonaparte used a novel form of offensive defense, which led to the Battle of Arcola.

General Würmster did not learn from his mistakes. His plan for the relief of Mantua involved splitting the Austrian army into two unsupported columns; his own men would advance

Napoleon Bonaparte on the bridge at Arcola by Antoine Jean-Gros.

on Mantua from the east, while a force led by General Davidovitch attacked from the north. Bonaparte launched a pre-emptive assault on Davidovitch, driving him out of the Trent valley

(September 4–5, 1796), before turning on Würmster at Bassano (September 8). Both Austrian forces were defeated, while French losses were minimal. It took almost a month for the Austrians to recover and for Würmster to ready his army for offensive. Bonaparte had bought time, raising his army's morale in the process.

The Mantuan garrison had swollen to over 28,000 men, due to Würmster's complement of men, making a successful relief imperative to avoid starvation. This next attempt was to be made by General Alvintzi, who had defeated the French Revolutionary Army in 1793 at Neerwinden (*see page 13*). He was to push on Mantua from the east with 28,000 men, while Davidovitch marched down the eastern side of Lake Garda with 18,000 men.

Bonaparte responded by sending Massena and Augereau to hold off Alvintzi, while he massed the rest of his army to strike Davidovitch; 9,000 men were left to screen Mantua. Alvintzi moved quickly and the Austrians defeated Bonaparte's subordinates at Caldiero on November 12. The French commander switched his force to meet Alvintzi, leaving General Vaubois with 10,000 men to block Davidovitch near Rivoli, between Lake Garda and the Adige.

Alvintzi was not the only commander to move quickly. Instead of simply reinforcing Massena and Augereau around Verona, Bonaparte left a screening force in the city to face the Austrians, then moved the bulk of his army south down the Adige. His aim was to halt the Austrian advance by launching a maneuver in the rear, threatening Alvintzi's lines of communication, which stretched east toward Vicenza.

Struggle for a costly victory

On the night of November 14, French engineers threw a pontoon bridge across the Adige near the town of Ronco. A series of causeways led over the flooded eastern bank to the northwest and north, the latter following the course of the Alpone toward the village of Arcola. Bonaparte planned to cross the river, then use Massena's division to screen the approaches to the northwest, while the bulk of his army crossed at Arcola. It would then be free to cut the Austrian lines of communication by seizing the town of Villanova, three miles to the north.

While Massena's advance went according to plan,

Augereau was pinned down at Arcola by heavy fire from the far side of the river. Attempts by Bonaparte and Augereau to storm the bridge were forced back with heavy casualties. Bonaparte sent a small force back to Ronco to cross the Adige further downstream and fall on the Austrian flank. Meanwhile, his army was stuck, buying time for Alvintzi to pull his troops back from Verona to Villanova. By nightfall, Massena was forced back by Austrian General Provera, while the diversionary force failed to appear by nightfall.

Bonaparte ordered a general withdrawal. His army needed to regroup, and he was unsure whether Vaubois would hold off Davidovitch in the north. On November 16 Massena and Provera fought a see-saw battle along the causeways south of Porcile, and Augereau attempted to storm the bridge at Arcola. Little progress was made.

With the prospects of catching Alvintzi's army receding, Bonaparte launched a third attack on November 17. This time Massena split his forces, assuming responsibility for the Porcile and Arcola sectors, while Augereau attempted an outflanking maneuver by crossing the Alpone further downstream. A rash attack across Arcola bridge only pinned the Austrians down, while Augereau appeared on their left flank. The Arcola garrison retreated, leaving the French to count the cost of their victory. While Alvintzi's army escaped to Vicenza, Bonaparte had prevented the Austrian relief of Mantua.

French engineers constructed a pontoon bridge across the Adige, close to the village of Ronco, in order to attack the Austrian garrison at Arcola, just under two miles to the north. Although the French eventually triumphed, it was a Pyrrhic victory.

Rivoli: The Battle for Italy

The hard-fought battle of Arcola had cost the lives of 7,000 Austrians and 4,500 Frenchmen, but achieved little. The Mantuan garrison was now in dire straits, its numbers reduced by starvation and disease. The fate of Italy now rested in one last roll of the die.

General Alvintzi gathered an army of 43,000 men, and in January 1797 was ready to launch the fourth relief attempt of Mantua. This time the bulk of the army would operate together, marching down the Adige valley toward Verona, while 15,000 men were used on diversionary operations to the east and southeast. The diversions kept Bonaparte guessing and, while he placed General Joubert in command of a blocking force along the low Trombalore Ridge to the north of Rivoli, he kept the bulk of his 55,000-man army around Verona.

By January 8 General Provera had driven Augereau back near Legnano, and for a few days Bonaparte feared the main Austrian attack might come from the east. He moved his headquarters to Verona, where an Austrian force of 6,000 men threatened the city. He was reluctant to commit the main army until he discovered the direction of the main attack.

Finally, on January 13, Bonaparte learned that Alvintzi was in the Adige valley. That evening he joined Joubert and saw six groups of Austrian camp fires burning to the north. Clearly the main Austrian thrust would be directed against Joubert at Rivoli. Bonaparte sent for reinforcements and by dawn the bulk of the French army was marching north.

Alvintzi had formed his army into six columns, three of which (the columns of generals Liptay, Koblos, and Ocksay) were to attack the Trombalore Ridge held by Joubert's division, while a fourth group commanded by General Quasdanovitch planned to march along the west bank of the Adige, then attack Joubert's force in the flank where the river road rose to the Rivoli plateau, via the Osteria gorge. A fifth column on the east bank was to support the main attack and establish a battery to provide support to Quasdanovitch. The sixth column, commanded by General Lusignan, was ordered to make a wide, sweeping flank march to the west and fall on the rear of the French force. Only Quasdanovitch's column contained more than 5,000 men, and none was ordered to support neighboring formations.

A contemporary engraving shows the rugged terrain that formed the battlefield of Rivoli in 1797.

Master of Italy

Shortly before dawn the Austrians attacked. Joubert held off the main attack with the aid of leading units from Massena's division, which had force-marched to Rivoli during the night. While the Austrians at Rivoli faced 10,000 French at dawn, reinforcements meant that number rose to 17,000 by 8am and 20,000 men by mid-afternoon.

To the northwest Quasdanovitch's column was separated by Monte Magnont, a virtually impassable rock outcrop that split the battlefield. The French therefore enjoyed interior lines of defense and rushed troops from one sector to the other, while the three Austrian columns attacking the Rivoli ridge were unable to support Quasdanovitch. Reinforcements, augmented by part of Joubert's force, repulsed Quasdanovitch as he reached the top of Osteria Gorge and a crisis was averted.

As Lusignan's column neared Rivoli, it was attacked by the troops of generals Rey and Victor, who had reached the battlefield with Massena. Meanwhile, Bonaparte diverted the rest of his army to the Trombalore Ridge, to ward off any renewed threat from the north. Outmaneuvered at every turn, Alvintzi had little option but to call off the attack.

As night fell, Bonaparte raced south with Massena's division to prevent the fall of Verona, and the following day Joubert counterattacked Alvintzi's main force. The demoralized Austrians broke and fled to the north, pursued by the French cavalry. The last attempt to relieve Mantua had failed.

With no relief in site, Mantua capitulated on February 2. Over the next six weeks the French advanced into Austria via the Tyrol, but the Austrians were reluctant to risk another defeat. With Bonaparte less than a hundred miles from Vienna, the Austrian emperor sued for peace. An armistice was signed on April 18, and the peace treaty of Campo Formio ended hostilities on October 17, 1797.

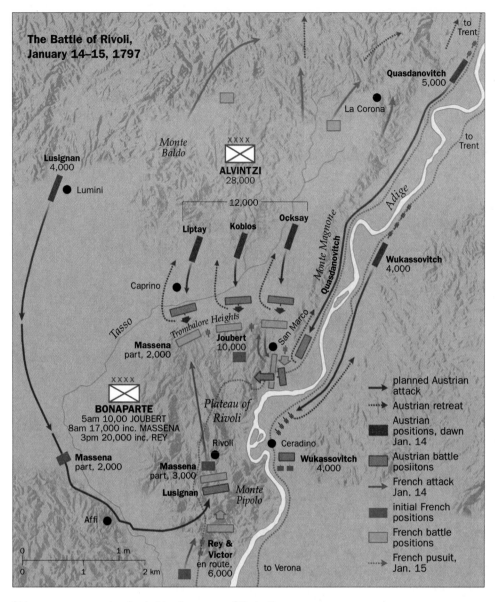

The Battle of Rivoli, January 14–15, 1797

Applauded in the streets of Paris, Bonaparte was a national hero, and posed a serious political headache for the Directoire. The most successful general in France would have to be given an assignment worthy of his talents.

The Citizen General dictates peace terms to the Austrians at Campo Formio (1797).

The New Alexander

Egypt, 1798–1800

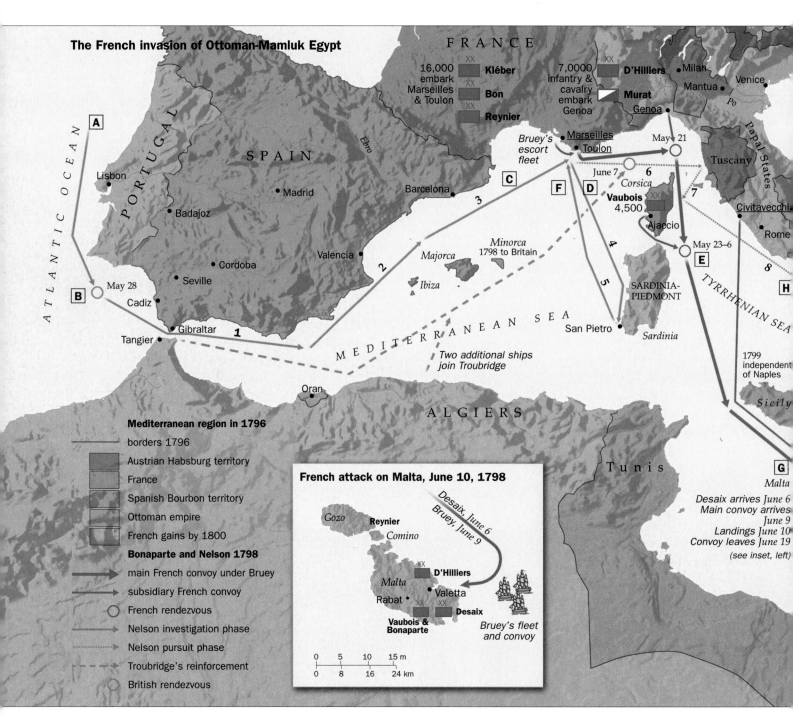

The French invasion of Ottoman-Mamluk Egypt

16,000 embark Marseilles & Toulon — **Kléber**, **Bon**, **Reynier**

7,0000 infantry & cavalry embark Genoa — **D'Hilliers**, **Murat**

FRANCE · Milan · Venice · Mantua · Po · Tuscany · Papal States

Bruey's escort fleet · Marseilles · Toulon · Genoa

May 21 · June 7 · **6** · Corsica · **Vaubois 4,500** · Ajaccio · **7** · Civitavecchia · Rome

C · **F** · **D** · **8**

May 23–6 · **E** · **H**

SARDINIA-PIEDMONT · San Pietro · Sardinia · TYRRHENIAN SEA

3 · **2** · Majorca · Minorca 1798 to Britain · Ibiza · **4** · **5**

MEDITERRANEAN SEA

Two additional ships join Troubridge

ATLANTIC OCEAN · PORTUGAL · SPAIN · Lisbon · Madrid · Badajoz · Barcelona · Ebro · Valencia · Cordoba · Seville · Cadiz · Gibraltar · Tangier · Oran

A · **B** May 28 · **1**

ALGIERS · Tunis

1799 independent of Naples · Sicily · **G** · Malta

Desaix arrives June 6
Main convoy arrives June 9
Landings June 10
Convoy leaves June 19
(see inset, left)

Mediterranean region in 1796

— borders 1796
▢ Austrian Habsburg territory
▢ France
▢ Spanish Bourbon territory
▢ Ottoman empire
▢ French gains by 1800

Bonaparte and Nelson 1798

→ main French convoy under Bruey
→ subsidiary French convoy
◯ French rendezvous
→ Nelson investigation phase
⋯→ Nelson pursuit phase
--→ Troubridge's reinforcement
◯ British rendezvous

French attack on Malta, June 10, 1798

Gozo · **Reynier** · Comino · *Desaix, June 6* · *Bruey, June 9*

D'Hilliers · *Malta* · Rabat · **Valetta** · **Vaubois & Bonaparte** · **Desaix**

Bruey's fleet and convoy

0 5 10 15 m
0 8 16 24 km

By 1798 France had defeated the combined armies of Europe and her troops were encamped outside the Channel ports, waiting for the opportunity attack Britain. The Directory sent Bonaparte to inspect the situation, but he considered a cross-Channel invasion to be impractical. With the French fleet scattered between Toulon and Brest, and any attempt to unite the two portions fraught with difficulty, it was impossible for the French navy to safeguard the invasion force.

Instead, Bonaparte proposed a plan that would allow France to seize the strategic initiative. He advocated an attack on Egypt, which would threaten British control of India, tie up British naval resources, and sever Britain's trade with the East. At the least it would make up for the French colonies lost to the British in the West Indies.

This scheme was approved by the Directoire in Paris, probably because it removed a man, who was coming to be viewed as dangerous, further from the seat of power. Bonaparte saw things differently:

of the French Army of the Orient. With the British fleet temporarily absent from the area because of a bad storm, the French fleet under the command of Admiral Brueys sailed from Toulon without hindrance. It sailed to Malta, where Bonaparte captured the island before sailing on east toward Egypt.

Vice Admiral Jervis (now Lord St. Vincent) sent

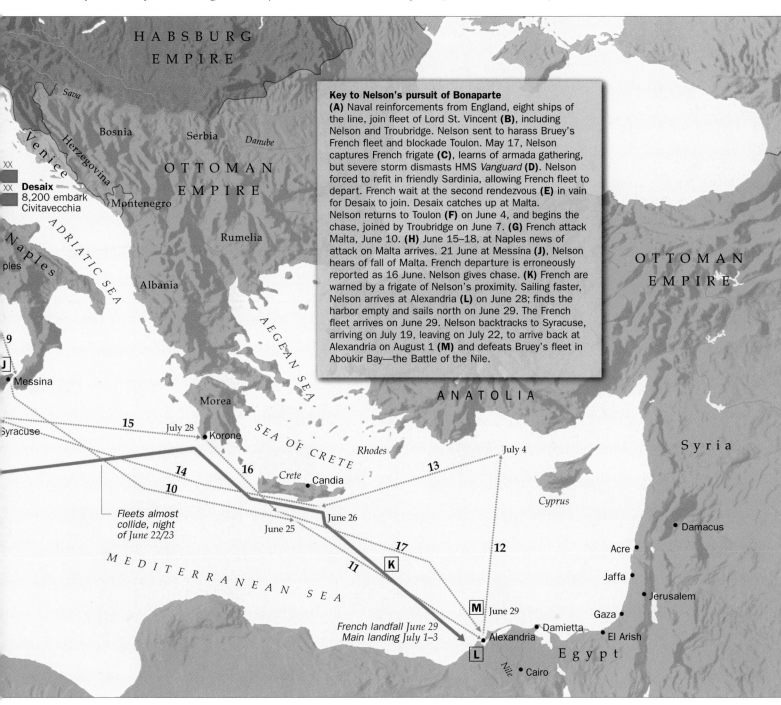

Key to Nelson's pursuit of Bonaparte
(A) Naval reinforcements from England, eight ships of the line, join fleet of Lord St. Vincent **(B)**, including Nelson and Troubridge. Nelson sent to harass Bruey's French fleet and blockade Toulon. May 17, Nelson captures French frigate **(C)**, learns of armada gathering, but severe storm dismasts HMS *Vanguard* **(D)**. Nelson forced to refit in friendly Sardinia, allowing French fleet to depart. French wait at the second rendezvous **(E)** in vain for Desaix to join. Desaix catches up at Malta. Nelson returns to Toulon **(F)** on June 4, and begins the chase, joined by Troubridge on June 7. **(G)** French attack Malta, June 10. **(H)** June 15–18, at Naples news of attack on Malta arrives. 21 June at Messina **(J)**, Nelson hears of fall of Malta. French departure is erroneously reported as 16 June. Nelson gives chase. **(K)** French are warned by a frigate of Nelson's proximity. Sailing faster, Nelson arrives at Alexandria **(L)** on June 28; finds the harbor empty and sails north on June 29. The French fleet arrives on June 29. Nelson backtracks to Syracuse, arriving on July 19, leaving on July 22, to arrive back at Alexandria on August 1 **(M)** and defeats Bruey's fleet in Aboukir Bay—the Battle of the Nile.

"Europe is but a molehill… all the great reputations have come from Asia." The Orient was a suitably large target for a man with an immense sense of ambition and self-worth.

In great secrecy, a force of almost 40,000 men marched south to Toulon. While preparations were underway, Bonaparte was nominated General in Chief

the newly promoted Rear Admiral Nelson in pursuit. As the secrecy surrounding the expedition had been complete, the British had no real idea where Bonaparte was heading. For a few weeks the Royal Navy chased the French force through the eastern Mediterranean but were unable to intercept, or to prevent Bonaparte from landing his army on the shores of Egypt.

Nelson and the British Navy

The British Royal Navy was the largest sea-borne force in the world, but it needed skilled leaders to contain its rivals. Fortunately Britain had great naval commanders in abundance, none more gifted than Horatio Nelson.

With Nelson absent from the southern French coast, and thus loosed from Toulon, Bonaparte's Army of the Orient landed in Alexandria at the start of July 1798. The excitement of the occasion is caught by Jean-Leon Gerome's famous painting "Napoleon and His General Staff in Egypt."

*B*orn into minor Norfolk gentry on September 29, 1758, the frail Horatio Nelson was sent to join the navy at the age of 12, under the protection of his uncle, Captain Maurice Suckling. Over the next few years he served on Suckling's ship, was the clerk on a merchantman, and joined a survey ship operating in the Arctic. At 18 he passed the fleet board, becoming a lieutenant in 1775.

Nelson was made Post Captain in 1778, becoming what one contemporary called "the merest boy of a captain." He excelled at the job, and within a year he was given command of the frigate HMS *Hinchinbrook*, then commanded HMS *Albermarle* during the last years of what the British called the American Revolutionary War. When what the New World colonists called the American War of Independence ended and the Royal Navy reduced its strength, Nelson was forced to survive on shore at half-pay for most of the 1780s.

He was saved from obscurity by the French Revolution. The navy needed gifted captains, and in 1793 Nelson was given command of the ship-of-the-line HMS *Agamemnon*. He participated in the capture of Toulon (1793), helped the Neapolitans liberate Corsica, but lost an eye in a skirmish at Calvi. In March 1795 he fought the *Ca Ira* and *Sans Culotte*, forcing the larger *Ca Ira* to surrender. He was duly given the rank of commodore.

In 1797 he played a major part in the Battle of Cape St. Vincent. When it looked as if the Spanish might escape from the British fleet commanded by Admiral Sir John Jervis, Nelson broke formation in HMS *Captain* and sailed to intercept a portion of the Spanish fleet. He captured the larger *San Nicolas* by boarding, then used his prize to capture the even bigger *San Josef*, which had ranged alongside. Nelson's own invention of a boarding bridge turned an ignominious battle into a substantial victory and won him promotion to flag rank. Months later he lost an arm during a skirmish on Santa Cruz de Tenerife, but by mid-1798, Rear Admiral Nelson was sent to the Mediterranean, charged with blockading the French fleet in Toulon.

Horatio Nelson, portrait by Leonardo Guzzardi. The British admiral proved to be Bonaparte's nemesis at sea, destroying his fleet and cutting his communications with France.

Breaking through the lines

The tool at Nelson's disposal was a powerful one. Since the outbreak of the French Revolutionary War, the British had maintained a blockade of French ports, isolating the French fleets in Brest and Toulon to prevent their amalgamation into a single powerful armada. The bulwark of the fleet was the ship-of-the-line, a floating gun battery carrying 50–130 large guns and crewed by 400–900 men. These vessels were divided into Rates, ranging from the largest First Rates (carrying over a hundred guns) down to Fourth Rates (50 guns). By far the most common type was the Third Rate, armed with 74 guns.

Tactics revolved around the formation of a line-of-battle, where ships-of-the-line deployed in line astern, so that each ship supported its neighbors, creating a wall of guns. For a century, a rigid adherence to line-of-battle tactics had led to a stalemate, but by 1798 things were changing. Innovative British admirals such as Rodney and Howe were prepared to try to break through the enemy line. The result was either an impressive victory or a severe defeat. Nelson developed their tactics into a battle-winning formula.

The storm that drove Nelson's Mediterranean fleet away from Toulon in mid-May 1798 also allowed the French invasion fleet to slip out to sea in its wake. After a brief halt at Malta, where the island surrendered to the French, Bonaparte ordered his armada to steer east toward Egypt. The army disembarked at Alexandria on July 1, one month before Nelson, commanding 14 ships-of-the-line, caught up with the French. The Mamluk kingdom of Egypt put up little resistance against this invasion, and the country lay open to Bonaparte's land forces.

Battle of the Pyramids

With the Army of the Orient on African soil, Bonaparte set out to conquer the Mamluk kingdom of Egypt. Between the French and Cairo lay a Mamluk army. In a clash of two worlds, a modern European army fought a host hardly altered since the end of the Crusades.

*T*he French landings were achieved with few casualties, and Alexandria's capture secured the French a Mediterranean base. Bonaparte marched toward Cairo within two days of arriving. The light resistance was confined to a few skirmishes with Bedouin horsemen—the real enemy was the desert. Morale plummeted as the French troops became worn down by the heat, wracked by dysentery, and plagued by thirst. It was so bad that several, including the experienced General Mireur, committed suicide.

The conqueror of Egypt, "Napoleon Bonaparte in Cairo." Painting by Henry Levy.

Finally, on July 20, 1798 scouts reported that they were close to the Nile. They also brought news that a Mamluk army under the command of joint-ruler Murad Bey lay encamped to the south.

The typical Mamluk warrior was a mounted swordsman, who rode into battle followed by slaves carrying his weapons. Some 10,000 warriors formed the core of Murad Bey's army, supported by allied Ottoman cavalry and mounted servants. A force of 15,000 *fellahin* (followers) under the other joint-ruler, Ibrahim Bey, protected the east bank of the Nile north of Cairo, and guarded a fortified bridgehead on the western bank at Embabeh.

When the French reached the Nile, Murad Bey advanced. It was just past noon on July 21. Faced with a battle, Bonaparte made a speech, inspired by the pyramids clearly visible in the distance: "Soldiers! From the summit of yonder pyramids, forty ages look down upon you!" He ordered his army into five divisional-sized squares, each of 5,000 men, their walls bristling with bayonets. The squares of generals Vial and Bon formed up close to the river, while those of Dugua, Reynier, and Desaix spread westward across the desert for almost two miles. Bonaparte took up position in Dugua's central square, while he held the small French cavalry in reserve behind the center.

Defenders on the run

About 3.30pm, the Mamluk cavalry charged against the western squares of Desaix and Reynier. Unable to break in, the Mamluk cavalry split into three columns, which were fired on from all sides as they surged around the French infantry. Despite heavy losses, they rallied and charged again, this time concentrating on Desaix's division. An advanced guard of the division had barricaded itself in the nearby village of Biktil, and the Mamluks surrounded the settlement, as French troops fired from the rooftops. Desaix and Reynier's forces crept across the desert to lend their support.

Eighteenth-century Egypt

Although part of the Ottoman Turkish Empire, the Mamluk state was virtually independent, as it had been since the 13th century, when the mamluk slave caste of warriors rose up against their Ayyubid rulers toward the end of the crusading era. In Mamluk society, power was concentrated in the hands of a ruling warrior elite, who relied on native Egyptians to provide everything. The powerful army ensured loyalty to the ruling minority; without it the system would crumble.

"Battaille des Pyramides" by the French artist Pellerin shows Murad Bey's cavalry preparing to charge the French infantry, with the pyramids at Giza in the background.

While the bulk of the Mamluk cavalry was locked in combat, Bonaparte launched Vial and Bon's divisions against the fortified village of Embabeh, which guarded the main crossing point over the Nile. A small flotilla of French gunboats supported the attack, driving off the Mamluk *dhows* that thronged the river. At about 4pm the French charged the Mamluk entrenchment, and within minutes the defenders were in full retreat. Many attempted to escape across the river, and over a thousand drowned in the shallows, while others fled south.

Bonaparte led the French south, supporting the

flank of their assault, and cornered the Mamluk cavalry to the west. By 4.30pm all resistance had crumbled. The horsemen who remained in their saddles broke and fled into the desert, leaving 2,000 of their compatriots lying where they had fallen. Losses to the *fellahin* probably exceeded 4,000. By contrast, French casualties were minimal: 29 dead and 260 wounded. Bonaparte entered Cairo the following day, July 22. His triumph was short-lived, however. The Royal Navy arrived off the coast near Alexandria only nine days later.

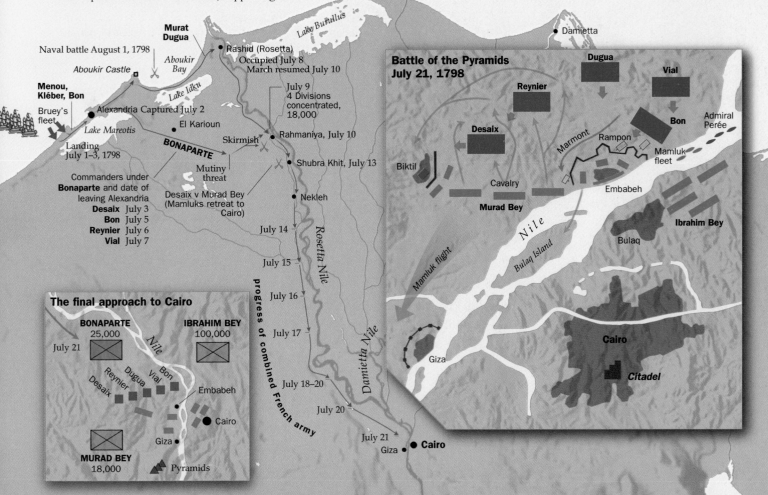

Battle of the Nile

The French fleet that had escorted Bonaparte's army to Egypt lacked the experience to engage in a full-scale sea battle, so it was anchored in a defensive line inside a protective bay guarded by shore batteries.

*T*he French naval commander Admiral Brueys decided that Alexandria was too poorly defended against attack from the sea, so he moved the fleet 13 miles to the east to anchor in Aboukir Bay. He arrayed the fleet in a line, close to shore, while to the west the guns of captured Castle of Aboukir were deployed to protect the anchorage. Smaller warships anchored between the main battle-line and the shore.

For the past four months, Nelson's fleet of 14 ships-of-the-line had searched in vain for the French,

This contemporary engraving shows survivors of *L'Orient* struggling into a boat while their flagship burns and sinks.

but early on August 1, a scouting ship spotted some French transports in Alexandria. Hours later, another frigate sighted the main French fleet in Aboukir Bay. Although Brueys had had weeks to prepare for battle, he was taken by surprise. Over 3,000 French sailors were on the shore collecting water. The French flagship *L'Orient* was anchored in the center of the French line when the British appeared at about 4pm. Because of the late hour, Brueys anticipated no attack until the next morning. Nevertheless, he immediately ordered his ships to be ready to raise anchors on his command and the ships remained where they were.

An unconventional commander, Nelson had no intention of waiting. His plan was to concentrate his fleet against the front of the French line, then to work his way down its length, overpowering each still-anchored ship in turn. As the sun began to set at about 6.30pm, the British rounded the shoal waters protecting the western edge of the bay and closed with the enemy. Although HMS *Culloden* ran aground in the shallow water, the remainder continued. As the lead ships passed the first few French ships, they began firing to either side as they ran through the enemy line.

Victory not a strong enough name

Captain Foley in the leading ship HMS *Goliath* passed the bow of the *Guerrier*, followed by four more Third Rates. Working their way between the French line and the shore, they teamed up with Nelson's rearward ships, who engaged the French from the seaward side. The French fought with incredible bravery and skill, but the odds were against them. Under fire from both sides and from astern, the *Guerrier*, *Conquérant*, and *Spartiate* were battered into submission and, with their decks filled with dead and wounded, hauled down their colors.

HMS *Bellerophon* took on *L'Orient*, but the French flagship pummeled the British Third Rate, dismasting her and leaving her a drifting hulk. By 9pm, the French vanguard had been overrun, but the rest of the line held its own. The *Peuple Souverain* cut her anchor cables and drifted out of the line, and HMS *Leander* moved into the vacant space, anchoring and firing broadsides into *Aquelon* and *Franklin* to either side. The fighting raged on, until suddenly, at about 10.30pm, *L'Orient* blew up, taking Admiral Brueys and most of his crew with her. The French three-ship

rearguard under Rear Admiral Villeneuve cut their anchor cables and escaped; Villeneuve would face Nelson at Trafalgar seven years later.

Nelson's victory was complete. As dawn rose over a bay filled with debris and bodies, he counted the cost. For a mere 218 British dead, he had virtually destroyed the French fleet, capturing 11 ships-of-the-line in a dangerous and somewhat reckless night action, fought at point-blank range. As Nelson himself put it, "Victory is not a name strong enough for such a scene." Without his fleet, Bonaparte's army was stranded in Egypt. Without setting foot ashore, Nelson had decided the fate of the Orient.

"Battle of the Nile" painted by L. Whitcombe and printed by J. Jenkins in 1816.

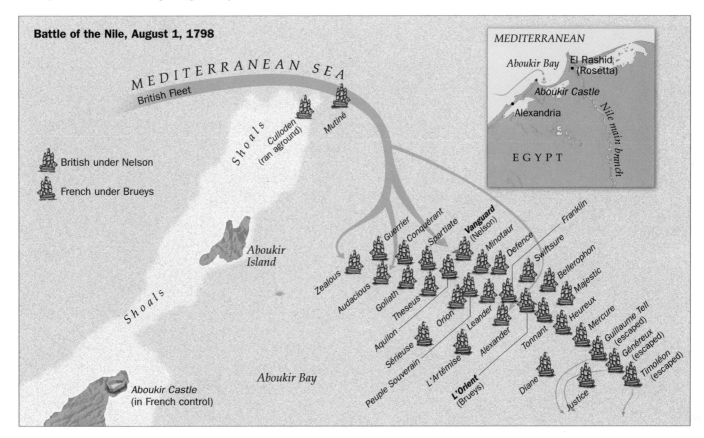

Battle of the Nile, August 1, 1798

Death and Failure at Acre

The loss of Admiral Brueys' fleet stranded Bonaparte's Army of Egypt in Cairo, surrounded by enemies. Should he continue the campaign into the Ottoman heartland, or watch his army evaporate through inactivity and disease? Bonaparte went on the offensive.

Detail from the painting of 1804 by Antoine Jean Gros of "Napoleon Visiting the Plague-Stricken at Jaffa."

*I*n the summer of 1798, Bonaparte was becoming increasingly isolated. Sultan Selim I of Turkey had declared a *jihad* (holy war) against him. A Turkish army commanded by Achmed Pasha (nicknamed "the Butcher") was moving south through Syria toward Egypt, while another was gathering on Rhodes, and with British help it could land anywhere on the Egyptian coast.

While French scientists scoured Egypt for cultural information (discovering the famous Rosetta Stone in the process), Bonaparte laid plans for even greater conquests. In late 1798 he led his army east and crossed into Sinai. Advancing through El Arish, he captured Jaffa on March 7, 1799. Bonaparte ordered the execution of 3,000 captured Turkish soldiers to discourage any further resistance.

In the French path lay the crucial port of Acre. Ironically, the city's Turkish garrison was under the command of French *émigré* Louis Phélipeaux. Confronted by his own kin, he remained undaunted. As Achmed Pasha halted his advance to gather numerical strength, and Phélipeaux strengthened Acre's defenses, fortune was on the Turkish side. A plague epidemic delayed the French advance from Jaffa for ten days. Bonaparte was only able to lay siege to a well prepared Acre on March 18, having positioned an outlying force under General Kléber 25 miles away at Mount Tabor.

From the start, Bonaparte's efforts were confounded by the spirited Ottoman defense and a British naval squadron under the command of the

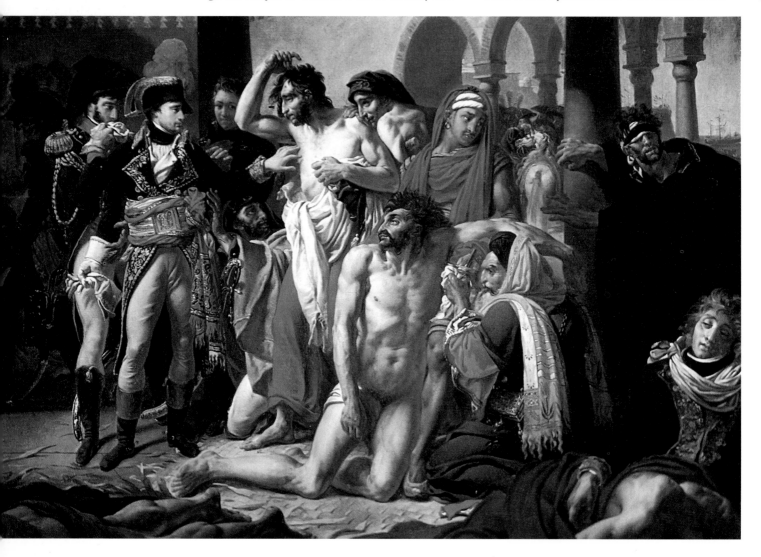

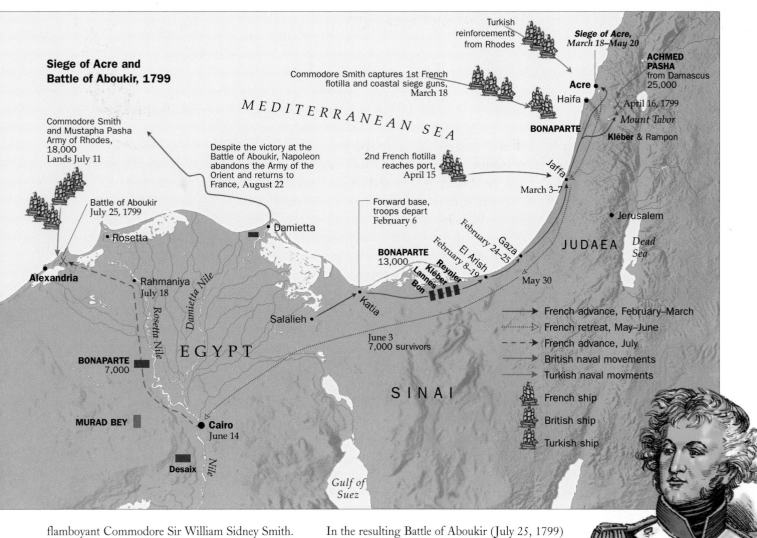

Siege of Acre and Battle of Aboukir, 1799

Turkish reinforcements from Rhodes

Siege of Acre, March 18–May 20

Commodore Smith captures 1st French flotilla and coastal siege guns, March 18

ACHMED PASHA from Damascus 25,000

Acre

Haifa

April 16, 1799

Mount Tabor

BONAPARTE

Kléber & Rampon

Commodore Smith and Mustapha Pasha Army of Rhodes, 18,000 Lands July 11

Despite the victory at the Battle of Aboukir, Napoleon abandons the Army of the Orient and returns to France, August 22

2nd French flotilla reaches port, April 15

Jaffa

March 3–7

MEDITERRANEAN SEA

Battle of Aboukir July 25, 1799

• Damietta

• Rosetta

• Jerusalem

February 24–25

Gaza

El Arish

JUDAEA *Dead Sea*

Alexandria

BONAPARTE 13,000

Reynier
Kléber
Lannes
Bon

February 8–19

May 30

Rahmaniya July 18

Rosetta Nile

Damietta Nile

Salalieh •

• Katia

EGYPT

BONAPARTE 7,000

June 3 7,000 survivors

→ French advance, February–March

┈▷ French retreat, May–June

-→ French advance, July

→ British naval movements

→ Turkish naval movments

SINAI

🚢 French ship

🚢 British ship

🚢 Turkish ship

MURAD BEY

● **Cairo** June 14

Desaix Nile

Gulf of Suez

flamboyant Commodore Sir William Sidney Smith.

Smith's squadron captured the French siege train, which forced Bonaparte to storm the city. Several attacks made during March and early April were all repulsed. On April 16 Achmed Pasha pounced on General Kléber's isolated force at Mount Tabor. Kléber held out against overwhelming odds until Bonaparte came to his relief. The Ottoman host was scattered, with French losses of around 300 men. Despite this success, Acre continued to defy him.

Fleeing disaster

The siege continued, while losses from disease continued to mount; but help was at hand. On May 20, word reached Bonaparte that the British and Turks planned to land an army in Egypt. He had no option but to call off the siege and march south. By this time the French had been reduced to an operational strength of a mere 7,000 men; barely enough to meet the new British threat. Over 2,200 French graves marked the furthest extent of the French advance into Palestine and Syria. Bonaparte needed a victory to restore his men's faith in his generalship.

In mid-July, an 18,000-strong Turkish army commanded by Mustapha Pasha landed at Aboukir. Incredibly, instead of advancing, Mustapha dug in, allowing Bonaparte the time to race across the delta.

In the resulting Battle of Aboukir (July 25, 1799) Turks were slaughtered in their thousands, for the loss of under a thousand Frenchmen. Despite this victory, Bonaparte was aware that his Egyptian gamble had failed. Back in Europe, Austria, Russia, and Naples had joined the Anti-French Coalition. To remain in Egypt was to invite disaster, while to return to Europe opened the possibility of further conquests.

On August 22 Bonaparte passed on the command of the Army of the Orient to General Kléber. Boarding a frigate packed with Egyptian antiquities and senior French commanders, he slipped through the patrolling British warships and escaped to France, leaving behind the remnants of a dispirited army.

Landing in France on October 9, Bonaparte was fêted as a hero, arriving in time to command a new army. Back in Egypt, Kléber called him *ce petit bougre*; army veterans were even more vociferous in their criticism. Kléber was assassinated in June 1800 and, following a British invasion of Egypt in March 1801, his successor, General Menou, surrendered the army in return for a passage home. The Oriental dream was over, but by the time the campaign ended, the instigator was embroiled in ever-greater schemes in Europe.

Jean Baptiste Kléber (1753–1800), a veteran of the Revolutionary Wars who thought Bonaparte a callow upstart (top), and (below) young William Sidney Smith (1764–1840), who in 1793 had scuttled the bulk of the French ships at Toulon before the British withdrawal (*see page 17*).

Bonaparte as First Consul

Having abandoned his Army of the Orient in Egypt, Bonaparte returned to Paris in August 1799 to find he was the toast of the city. This popular support proved crucial in his seizure of political power

Jacques-Louis David's famous painting of 1801 depicts Napoleon Bonaparte on horseback at the St. Bernard Pass, from where he led his forces across the Alps in 1800 to attack the Austrian army besieging Genoa. This neoclassical equestrian portrait was painted in several versions.

When Bonaparte returned from Egypt, the Directory was in turmoil. Conspirators within its ranks such as Talleyrand, Sieyès, Barras, and Ducos were planning a *coup d'état*, and asked the young general to act as their military figurehead. He was not their first choice: General Barthelemy Joubert (1769–99) had been the prime candidate until his death at Novi (August 15, 1799), when a combined force of Russian and Austrian allies defeated the French in Italy, overturning everything Bonaparte had achieved there earlier. Barras and Ducos, who were the *de-facto* leaders of the Directory, planned to share power with Bonaparte because they believed he would have little political interest or ability. They soon learned it was unwise to underestimate the "little corporal."

On the night of November 9–10, 1799, the three seized power in Paris, evicting the other members of the Directory and dissolving it as a means of government. Known as the coup of 18th Brumaire (the date of the event in the new Republican calendar), the *coup d'état* was achieved by force of arms—Bonaparte at the head of 10,000 troops.

Although selected members of the old administration such as the Council of Five Hundred and the Directory were formed into new supporting bodies, true power was now shared by Sieyès, Ducos, and Bonaparte, who referred to themselves as "consuls." The coup was an immense gamble for Bonaparte, but with the support of the army and the majority of the citizens, he was able to ignore carping declarations that he was being a traitor to the Revolution and its principles.

A new Bonaparte had emerged. To all intents, he had become a military dictator. Although power was still theoretically shared with his fellow members of the triumvirate, Bonaparte became First Consul. Sieyès and Ducos were later replaced by the royalist Lebrun and the republican Cambacérès, but these secondary consuls held nothing more than titular authority in the new France. Bonaparte was the unopposed head of state.

Tired of war

To ensure his hold on power, the First Consul instigated a series of constitutional, administrative, and military reforms. He created the Consular Guard, charged with his own security, which eventually developed into the French Imperial Guard. The army was reorganized into a "proto-corps" (the term "corps" would not come into effect until after the 1800 campaign), and he ensured that all senior army commanders were loyal to the newly formed state.

His spectacular victory at Marengo in 1800 (*see following page*) was another gamble. A defeat would have led to his fall from grace, the loss of popular support, and his removal from power. But the victory ensured his position as unrivaled head of France. General Moreau, who defeated the Austrian army in Germany at Hohenlinden on December 2, 1800, was his only real military rival. These two defeats knocked Austria out of the war, and by mid-February 1802 only Britain remained at war with France.

Britain continued to fight alone, although the political waters were muddied by the erratic Czar Paul I of Russia, who organized the Baltic League to oppose both British and French initiatives in the region. This alliance was unacceptable to Britain, which relied on Baltic trade for much of the timbers required for ship-building and naval refurbishment. The Royal Navy responded with a spirited attack on the Danish fleet at Copenhagen (1801), removing the threat to British naval supremacy and disintegrating the league.

Britain's minor success did little to offset France's dominant military position in Europe, but the two nations were locked in stalemate. As the dominant maritime power, Britain was unable to do more than attack the fringes of French power in Europe. For her part, France was unable to break the maritime and economic stranglehold imposed by the Royal Navy in the Mediterranean, Atlantic, and Baltic.

The impasse was broken by a general war-weariness, particularly on the part of the British public. After prolonged negotiation, Britain and France signed the Peace of Amiens on March 27, 1802. The French Revolutionary Wars had ended, and the First Consul was left in peace to complete his transformation of the French state from a republic into a dictatorship.

Battle of Marengo

The young Bonaparte was never afraid to take an essential gamble, but his first act as First Consul was to stake everything on a spectacular defeat of the Austrians in Italy. It almost failed.

The Second Coalition of Britain, Austria, Russia, and other minor states had formed in December 1798, while Bonaparte was occupied in Egypt. This time, the allies co-ordinated their attacks on revolutionary France; an Anglo-Russian drive south from Holland, Austro-Russian forces pressing west through Italy, and an Austrian offensive along the Rhine, all undertaken simultaneously.

While the campaigns in Holland and on the Rhine achieved little, the Italian campaign was a resounding success. This was largely due to Russian Field Marshal Alexander Suvarov (1729–1800), an old but gifted commander, and a great advocate of the bayonet. With the help of Austrian allies, his small Russian force defeated two French armies in a brilliant campaign that culminated in an allied victory at the Battle of Novi (August 15, 1799). In a single campaign he ejected the French from Italy, overturning Bonaparte's achievements from the 1796–7 campaign. A jealous czar recalled him, and although his old army was defeated at Zurich (September 25–26, 1799), the strategic situation remained bleak for the French.

Following his appointment as First Consul in

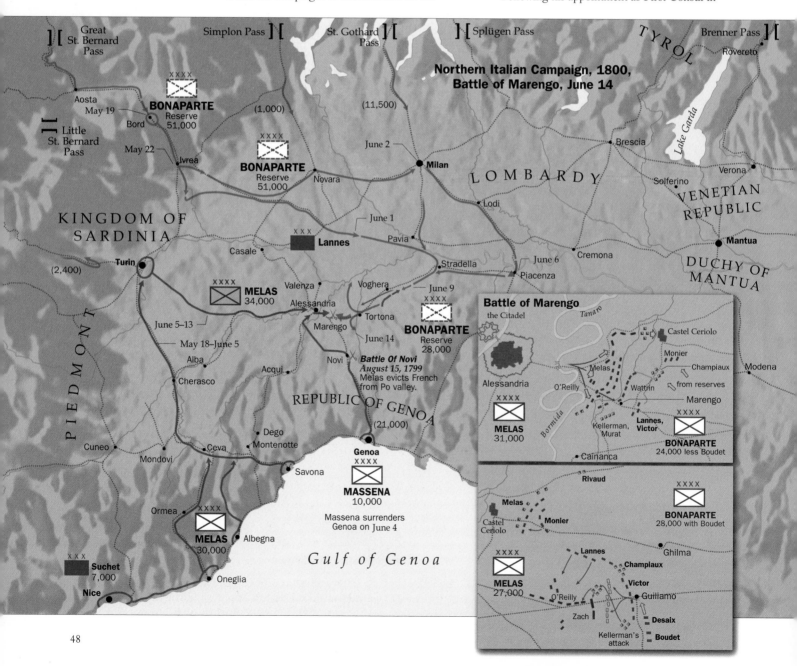

November 1799, Bonaparte set about redressing the balance. He tried to restore morale in the French Army of Italy, and created a new Army of the Reserve based in Dijon. He decided that in the coming campaign, Italy would be the decisive theater.

The Army of Italy contained two divisions; those of General Massena near Genoa and General Suchet near Nice. The aggressive Austrian commander General Michael Melas occupied a central position near Turin. Bonaparte's plan was for Massena to pin the bulk of Melas's army, while the Army of the Reserve marched southeast through the Alps to enter Italy behind the Austrians. The plan went awry when Massena was forced to surrender Genoa on June 4, leaving Bonaparte to face Melas alone.

Saved by Desaix and Kellerman

During May, Bonaparte's 51,000 troops marched through the snow-filled Alpine passes. This bold undertaking paid off, and by early June Bonaparte was in the Po valley. Melas had no option but to turn northward to fight. By June 13 the two armies lay close to each other, in the flat lands east of Alessandria.

Early in the morning of June 14, 1800, several columns of Austrian troops crossed the Bormida river to attack the isolated French force to the east. Bonaparte's army was scattered, giving the Austrians an opportunity to defeat their enemy in detail. General O'Reilly's column clashed with General Victor's division near Marengo village around 10am. Victor was supported by French cavalry led by

Brigadier Kellerman (son of the general who fought in the Battle of Valmy), who helped stave off disaster by launching charges to slow the attackers.

More Austrian columns entered the fight, and the French began to give ground. Bonaparte still thought the Austrian attack was a diversion, and refused to march reinforcements "to the sound of the guns." Disaster was averted by the arrival of General Lannes' division, but the French still lacked the strength to halt the Austrians. When Lannes was outflanked to the north by two more Austrian columns, the French fell back even further. By noon it looked as if they would be crushed, having retreated over three miles.

Lannes was saved by Bonaparte's realization that Victor and Lannes faced the main Austrian army, not just a diversionary force. He recalled all of his scattered divisions, throwing them piecemeal into the fight as they arrived. Just when defeat seemed certain, the divisions of generals Desaix and Boudet reinforced the French. These reinforcements turned the tide of battle. Although Desaix was killed during the counterattack, Austrian momentum was halted. Another cavalry charge by Kellermann turned stalemate into victory, and within an hour the Austrians were in full retreat.

The victory at Marengo led to Austria's retreat from Italy, and peace was secured at the Treaty of Luneville (February 1801). Once more, Bonaparte had emerged from a disaster with an enhanced reputation, and consolidated his grip on France.

An engraving depicts the Battle of Marengo, fought on a rolling plain outside Alessandria.

Louis Desaix (1768–1800) and François-Etienne Kellerman (1770–1835), whose actions turned the tide of battle.

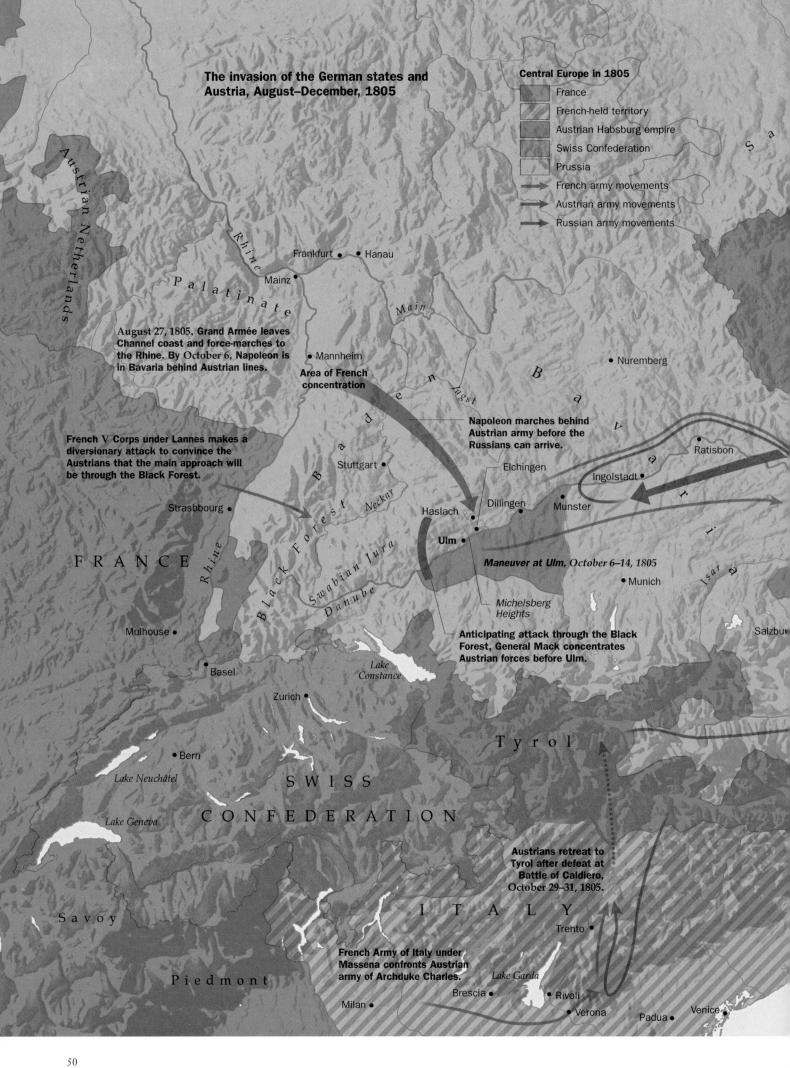

The invasion of the German states and
Austria, August–December, 1805

Central Europe in 1805
- France
- French-held territory
- Austrian Habsburg empire
- Swiss Confederation
- Prussia
- → French army movements
- → Austrian army movements
- → Russian army movements

Austrian Netherlands

Frankfurt • • Hanau

Palatinate

• Mainz

Rhine

Main

**August 27, 1805, Grand Armée leaves
Channel coast and force-marches to
the Rhine. By October 6, Napoleon is
in Bavaria behind Austrian lines.**

• Mannheim

**Area of French
concentration**

Jagst

• Nuremberg

**Napoleon marches behind
Austrian army before the
Russians can arrive.**

B a v a r i a

• Ratisbon

**French V Corps under Lannes makes a
diversionary attack to convince the
Austrians that the main approach will
be through the Black Forest.**

Stuttgart •

B a d e n

Elchingen

Ingolstadt •

• Strasbbourg

Neckar

Haslach

Dillingen •

• Munster

Rhine

F R A N C E

Black Forest

Swabian Jura

Ulm •

Maneuver at Ulm, *October 6–14, 1805*

Isar

• Munich

Danube

*Michelsberg
Heights*

Salzbu

• Mulhouse

**Anticipating attack through the Black
Forest, General Mack concentrates
Austrian forces before Ulm.**

• Basel

*Lake
Constance*

Zurich •

• Bern

Lake Neuchâtel

T y r o l

Lake Geneva

S W I S S

C O N F E D E R A T I O N

**Austrians retreat to
Tyrol after defeat at
Battle of Caldiero,
October 29–31, 1805.**

Savoy

I T A L Y

Trento •

**French Army of Italy under
Massena confronts Austrian
army of Archduke Charles.**

Lake Garda

Piedmont

Brescia •

• Rivoli

Milan •

• Verona

Padua •

Venice •

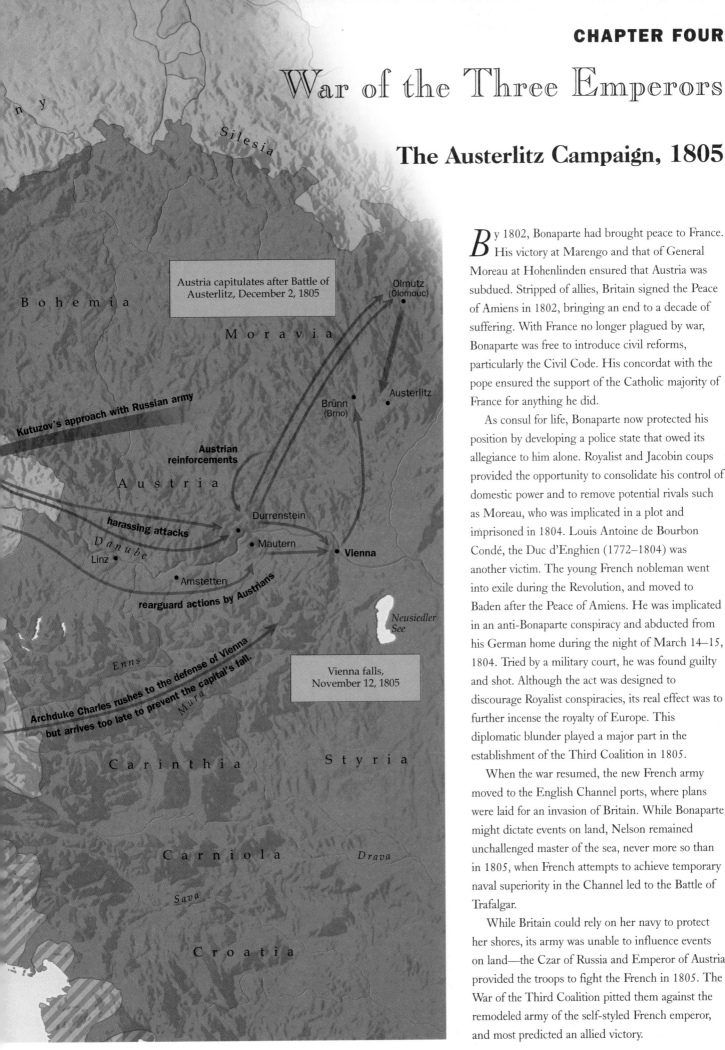

CHAPTER FOUR

War of the Three Emperors

The Austerlitz Campaign, 1805

Silesia

Bohemia

Moravia

Austria capitulates after Battle of
Austerlitz, December 2, 1805

Olmutz
(Olomouc)

Austerlitz

Kutuzov's approach with Russian army

Brünn
(Brno)

Austrian
reinforcements

Austria

Durrenstein

harassing attacks

Danube

Mautern

Linz

Vienna

Amstetten

rearguard actions by Austrians

Neusiedler
See

Vienna falls,
November 12, 1805

Enns

Archduke Charles rushes to the defense of Vienna
but arrives too late to prevent the capital's fall.

Mura

Carinthia

Styria

Carniola

Drava

Sava

Croatia

*B*y 1802, Bonaparte had brought peace to France. His victory at Marengo and that of General Moreau at Hohenlinden ensured that Austria was subdued. Stripped of allies, Britain signed the Peace of Amiens in 1802, bringing an end to a decade of suffering. With France no longer plagued by war, Bonaparte was free to introduce civil reforms, particularly the Civil Code. His concordat with the pope ensured the support of the Catholic majority of France for anything he did.

As consul for life, Bonaparte now protected his position by developing a police state that owed its allegiance to him alone. Royalist and Jacobin coups provided the opportunity to consolidate his control of domestic power and to remove potential rivals such as Moreau, who was implicated in a plot and imprisoned in 1804. Louis Antoine de Bourbon Condé, the Duc d'Enghien (1772–1804) was another victim. The young French nobleman went into exile during the Revolution, and moved to Baden after the Peace of Amiens. He was implicated in an anti-Bonaparte conspiracy and abducted from his German home during the night of March 14–15, 1804. Tried by a military court, he was found guilty and shot. Although the act was designed to discourage Royalist conspiracies, its real effect was to further incense the royalty of Europe. This diplomatic blunder played a major part in the establishment of the Third Coalition in 1805.

When the war resumed, the new French army moved to the English Channel ports, where plans were laid for an invasion of Britain. While Bonaparte might dictate events on land, Nelson remained unchallenged master of the sea, never more so than in 1805, when French attempts to achieve temporary naval superiority in the Channel led to the Battle of Trafalgar.

While Britain could rely on her navy to protect her shores, its army was unable to influence events on land—the Czar of Russia and Emperor of Austria provided the troops to fight the French in 1805. The War of the Third Coalition pitted them against the remodeled army of the self-styled French emperor, and most predicted an allied victory.

Emperor Napoleon

With methods reminiscent of Julius Caesar's almost 1900 years before him, Bonaparte persuaded others to shower him with the offices of government. In less than two years he moved from general to absolute ruler.

Contemporary engraving showing the procession for Napoleon's coronation, which took place in Paris on December 2, 1804.

With the end of the French Revolutionary War in 1802, Bonaparte was the undisputed leader of France. While in theory he shared power with Jean-Jacques Régis de Cambacérès (Second Consul from 1799) and Charles François Lebrun (Third Consul from 1799), in reality Napoleon controlled the French state. Ironically, both men remained loyal to Bonaparte throughout their lives, serving as court administrators and legal advisors.

The first triumvirate of consuls consisted of "Brumaire" conspirators Pierre-Roger Ducos and Emmanuel-Joseph Sieyès, and Bonaparte. Both late revolutionary figures voted for the execution of Louis XVI and served as members of the Directoire. They represented the spirit of the Revolution, and although their political manipulation placed Bonaparte among the leading men in France, it also threatened the stability of his grip on power. He managed to secure their replacement by the more malleable Cambacérès and Lebrun.

The consulate was formalized under the Constitution of Year VIII, on December 14, 1799, but Bonaparte had little intention of sharing power, or even handing over control to a successor. His victory at Marengo in 1800 and the collapse of the Second Coalition gave Bonaparte the opportunity he needed. Already First Consul, he worked to limit the influence of rival military commanders and increase his hold on power. Following the Peace of

Amiens, this power had almost become absolute, and in May 1802 his "acceptance" of the position of (First) Consul for Life was little more than tacit recognition of the political situation.

A national plebiscite held three months later confirmed his selection by an overwhelming majority. The victor of Rivoli, the pyramids, and Marengo was the virtual monarch of a France, which was rapidly abandoning its Revolutionary principles. The plebiscite also included the approval of a special constitutional amendment drafted by Cambacérès. Consul Bonaparte was given the right to nominate his own successor. Former joint consul Cambacérès was later rewarded with the title Duke of Parma, President of the Senate, and Arch Chancellor of the Empire.

A self-crowning ceremony

It took just over 20 months to prepare the public for this amazing change in their political course. Bonaparte was seen as the peacemaker, but not everyone was happy with this drift toward absolutism, and attempts were made against his life by Jacobin and Royalist sympathizers. These plots were manna from heaven for Bonaparte, who preyed on French fears that his death would leave a dangerous political vacuum.

More power was devolved to him, including a more powerful state police service, the establishment of a Consular Guard, and restrictions on the freedom of the press. The execution of the Duc d'Enghien was simply the most notorious in a number of actions by Bonaparte to ensure the stability of his position. While the French population was aware of these activities, most were also impressed by his civic and military reforms.

Pressure was exerted on the senate to nominate Bonaparte to be emperor and, on May 18, 1804 the legislation was formally passed, subject to ratification by plebiscite, held on November 6. The public apparently gave overwhelming support for the creation of an imperial form of government, but as it was Bonaparte's officials who counted the votes, any other result was probably unlikely. France had turned full circle, and the days of the Revolution were officially over.

On December 2, 1804, the First Consul ascended the steps of the throne as Bonaparte, but walked down again as Napoleon I, Emperor of France. In a lavish civic coronation he placed the imperial crown on his own head before crowning his wife Josephine as his empress. Officially, France was delighted with its new-found order, but the rest of Europe was horrified that a "jumped-up" Corsican general could elevate himself above the crowned heads of Europe. To the French, he became *l'Empereur*; to the British and their allies, he remained General Bonaparte.

François Le Villain's semi-comic portrait of Napoleon shows him preparing to place the crown on his own head. The symbolism of this arrogant ceremony was not lost on the monarchs of Europe.

The Grande Armée

In 1802, Napoleon created the instrument that would make him the Master of Europe. The Grande Armée's centralized military structure permitted the French to campaign efficiently and, when needed, to concentrate its force to achieve victory.

*C*onsul Napoleon Bonaparte used the Peace of Amiens to overhaul the French army. At Marengo the army had faced defeat due to poor co-ordination between its various divisions. Napoleon proposed permanent higher formations, an innovation first considered by French reformer Marshal Broglie in 1761.

French military efficiency had been reduced by old rivalries between armies and commanders, and the differences between arms of the service. The size of armies in the field had increased during the Revolutionary Wars, and this trend continued, further hindering control and administration. The introduction

of a permanent corps system was the best way to solve these problems and forge the army into a tool suited to Napoleon's style of command. Due to his reformative zeal and command of detail, this process was completed within three years. The French army that marched off to war in 1805 was the best organized and most efficient military force in Europe.

The cornerstone of the Grande Armée was the *corps d'armée*. The genius of the corps system was that each was a self-contained army of its own, with formations ranging between 12,000 and 40,000 men. Each had its own staff officers, engineering units, supply and transport cadres, light cavalry regiments, and artillery batteries. In military terms, this was indeed a revolutionary concept. It was the forerunner of the armies of the 20th century, and is still pretty much the way things are organized today.

Each of the seven corps was commanded by a trusted general, men who would soon be elevated to the rank of Marshal of France—18 marshals were created in 1804, and eight more joined during the Napoleonic Wars. In most cases, a corps consisted of at least two divisions, which in turn were divided into two or more brigades. Each brigade contained three or more infantry battalions, or at least two cavalry

Europe's new model army. Elements of the Imperial Guard engage in maneuvers before Napoleon.

regiments. The corps had a pyramidal command structure, the marshal supervising the actions of his immediate subordinates, and so on down the line to the battalion commanders. The key was flexibility. A single corps could operate independently from the rest of the army, and several could be concentrated with relative ease, as the strategic situation demanded.

The army within the Armée

Napoleon kept three formations outside the corps structure. The heavy cavalry reserve was to be unleashed only at a decisive moment on the battlefield. Similarly, the army artillery reserve permitted the concentration of massed (grand) batteries of guns. Napoleon's maxim that "It is with cannon that one makes war" was demonstrated in many of the battles that followed. Finally, the newly created Imperial Guard comprised elite soldiers who protected the emperor. Within the Imperial Guard, a hand-picked regiment of veterans, called the Old Guard, became the most pretisgious unit. More regiments were added to the Imperial Guard, which soon became an army within the army. These included the Young Guard, Guard Cavalry (*Chasseurs* and *Grenadiers à Cheval*), Guard Artillery, Guard Marines, and even a squadron of Egyptian mamluks.

However, there was a weakness in Napoleon's thinking: logistics. Rooted in its Revolutionary Army beginnings and reinforced by the success of Napoleon's Italian campaigns, the French avoided fixed supply depots and artillery magazines, living off the land instead and foraging for provisions as it marched. This somewhat medieval approach was not a significant problem when forces numbered less than 50,000, but by the time of the Austerlitz campaign the Grande Armée had swelled to three times this size. An army this huge could strip a region of food in no time. Napoleon came increasingly to rely on fixed supply magazines, but the army still had to augment its food supplies by foraging, which inevitably caused resentment, particularly in Spain (*see Chapter Seven*).

Napoleon stood at the tip of the Grande Armée's pyramid together with his Chief of Staff, Marshal Berthier. While on campaign, Napoleon devised the strategy and Berthier set the army in motion. While the *corps d'armée* system made it far easier to move large groupings of men, Napoleon still relied on his staff to carry out his orders, which demanded much of communications. This involved a string of high-ranking messengers who ensured everything worked as smoothly as possible. During the Austerlitz campaign, the Grande Armée and the *corps d'armée* systems worked perfectly, helping Napoleon's first imperial campaign toward success. But in 1805, the new military machine's first objective lay in the opposite direction—Britain.

Detail of an engraving depicting Napoleon and General (later Marshal) Berthier during the Battle of Marengo in 1800.

Invasion of England

In 1805, Napoleon and the Grande Armée stood on the shores of the Channel, waiting for the opportunity to launch the much-delayed invasion of England. Only the Royal Navy stood between them and their goal.

In England, newspapers provided alarming and futuristic notions of what form a French invasion might take.

Napoleon's was not the first French attempt to invade the British Isles. In December 1796 an invasion of Ireland had been thwarted by bad weather and indifferent leadership. A second invasion plan drawn up in 1798 was shelved after Napoleon toured the Channel ports, while the Royal Navy drove off a secondary Irish invasion fleet. A new fleet was gathered in 1801, but the project abandoned after the Peace of Amiens in 1802. This, however, was little more than a temporary respite, and war broke out again in May 1803. Napoleon determined to carry out the invasion of his last effective European enemy. During the remainder of 1803 and 1804, an army of 146,862 men and 9,059 horses was gathered in camps outside the Channel ports. Meanwhile, a new invasion flotilla was readied: 2,293 large gunboats, unarmed transport vessels, and *prames* (flat-bottomed gunboats), crewed by 16,783 sailors. The latter type of vessel was designed to carry a single gun (although some carried three or four) and could transport a hundred men.

All of France supported the project; each village or small town sponsored a *prame*, while larger communities provided funds for the construction of bigger warships. Built on any piece of water with a depth of over three feet, these invasion craft gathered in the Channel ports using France's river network. Even Paris became a shipyard port. Two slips were built there and used to produce a string of gunboats. In Antwerp (or Anvers) on the Scheldt estuary, keels were laid for frigates and ships-of-the-line. The dockyards of Brest, Lorient, Rochefort, and Toulon also teemed with newfound energy, under the guidance of Napoleon and his ministers.

Dividing the grand plan

In late 1804, an inspection of the seven Channel ports of Etaples, Boulogne, Vimereux, Ambleteuse, Calais, Dunkirk, and Ostend showed that all was ready. There were 578 gunboats and *prames* in Boulogne alone, while another 526 transports crowded the harbor.

During this period, the Royal Navy carried out a series of harassing coastal raids, cutting-out expeditions, and hostile patrols designed to prevent the invasion build-up. It was clear to Napoleon that the armada would fail without adequate naval flank protection. To reinforce the smaller Channel fleet, he

The flotilla was organized into six "grand divisions." The first (designated the left wing) was stationed at Etaples and earmarked to carry the troops of Marshal Ney's corps, camped nearby in Montreuil. The second and third divisions (the left and right divisions of the central flotilla) were based in Boulogne and created to transport Marshal Soult's troops, whose camps surrounded the port. The fourth grand division (designated the right wing), based in Vimereux, was for Marshal Lannes' corps, which included most of the invasion force's light infantry and grenadiers, grouped into their specialist formations. The Franco-Batavian (Dutch) division assembled at Ambleteuse. This fifth flotilla was earmarked to transport the troops of Marshal Davout. Finally, the sixth (or reserve) grand division, lying in the port of Calais, was to transport the cavalry, plus a supporting Italian division of infantry.

ordered those of the Mediterranean and his newfound Spanish allies to sail for the Atlantic and to pass into the Channel. But Britannia ruled the waves, and the French naval maneuvers only precipitated the Battle of Trafalgar.

France's defeat at Trafalgar meant that an invasion of England was no longer practicable. As American naval historian Alfred Mahan put it, "Those far-distant, storm-beaten ships upon which the Grand Army never looked, stood between it and the domination of the world." The Grande Armée packed its transports and left the Channel ports to march east, to do battle with the combined armies of Austria and Russia. Although the Battle of Austerlitz would ensure that Napoleon became Master of Europe on land, he had lost the campaign for naval supremacy. The abandoned invasion flotilla simply rotted away at its moorings.

The cartoon "The Consequences of a Successful Invasion" shows French soldiers dominating an enslaved English population.

Expecting Every Man to do His Duty

The Battle of Trafalgar was the most decisive naval engagement of the age of fighting sail. Vice Admiral Horatio Nelson's victory guaranteed his posthumous national hero status and ensured Britain's survival in the climactic battle with France.

Above: Admirals Pierre Charles Villeneuve and Federico Carlos Gravina.

Below: "Battle of Trafalgar" as depicted in 1816 by L. Whitcombe and J. Jenkins.

*I*n February 1805, Napoleon ordered his navy to concentrate in the Channel to support the invasion of Britain. The operation involved the French fleets of admirals Villeneuve and Ganteaume, and the Spanish fleet of Admiral Gravina. Villeneuve was ordered to rendezvous with the Spanish, then meet Ganteaume's fleet in the West Indies before sailing toward the Channel. The combined fleet would then sail to the Channel. The plan fell apart immediately.

In late March, Villeneuve and Gravina sailed to the West Indies, but with Nelson in pursuit. When Villeneuve learned that Ganteaume's ships were still in port at Brest, he returned to Spain. Again, Nelson followed close behind. By August the allied fleets were at anchor in Cadiz harbor, effectively hemmed in by the Royal Navy. After a brief visit to England in September, Nelson sailed toward Cadiz with 27 ships-of-the-line.

Villeneuve was ordered to Toulon and sailed in his flagship *Bucentaure* on October 19, with 33 ships-of-the-line (18 French, 15 Spanish), while Admiral Gravina commanded the Spanish from the *Principe de Asturias*. By dawn on October 21, the British fleet sighted the allies and closed as quickly as the light winds allowed.

Nelson planned to form his fleet into two columns, approach the Franco-Spanish fleet at right angles, then cut its line. He told his captains: "It is annihilation that the country wants, and not merely a splendid victory." He led the first column of 12 ships-of-the-line in his flagship *Victory*, while Vice Admiral Collingwood in *The Royal Sovereign* led the second column of 15 ships.

At 11.45am, Nelson ordered a signal to be hoisted. Shortly before noon, the Spanish *Santa Ana* and the French *Fougueux* opened fire on *The Royal Sovereign*. Collingwood's flagship was battered but held its course, passing between the two allied ships before delivering a broadside on both. It then turned to fight the *Santa Ana*. The *Belleisle* and *Mars* were next to pierce the line, and then turned north to engage the allied center. The fight soon devolved into a brutal close-range mêlée between two evenly matched groups.

A historic victory

To the north, at about 12.30pm, Nelson's *Victory* came under fire from the Spanish *Santissima Trinidad* and Villeneuve's flagship *Bucentaure*, supported by the *Redoutable*. Once *Victory* passed between the enemy ships it turned to starboard to fight the *Redoutable*.

For the rest of the battle, the *Victory* lay with a French ship on either side. Behind her came HMS *Téméraire*, which wedged between the *Redoutable* and *Fougueux*. The rest of the column followed on behind, splitting the allied fleet at two points. Captain Lucas of the *Redoutable* sent marksmen into the rigging to fire down onto the deck of the *Victory*. Shortly after 1.15pm, a sharpshooter hit Nelson as he paced his quarterdeck. The wound was mortal, passing through his shoulder and down through his body, and he was taken below.

On deck, both the *Victory* and *Redoutable* were battered, but the French ship was sinking. On the other side of *Victory*, Villeneuve's *Bucentaure* had been battered by the *Britannia* and surrendered soon after 3pm. The allied vanguard failed to come to the assistance of the center, since too many British ships blocked the way. Its commander therefore ordered a retreat to Cadiz, leaving the rest of the allied fleet to its fate.

The fighting was drawing to a close. The *Santa Ana* surrendered to Collingwood at 2.30pm, followed by the remainder of the rearguard. Shortly before he died at 4.30pm, Nelson was told that he had won a brilliant victory. Eighteen ships-of-the-line were captured or destroyed, Villeneuve was a prisoner, and Gravina seriously wounded. Ten days later, four allied ships that had escaped the fighting were captured as they made their way home.

With his entire force of fighting ships lost in a single day, Napoleon's dreams of conquering Britain had been dashed. Nelson's death was a severe blow to the British, but his last and greatest victory established him as the country's most celebrated naval commander. By the complete annihilation of the French fleet (and most of the Spanish), Nelson secured the supremacy of British seapower during the Napoleonic Wars.

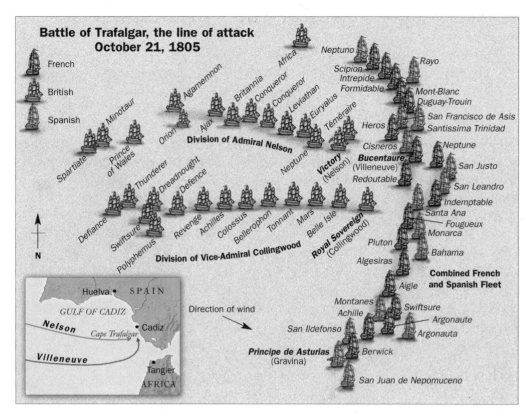

Battle of Trafalgar, the line of attack
October 21, 1805

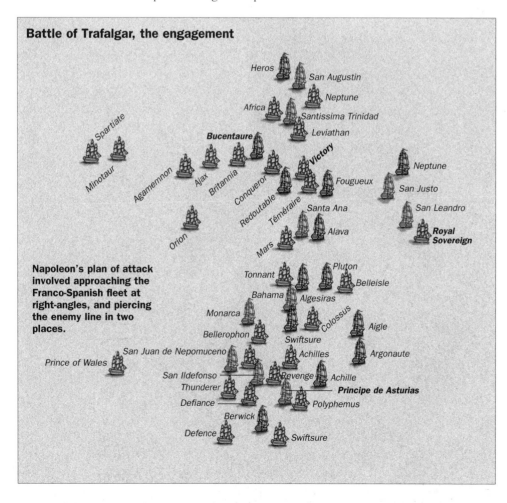

Battle of Trafalgar, the engagement

Napoleon's plan of attack involved approaching the Franco-Spanish fleet at right-angles, and piercing the enemy line in two places.

The Strategic Situation in 1805

After the Peace of Amiens was broken, Britain was prepared to go to any lengths to form a workable anti-French coalition. While the Royal Navy guarded the Channel against a French invasion, diplomats and bankers helped raise a new continental army.

*T*o the established monarchs of Europe, the fact that the French had executed their king was bad enough; to have a French general crown himself "emperor" was insufferable. Napoleon's heavy-handed policy in central Europe made him more enemies, propelling potential allies into the British camp.

At this time, there was no unified German nation. For centuries, Austria had dominated the patchwork of German states known as the Holy Roman Empire. The old adage that it was neither holy, Roman, nor an empire is largely true, but Emperor Francis I of Austria continued to exert at least partial control over this loose alliance until the aftermath of

the Treaty of Lunéville in February 1801. From that point, French diplomatic and military pressure forced many of the larger German states, such as Bavaria, Saxony, and Württemberg, to press for a restoration of lost territories at the expense of smaller states.

The result was the collapse of the Holy Roman Empire and a reorganization of the smaller German states. Many were absorbed into larger neighbors, and the Confederation of the Rhine was created to replace the old imperial grouping. France occupied the British-allied northern state of Hanover and it lost its independence completely. The French-dominated confederation turned most of Germany into a patchwork of client states, dominated by Bavaria and Württemberg. This did little to improve relations between France and Austria.

Napoleon ensured control over the Italian peninsula by turning the Northern Italian Cisalpine Republic into the Kingdom of Italy, and appointed his stepson, Prince Eugène de Beauharnais, to be the kingdom's first viceroy. While British diplomats and financial incentives did much to encourage a new anti-French

coalition, Napoleon himself was largely responsible for the resurgence of opposition to French policies.

Turning to target France

Britain's staunch anti-French stance was encouraged by the efforts of William Pitt (1759–1806), who opposed French expansionism vigorously. In 1804, when he became Prime Minister for a second time (having resigned as a result of George III's refusal to accept Catholic emancipation), he unleashed the diplomatic initiative that led to the formation of the Third Coalition.

When the war resumed, the Royal Navy returned to blockade the French coast, and secret negotiations took place between London, St. Petersburg, and Vienna. Czar Alexander I was already inclined to renew his war with France after the Duc d'Enghien incident (*see page 51*). In Austria, Francis I assumed the honorary title of emperor, following the dissolution of the Holy Roman Empire. He wanted to restore his position in Germany, while his people wanted to avenge the humiliation inflicted upon them at Rivoli and Marengo. Both countries agreed to join the Third Coalition. Also horrified by the murder of the Duc d'Enghien, King Gustavus IV of Sweden overruled his ministers—who counseled a neutral policy—and joined the coalition.

While Austria provided the bulk of the land forces, Russia sent another 20,000 men, and Britain provided financial backing, placing £12.5 million (approximately $20 million, a colossal amount at the time) at the disposal of the allies. By summer 1804, the new battle lines were set.

The allies devised an ambitious scheme. An Austro-Russian army under General Mack would move into France from Bavaria. A secondary offensive would sweep through northern Italy from the Tyrol, while an Anglo-Neapolitan invasion of southern Italy would divert French attention from the main offensive. A third offensive was planned in the Baltic, where a small Anglo-Swedish army would land on the north German coast to incite a rebellion among the northern states in the Confederation of the Rhine. The allies hoped that, with success, Prussia would join the Coalition.

With the loss of his main naval force at Trafalgar and faced with this degree of opposition, Napoleon had little choice but to abandon the invasion of England. He may even have been relieved. Faced with the uncertainties of a costly invasion across waters now firmly in British hands, a tangible enemy on land presented much better opportunities for success. With his newly reorganized Grande Armée, Napoleon made a dramatic about-face and led his troops across Europe with a speed that dumbfounded his relatively pedestrian opponents.

The main protagonists in the coming war. **Facing above:** Francis II (1768–1835) is the last Holy Roman Emperor (r.1792–1806), and also Francis I of Austria (r.1804–35). In 1810 he married his daughter Marie-Louise to Napoleon. **Facing below:** Czar Alexander I of Russia. **Above:** A British political cartoon depicts William Pitt (left) and Napoleon dividing up the globe. The captions reads: "The plum-pudding in danger, or State Epicures taking un Petit Souper, the great Globe itself and all which it inherits is too small to satisfy such unsatiable appetites."

Maneuver at Ulm

An Austrian army moved into Bavaria, while three columns of Russian troops headed through eastern Europe toward the French border. In the campaign that followed, Napoleon's Grande Armée moved with such speed they seemed to leave their opponents standing.

On August 27, 1805, the Grande Armée left its encampments on the Channel coast and headed eastward to meet the allied threat. Some 40,000 Russians were poised to invade northern Germany, while 100,000 Austrians stood on the borders of Italy. To Napoleon, these were secondary threats, and the prospect of allied diversionary raids on the Baltic and Mediterranean coasts did little to influence his strategy.

The main enemy thrust was in Bavaria, where an Austrian army of 89,000 men commanded by Archduke Ferdinand was already in the field. It would take another two months for General Kutuzov's Russian army of 55,000 men to reach Bavaria and influence the campaign. Napoleon needed to strike quickly before the Austrian army in southern Germany was reinforced. Prussia remained uncertain of what

stance to take, so to prevent its involvement, Napoleon handed over Hanover to bribe King Frederick Wilhelm III—an action with later consequences.

Most allied military analysts considered it unlikely that the Grande Armée could intervene in Bavaria before the arrival of Kutuzov in mid-October. This proved to be a fatal miscalculation. The entire Grande Armée of seven corps plus the Imperial Guard and the reserve artillery force-marched east along pre-assigned roads, their movement screened by six divisions of reserve cavalry under the command of Marshal Murat.

A diversion by Marshal Lannes's V Corps was made to convince the Austrians that the French would approach through the Black Forest. Instead, Napoleon planned to mass the bulk of his 200,000 men along the Rhine south of Mannheim, then advanced east through Baden and Swabia before descending into Bavaria behind the Austrian army.

Loss of a force

General Karl Mack took over command of the Austrian army and concentrated his forces near the city of Ulm, where it could cover both sides of the

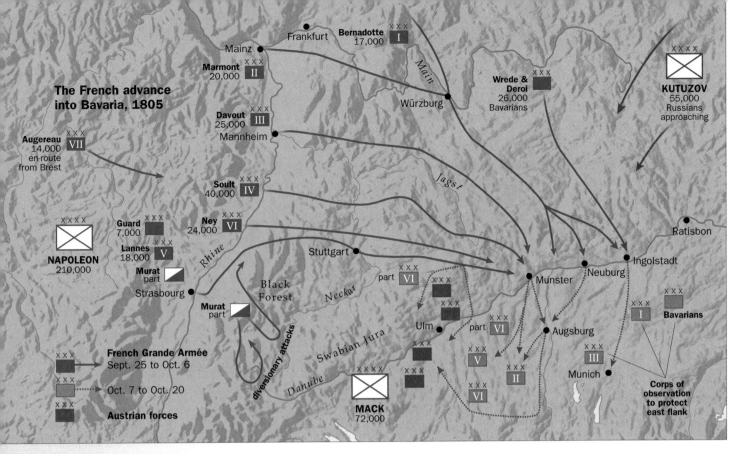

The French advance into Bavaria, 1805

Frankfurt

Mainz

Bernadotte
17,000 — I

Marmont
20,000 — II

Davout
25,000 — III
Mannheim

Augereau
14,000
en-route
from Brest — VII

Soult
40,000 — IV

Guard
7,000

Ney
24,000 — VI

NAPOLEON
210,000

Lannes
18,000 — V

Murat
part

Strasbourg

Murat
part

Rhine

Black
Forest

Neckar

Stuttgart

Main

Würzburg

Wrede & Deroi
26,000
Bavarians

KUTUZOV
55,000
Russians
approaching

Jagst

Ratisbon

Munster

Neuburg

Ingolstadt

part — VI

Ulm

part — VI

Augsburg

I

Bavarians

III

Munich

Corps of
observation
to protect
east flank

V

II

VI

diversionary attacks

Swabian Jura

Danube

MACK
72,000

French Grande Armée
Sept. 25 to Oct. 6

Oct. 7 to Oct. 20

Austrian forces

Danube and the approaches through the Black Forest. On October 6, 1805, the Austrian commander was horrified to discover French units had reached the Danube to the east. Napoleon's strategy had paid off, and he now sat between the forces of Mack and Kutuzov, and could now concentrate on defeating the Austrians well before the Russians arrived.

The French continued their encirclement of Ulm

and thwarted an Austrian attempt to break out to the northeast on October 11–14. Archduke Ferdinand escaped from the city with his escort, leaving Mack to surrender his doomed army of 23,500 men. This classic example of maneuver in the rear of the enemy had saved France with hardly a shot being fired. As one veteran put it, "The Emperor makes war not with our arms but with our legs." Napoleon was now free to turn on the Russians and the Austrians to the east.

Much further south, Marshal Massena faced Archduke Charles in Italy. At the Battle of Caldiero (October 29–31) the Austrians were defeated and forced to retire into the Tyrol. With the two main Austrian forces captured or in full retreat, Napoleon pressed on along the Danube toward Vienna. It was up to the Russians to turn disaster into victory.

Despite the pleas of Francis I, General Kutuzov decided not to defend Vienna, but crossed to the north bank of the Danube in an attempt to link up with a column of Russian and Austrian reinforcements. Throughout November Kutuzov retreated along the river toward the east, fighting off the French columns that tried to delay him.

Vienna fell to the advancing French on November 12, but a skilled rearguard action by Kutuzov and his subordinate General Bagration bought time for the allies to regroup. A week after the city fell, a combined Austro-Russian force of 86,000 gathered at Olmütz, where Czar Alexander I arrived to assume command. There would be no more retreat. This time, the allies were eager to fight, and the army marched southward, toward the advancing French.

The capitulation of Ulm (1805). Napoleon seated on his horse watches as Mack's army surrenders to the French outside the Bavarian city of Ulm in October 1805. The defeat left Vienna open to capture by the French.

General Karl Freiherr von Leiberich Mack (1752–1828) was first condemned to death by the Habsburgs for his failure at Ulm, but then reprieved and imprisoned until 1809.

Battle of Austerlitz

The Battle of Austerlitz has been described as Napoleon's greatest triumph. Fought on a cold December day in 1805, it involved deception, massed attacks, and, ultimately, the virtual destruction of the allied army.

*I*n late November 1805, Napoleon gathered most of his army near Brünn, 60 miles north of Vienna, while his Austro-Russian opponents were camped to the northeast, outside Olmütz. After detaching troops to guard Vienna and his long lines of communication along the Danube, Napoleon could only muster 70,000 men, while the allies exceeded 85,000 combatants, and a second Austrian army under Archduke Charles lay to the south of Vienna. Napoleon needed to defeat his nearest foe or risk being caught between the two forces. And he calculated that one decisive victory should be sufficient to destroy the will of coalition members to continue the war.

Napoleon was in a position to choose where to fight this decisive battle. He selected an area of hills and woodland 14 miles east of Brünn. He wanted the enemy to mass its forces, then attack the troops of his front line. Once the enemy was pinned, he planned to sweep the rest of his army around against the enemy flank, rolling up the allied army from north to south.

Like a good chess player, Napoleon enticed his opponents into this trap. He proposed an armistice on November 27, and withdrew his screen of scouting troops in what was intended to be a display of indecision and weakness. He even abandoned the dominant terrain feature of the Pratzen Heights as part of the deception. The allies were convinced that the Grande Armée planned to retreat. Czar Alexander demanded that the allies attack before the French withdrew completely, and his generals came up with a plan that involved the simultaneous advance of several allied columns.

At 4am on December 2, 1805, the allied army rolled forward: 71,000 Russians and 15,000 Austrians, with three korps-sized formations in the front line. The bulk of the army (some 40,000 men) concentrated on the southern flank, where Buxhöwden's Russians faced Soult's IV Corps. In the center, General Kollowrath's mixed force occupied

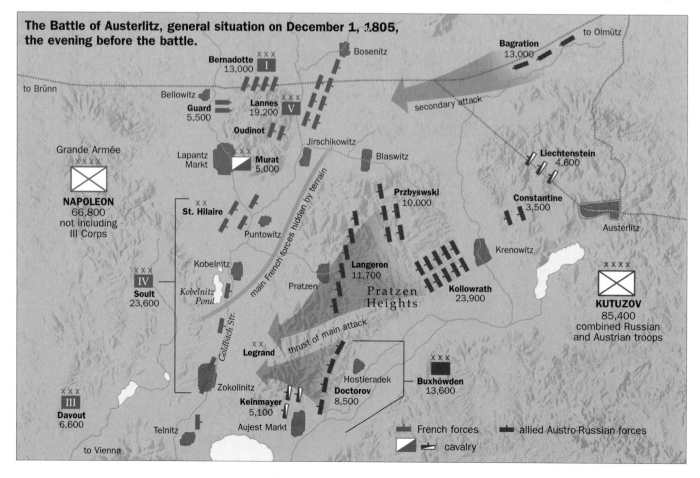

The Battle of Austerlitz, general situation on December 1, 1805, the evening before the battle.

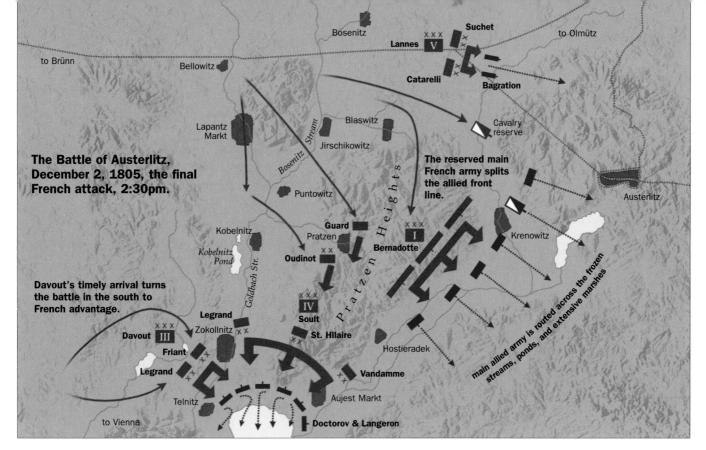

The Battle of Austerlitz, December 2, 1805, the final French attack, 2:30pm.

Davout's timely arrival turns the battle in the south to French advantage.

The reserved main French army splits the allied front line.

main allied army is routed across the frozen streams, ponds, and extensive marshes

the Pratzen Heights, supported by the Russian Guard. To the north, General Bagration commanded a Russian force that, along with the men to the south, was destined to attack Lannes' V Corps.

The sun of Austerlitz

Napoleon kept the bulk of his army in reserve, hidden by folds in the ground. The terrain also hampered the allied advance, and troops were bunched together by streams, small lakes, and woods. When Napoleon saw the allies advance obliquely from the Pratzen Heights toward his southern portion of this front line, he knew his deceptions had worked. With the bulk of the allied army pinned along the Goldbach stream to the south, its center was fatally weakened.

Soult bore the full brunt of the Austro-Russian advance, particularly in the southern section of his line, where the French were heavily outnumbered. Only the timely arrival of Marshal Davout's III Corps prevented a withdrawal on the French right flank. Somehow the line held, buying time for Napoleon to organize the counterattack.

At 8.30am, Napoleon ordered the northern portion of Soult's corps to advance against the weakened allied center on the Pratzen Heights. At that moment the sun broke through the clouds. By 9am Soult's men were in possession of the heights. A counterattack by the Russian Guard was met by the Imperial Guard and the cavalry reserve under Murat. Both formations had followed the advancing troops, and now held the Pratzen Heights

against all-comers, splitting the allied line in two.

Bernadotte's I Corps turned to face the trapped mass of allied troops to the south, pouring fire into their disorganized ranks. The allied left wing broke, and their retreat across the frozen lakes and marshes to the south became a panic-stricken rout. Thousands died as the frozen ice broke under the weight of men. By mid-afternoon only Bagration's Russians remained to face the French. His men retreated eastward from the field in good order, and by 4pm the fighting was over. France suffered 9,000 men killed and wounded, while allied losses were catastrophic: 16,000 casualties, and another 11,000 captured. Austria lay at the Napoleon's mercy, who dictated his own peace terms at the Treaty of Pressberg to a humiliated Francis I.

The meeting of two emperors: Napoleon meets Francis I of Austria on the field at Austerlitz after the French victory.

CHAPTER FIVE

Master of Europe

The Campaigns of 1806–7

Under the terms of the Treaty of Pressberg (September 26, 1805), Austria ceded Dalmatia and Istria to Napoleon's Italian allies and formally disbanded an already defunct Holy Roman Empire. With Austria neutralized in the east, Napoleon then secured his northwestern and southern frontiers by making his brother Louis king of Holland and his other brother Joseph king of Naples.

But trouble loomed in the northeast. With William Pitt's death, Napoleon saw a chance to secure a peace with the troublesome British, by offering to hand back to them the German state of Hanover. Unfortunately, this was the same bribe he had earlier offered to Prussia to stay neutral. The Prussian king, Frederick-Wilhelm III, was infuriated by this duplicity. But there was worse to come. Now, with Austria out of the picture and so less sure that he needed to placate the Prussians, Napoleon demanded that Prussia cede him the Swiss city of Neuchâtel, as well as other small parcels of Prussian land within the borders of the Confederation of the Rhine. As far as the Prussian king was concerned, France was meddling in German affairs, a political arena that had traditionally been dominated by Austria and Prussia. It seemed France was trying to replace Austria as champion of the western German states. After all, French troops occupied German cities from Westphalia to Bavaria.

Frederick-Wilhelm was encouraged in his new anti-French stance by his dominant and fervently anti-French wife, Louisa, who was described as "the only man in Prussia." Likewise, his advisers were dominated by a pro-war party and the military leaders—aged veterans of Frederick the Great—were adamant that the army was at the peak of its power. The king bowed to pressure and forged a secret alliance with Czar Alexander of Russia in July 1806.

While the Prussian army prepared for war, two large Russian armies gathered in Poland, earmarked for service on Prussian soil. Frederick-Wilhelm's troops advanced into blocking positions in Saxony and he issued an ultimatum to Napoleon on September 26, demanding that all French troops withdraw from German soil. The campaign for the control of Germany had begun.

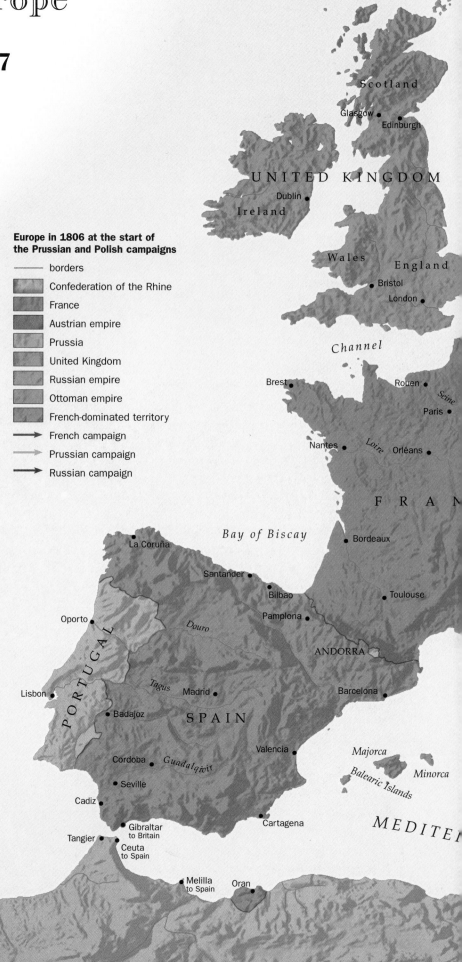

Europe in 1806 at the start of the Prussian and Polish campaigns

- —— borders
- Confederation of the Rhine
- France
- Austrian empire
- Prussia
- United Kingdom
- Russian empire
- Ottoman empire
- French-dominated territory
- → French campaign
- → Prussian campaign
- → Russian campaign

NORTH
SEA

Christiania

SWEDEN

Uppsala •

• Göteborg

DENMARK-NORWAY

• Copenhagen

Lübeck
Hamburg •
Bremen •

Amsterdam •

Holland

WESTPHALIA

...sels
Cologne •

Jena-Auerstädt
1806 ✕

Frankfurt •

Reims •

Mannheim •

Nancy •

...E

Geneva •

Lyon •

...vignon

Marseilles •

Toulon •

Corsica

Ajaccio •

Gulf of Bothnia

Helsingfors
(Helsinki) •

Reval
(Talinn) •

Estonia

• St. Petersburg

• Novgorod

Lake
Peipus

Gulf of Finland

BALTIC SEA

Stockholm •

Lake Vänern

Lake Vättern

Swedish
Pomerania

Eylau
1807

Pomerania

Danzig •

Königsberg •

East

Friedland
✕ *1807*

Prussia

• Riga

Western Dvina

Lithuania
and
Black Russia

• Smolensk

• Moscow

Berlin •

Brandenburg

Elbe

• Leipzig

SAXONY

Dresden •

PRUSSIA

Warsaw •

South Prussia

West Galicia

to Prussia, 1795

• Lublin

Vistula

Podlesia

RUSSIAN
EMPIRE

Silesia

Oder

• Prague

BOHEMIA

Moravia

Volhynia

• Krakow

Galicia and Lodomeria

• Kiev

Ukraine

Podolia

Rhine

Nuremberg •

Ratisbon •

Ulm •

Main

Danube

Austria

• Vienna

AUSTRIAN
EMPIRE

Bukovina

to Russia
1774

Bessarabia

Jedisan

Rhône

Bern •
SWISS
CONFEDERATION

BAVARIA

Munich •

Salzburg •

Styria

Carinthia

• Buda

Hungary

Moldavia

Transylvania

Sebastopol •

Tyrol

Piedmont

Turin •

• Milan

Mantua •

• Venice

Slavonia

Banat

Wallachia

• Bucharest

Danube

BLACK
SEA

...vignon

Genoa •

ITALY

Ligurian Sea

Florence •

Fano •

Tuscany

Elba

Papal
States

Rome •

Illyrian Provinces

Adriatic Sea

Herzegovina

Bosnia

Serbia

Bulgaria

Adrianople •

• Constantinople

*Tyrrhenian
Sea*

NAPLES

Naples •

Taranto •

Albania

MONTENEGRO

OTTOMAN

Rumelia

Thessalonica •

...RANEAN SEA

Sardinia

Caligari •

SICILY

Palermo •

Messina •

Syracuse •

Malta

Ionian islands
to France 1807

AEGEAN SEA

Athens •

Morea

EMPIRE

Sea of Crete

Crete

Rhodes

67

The Prussian Army

Although the Prussian army of 1806 was a powerful presence, it had changed little since the time of Frederick the Great half a century earlier. When it faced Napoleon's modern Grande Armée, it proved to be hopelessly outdated.

King Frederick-Wilhelm III at the Berlin Christmas Market with Queen Louisa, from an illustration of c.1810.

When France and Prussia went to war in September 1806, King Frederick-Wilhelm III of Prussia (r.1797–1840) had up to a quarter of a million men under arms. After deducting forces assigned to garrison duty throughout the kingdom, a field army of 171,000 remained, consisting of regular

Discipline was strict, drills rigorous, and punishment draconian. During training the Prussian aim was to transform recruits into military automatons; soldiers who would march, drill, and fight without questioning orders. This rigid discipline had brought Prussia a string of victories during the Seven Years War (1756–63), and several senior Prussian commanders were veterans of that conflict. Confidence ran high that the same qualities would guarantee Prussian victory in any war it fought in Europe.

This strict, staid approach was the complete opposite of the Grande Armée, forged from the egalitarian fervor of the French Revolution.

Prussian troops and foreign mercenary contingents (which made up over half of the army).

This was still very much the army created by Frederick the Great in the mid-18th century, in its time the most efficient military machine in Europe.

Napoleon had an army that had transformed battlefield tactics, and was capable of strategic maneuvers unimaginable to Frederick the Great and his veteran commanders under Frederick-Wilhelm, who now faced the French.

The Prussian army had been left behind by changes in warfare wrought during the late 18th century and the French Revolution. The only recent experience of the French had been during the campaigns of 1792–5, when Prussian forces had met a poorly disciplined army. This led the Prussians to underestimate French military ability in 1806, despite having witnessed French victories at Marengo, Hohenlinden, and Austerlitz. Of course, there had also been the Prussian defeat at the Battle of Valmy (1792), but this was explained away by the unusual preponderance of artillery gathered by the French army and the untypical timidity of the Prussian commander, Karl Wilhelm Ferdinand, Duke of Brunswick (1735–1806). Despite this failure, Brunswick was placed in command of the new campaign, assisted by aged Field Marshal Richard Mollendorf (1726–1806), who had learned the duties of command under Frederick the Great. Both generals were mortally wounded during the Jena campaign (1806), and Prussia would emerge from the war as a humiliated client state of France, shorn of over half her territory.

Patriotism and reform

This national humiliation inspired German nationalism in Prussia during the years that followed. Encouraged by the *Tugenbund* (League of Virtue), populist support for revenge on Napoleon led to new military doctrines. The architects of this reform were General Gerhard von Scharnhorst (1757–1831) and General Augustus von Gneisenau (1760–1831), who introduced modern tactics learned from the enemy based on columnar attacks, a corps system, and the use of *landwehr* (militia).

The Prussian army that emerged from this period of reorganization was a formidable military force. When King Frederick-Wilhelm III joined the Sixth Coalition against France in 1813, he possessed an army equipped and ready for the challenge. After six years of humiliation and occupation, the Prussians were driven by a deep hatred of the French and a desire for revenge.

The linear tactics espoused by Frederick the Great

were abandoned during the military reforms in favor of French tactics. Prussian soldiers were re-equipped and issued new uniforms through British financial subsidies. Improvements to logistics, artillery

equipment, and the cavalry also helped to transform the Prussian army into a force capable of matching the French. Although at its core it remained a conscript army, the influx of nationalist volunteers and *landwehr* ensured that morale remained high. After all, the Prussians were fighting a war of German national liberation, and in Prussia patriotism and the army were inextricably linked.

The departure of Prussian land forces in 1813. A young Jewish soldier (foreground) is among those saying goodbye to loved ones; from a wood engraving.

Campaigning in Prussia

In 1805, Prussia supported the Third Coalition against France, but had taken no offensive action. This changed in late September 1806 when the Prussian king initiated war in response to Napoleon's unreasonable demands and duplicity over Hanover.

*T*he Prussian campaign plan drawn up by Frederick-Wilhelm's veteran generals called for the augmentation of the Prussian army by contingents drawn from German allies, before moving south into Saxony, to ensure the compliance of the Saxon army. On September 12 the Prussian columns marched south through Leipzig to take up positions in central Saxony, across the most likely route of French advance. In overall command was the 71-year-old Duke of Brunswick, whose last encounter with a French army had resulted in a Prussian defeat at Valmy.

Le Bataillon Carré in action during the Jena campaign in Saxony, October 1806.

Following the end of the Austerlitz campaign, the bulk of the Grande Armée had remained in encampments in southern Germany, around Frankfurt-am-Main, Stuttgart, and Würzburg. Only the Imperial Guard had accompanied Napoleon back to Paris in early 1806, and in September they were shuttled to the Rhine in a series of wagon relays. By the time the Prussian ultimatum reached Napoleon, his army was ready for war.

He also had good intelligence from Saxony. It appeared that the main Prussian army of 70,000 men was based near Naumberg, while another 50,000 men under Prince Friedrich of Hohenloe (1746–1818) lay to the west, supported by 20,000 Saxons. Another force of 30,000 men under Gebhard Leberecht von Blücher, Prince of Wahlstadt (1742–1819), who was nicknamed "Marshal Forward," lay 30 miles northwest of Brunswick's main army. The Prussians had divided their force, inviting Napoleon to set his Grande Armée between Brunswick and Hohenloe: the classic maneuver of the central position that Napoleon used in Italy during the 1796–7 campaign.

The Grande Armée was divided into six corps, commanded by marshals Bernadotte (I Corps), Davout (III Corps), Soult (IV Corps), Lannes (V Corps), Ney (VI Corps), and Augereau (VII Corps). They were supported by 3,700 Imperial Guard, the reserve cavalry, and a Bavarian contingent commanded by General Wrede. In all Napoleon had over 180,000 men. The army formed into a *bataillon carré* arrangement; three long columns, each of two army corps, preceded by a cavalry screen of Murat's light horsemen. Napoleon marched in the central column, alongside the guard and the cavalry reserve.

Confusion leads to victory

The Thuringerwald—a chain of forest-clad mountains dividing the Danube valley from the Saxon plain to the north—lay between the two armies. Protected by the cavalry, the French army crossed this natural barrier and entered Saxony on October 8, less than two weeks after the Prussian ultimatum. The Prussian cavalry screen was brushed aside at Schleiz on the following day, and on October 10 Lannes defeated Hohenloe's advanced guard at Saalfeld, which prompted Brunswick to order the retreat of his entire army northward toward Leipzig.

A cavalryman of the French Imperial Guard, painted by Theodore Géricault in 1813.

Joachim Murat, who commanded the French cavalry during the Prussian campaign, was awarded with the title of Grand Duc de Berg. Murat was later raised higher, and became King of Naples, an appointment Napoleon would come to regret, as Murat switched sides between his emperor and the Allies depending on whose fortunes were brighter.

The French simply moved too fast. By October 12 the bulk of Napoleon's army had overtaken the two retreating Prussian forces and wheeled westward between Brunswick and Hohenloe. Napoleon made one mistake. He confused the two Prussian armies, assuming that the main force was at Jena and the smaller force further north at Auerstadt. He ordered Davout to pin what he assumed was the smaller army at Auerstadt, while he marched on Jena. In fact, he was facing Hohenloe's smaller force, while Davout faced almost twice as many Prussians. Bernadotte was ordered to support Davout, but failed to join either battle. Only the determination of Marshal Davout saved the day, and France won both battles of October 14 (*see following page*).

After Brunswick's fatal wounding, Frederick-Wilhelm took direct command of the shattered Prussian army. He ordered the action at Auerstadt to be broken off, and hoped to recover the army routed at Jena. Instead, Bernadotte moved to intercept the remains of Hohenloe's army as it retreated north, and the force disintegrated. Faced with disaster, Frederick-Wilhelm ordered a general retreat to Prussia, but his army melted away as isolated detachments were captured by Murat's cavalry while the French raced north.

In just over a week, Napoleon had shattered the mighty Prussian army. On October 24 he entered Berlin in triumph. All Napoleon now had to do to ensure lasting peace was drive off the Russians.

Jena-Auerstadt

With the Grande Armée positioned between the divided Prussian army, Napoleon left Marshal Davout to the smaller of the two forces and sent his main army to Jena. While Napoleon won a relatively easy victory, Davout's men fought for their lives at Auerstadt.

*M*arshal Lannes encountered a large Prussian force near Jena on October 13, 1806. His V Corps lay at the extreme left (southern) flank of the Grande Armée, which had marched up the eastern bank of the Salle before wheeling around to occupy a position between the two Prussian armies. Ney's VI Corps and Augereau's VII Corps were in a position to support Lannes, while Napoleon also led Soult's IV Corps, the Imperial Guard, and the reserve cavalry toward Jena. Davout's III Corps on the right (northern) flank, supported by Bernadotte's I Corps, was ordered to pin the Prussian force at Auerstadt, to prevent it intervening in the "main" battle at Jena.

Napoleon's miscalculation now pitted his 98,000 men against Prince Friedrich of Hohenloe's 52,000 near Jena, while Marshal Davout's 27,000 III Corps faced the Duke of Brunswick, who commanded 50,000 men, with a further 40,000 some distance to the north and east, and another 30,000 under Blücher 30 miles to the northwest.

Early on the morning of October 14 the leading French columns under Augereau and Lannes fought their way across the Saale into Jena, then spread out into line to the northwest, Augereau on the left, Lannes on the right. Hohenloe had only 38,000 men in the area and sent messengers instructing General Rüchel at Weimar to march toward the sound of the guns with his 15,000 men.

Meanwhile, Marshal Ney crossed the Saale to the north of Lannes' corps, hoping to work his way around the northern flank of Hohenloe. Instead his men were attacked by the massed ranks of the Prussian cavalry before his force could fully deploy. For a time it looked as if the corps would be lost, but Ney's men hung on, buying time with their lives. Napoleon sent part of Lannes' corps and the entire reserve cavalry, and disaster was averted.

Napoleon was also lucky that Hohenloe failed to support his counterattack with the rest of his army, and his infantry stood opposing the French VII and V Corps for two hours, exposed to artillery fire while they remained inactive. That was the way they had been trained; the way Frederick the Great fought. When the time came for the three French corps to advance, the line was too weak to resist. By 3pm the Prussians were in full retreat. Even the arrival of Rüchel's men from Weimar failed to stem the tide, and the Prussian survivors fled the battlefield toward the northwest. Hohenloe may have hoped to link up with the Duke of Brunswick's army at Auerstadt, but he was engaged in his own fight.

Marshal Ney narrowly avoided disaster when his VI Corps was attacked by massed Prussian cavalry before he had fully deployed his force.

Looking to the northwest, just beyond Jena, 1806, the French forces of V Corps press against the Prussian lines of Prince Friedrich of Hohenloe.

A humiliating defeat

Davout advanced toward Auerstadt, to find the main Prussian army waiting for him. He deployed his three divisions into a defensive line, and spent the morning fighting off repeated attacks by Prussian infantry and cavalry, hoping that Bernadotte would arrive on his left flank to relieve the pressure on III Corps. But Bernadotte never arrived. He was later court-martialed as a result of his non-involvement, although Napoleon absolved him of blame and Bernadotte was eventually reinstated.

At about 10am the Duke of Brunswick was wounded, and later died, while leading an attack. Brunswick's aide, General Mollendorf, was captured by the French, leaving the Prussian army leaderless. Although the king tried to co-ordinate their efforts, he proved unequal to the task. In lieu of any better ideas, he launched a series of poorly co-ordinated assaults that Davout's troops easily repulsed, and during which his son, Prince Louis, met his death. This pinned the Prussians against the French center, allowing Davout to move around the Prussian flanks in a double envelopment.

Frederick-Wilhelm tried to avert disaster by launching a cavalry counterattack, but his horsemen were turned by withering French musket fire. As the French advance resumed, the Prussian line broke under the pressure. The king was unable to stop the rout, and by late afternoon the Prussians were surrendering *en masse*. Against all the odds and a potentially disastrous error from their commander-in-chief, both the battles of Jena-Auerstadt resulted in decisive French victories.

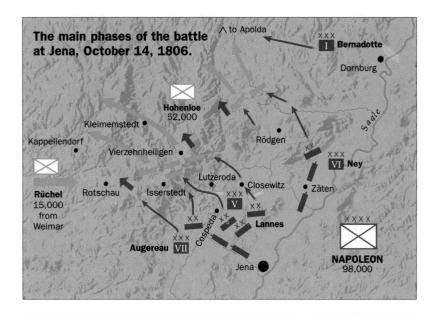

The main phases of the battle at Jena, October 14, 1806.

Bernadotte · Dornburg · Hohenloe 52,000 · Kleimemstedt · Kappellendorf · Vierzehnheiligen · Rödgen · Ney · Lutzeroda · Closewitz · Zäten · Rüchel 15,000 from Weimar · Rotschau · Isserstedt · Lannes · Cospeda · Augereau VII · Jena · NAPOLEON 98,000

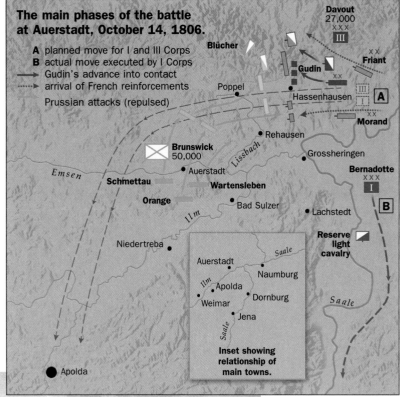

The main phases of the battle at Auerstadt, October 14, 1806.

A planned move for I and III Corps
B actual move executed by I Corps
→ Gudin's advance into contact
⋯▸ arrival of French reinforcements
Prussian attacks (repulsed)

Davout 27,000 · Blücher · Gudin · Friant · Poppel · Hassenhausen · Morand · Rehausen · Brunswick 50,000 · Lissbach · Grossheringen · Emsen · Auerstadt · Bernadotte · Schmettau · Wartensleben · Orange · Bad Sulzer · Lachstedt · Ilm · Reserve light cavalry · Niedertreba · Saale

Inset showing relationship of main towns.
Auerstadt · Saale · Naumburg · Ilm · Apolda · Dornburg · Weimar · Jena · Saale

Apolda

The Battle of Auerstadt, 1806. Brunswick (above), the Prussian commander, was killed, and the Prussian cavalry fled.

The Winter Campaign

The French swept north to take Berlin, forcing King Frederick-Wilhelm III toward Russia. Protected by two Russian armies, East Prussia remained a focal point for resistance. The campaign continued amid the snows of winter in what had previously been Poland.

Napoleon visits the siege lines outside the Baltic port of Danzig, from a print of 1807.

Facing: A French gouache of Napoleon during the Battle of Friedland (1807) in East Prussia.

Gebhardt Leberecht, Prince Blücher von Wahlstadt (1742–1819)

While Napoleon mismanaged the twin battles in Saxony, he made no mistakes in the weeks following his unexpected victories. His unrelenting pursuit of the remaining Prussian army gave the demoralized Germans no opportunity to rally. Marshal Murat's light cavalry was superbly handled during this pursuit phase, covering more than 400 miles in just over three weeks. While Louis Bonaparte advanced through Hanover toward the Elbe, Murat's horsemen raced northeast through Magdeberg and Potsdam toward Berlin, followed closely by the infantry. So complete was the Prussian demoralization that towns and fortresses surrendered at the first sight of French horsemen.

Davout's corps had the privilege of being the first French unit to enter Berlin (October 26), while Murat's cavalry raced on toward the Oder. The only Prussian force remaining in the field was that of Blücher, who retreated north toward Lübeck with 30,000 men, where he surrendered on November 7. Despite the loss of his country, Frederick-Wilhelm vowed to fight on from East Prussia.

By the time the French crossed the Oder into Poland, the Russians had 90,000 men on the banks of the Vistula, in two armies, commanded by General Count Bennigsen (1745–1826) and General Count Buxhöwden (1750–1811). As Napoleon advanced into Poland, Bennigsen retreated east across the Vistula to Pultusk. Although Napoleon tried to march his army between the two enemy forces in a manner similar to his maneuver in the rear in Saxony, the Russians fell back, avoiding the trap. The onset of winter and the poor state of Polish roads contributed to Napoleon's failure to force a decisive battle before the New Year. Instead, he set up court in Warsaw and recruited Polish troops for his army.

Victory follows defeat

This new force was commanded by Marshal Lefebvre, who was ordered to besiege Danzig. In January, Bennigsen attacked Ney and Bernadotte north of Warsaw, and Napoleon saw an opportunity to march the rest of his army around behind the Russians. Bennigsen realized the danger and retreated north, turning to face the pursuing French at Eylau, some 20 miles south of Königsberg. He hoped the French would attack piecemeal as they arrived, giving his men the opportunity to crush each corps in turn.

Instead, Napoleon kept his troops under control and launched a co-ordinated attack on February 8. The hard-fought Battle of Eylau was a French defeat, and both armies retired into winter quarters to recover from one of the bloodiest battles of the Napoleonic era (*see following page*). A fresh wave of French conscripts

was called to make up for the losses, and Marshal Massena's II Corps marched north from Italy. The emperor sent messages to Lefebvre, demanding that he bring the siege of Danzig to a speedy conclusion. The port surrendered on May 27, 1807.

The Russians had been busy recruiting, bringing the army to just over 100,000 men. It was June before Napoleon felt confident enough to resume the offensive, his army swelled by reinforcements to over 380,000 men. However, only a third of this force was available for offensive maneuvers; the remainder were scattered across Poland and Prussia, guarding the Grande Armée's long supply lines back to the Rhine.

After an initial clash at Heilsberg (June 10), Napoleon split his army, sending Soult and Murat to capture Königsberg on the Baltic coast, while the rest of the force probed the River Alle.

He found a 60,000-strong Russian army encamped around Friedland and launched an all-out attack, supported by massed artillery (*see pages 78–79*).

The hard-fought campaign ended on July 7, when Emperor Napoleon and Czar Alexander met on a raft moored in the River Niemen near Tilsit. After Friedland, Napoleon was at the height of his power, controlling Europe from the Channel to the Russian border.

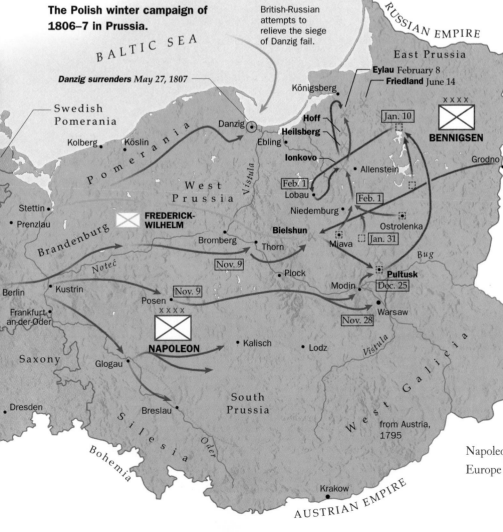

The Polish winter campaign of 1806–7 in Prussia.

British-Russian attempts to relieve the siege of Danzig fail.

BALTIC SEA

RUSSIAN EMPIRE

East Prussia

Danzig surrenders *May 27, 1807*

Königsberg

Eylau February 8
Friedland June 14

Swedish Pomerania

Danzig

Hoff
Heilsberg
Ebling

Jan. 10

XXXX
BENNIGSEN

Kolberg   Köslin

Ionkovo

P o m e r a n i a

Vistula

Allenstein

Grodno

Stettin

West Prussia

Feb. 1
Lobau

Feb. 1

Prenzlau

XX
FREDERICK-WILHELM

Niedemburg

Ostrolenka

B r a n d e n b u r g

Bromberg

Bielshun

Thorn

Miava

Jan. 31

Noteć

Nov. 9

Plock

Bug

Berlin   Kustrin

Modin

Pultusk
Dec. 25

Frankfurt-an-der-Oder

Posen

Nov. 9

Warsaw

XXXX

Nov. 28

W e s t   G a l i c i a

NAPOLEON

Kalisch

Lodz

Vistula

Saxony   Glogau

from Austria, 1795

Dresden

Breslau

South Prussia

S i l e s i a

Oder

B o h e m i a

Krakow

AUSTRIAN EMPIRE

Battle of Eylau

In late January 1807, Napoleon fought a running campaign across Poland and East Prussia that culminated in the Battle of Eylau. In a bitterly contested fight, Napoleon threw everything at the Russians, but his Grande Armée was unable to defeat them.

Napoleon and his generals amid the carnage on the snowbound battlefield of Eylau. In the right foreground, a Russian grenadier is being taken prisoner. Painting by Antoine-Jean Gros.

While Napoleon wintered in Warsaw, General Count Bennigsen clashed with the northern cantonments of the Grande Armée at Ionkovo, on the borders of East Prussia. Napoleon immediately went back onto the offensive, planning to catch the Russian army in the field before it could retreat north to its supply base at Königsberg, on the Baltic coast. The freezing weather and heavy snows delayed the French advance, and Bennigsen learned of the French plan in time to withdraw his army. Ney's VI Corps maintained contact with the retiring Russian army and, when Bennigsen turned around and offered battle at Preussisches Eylau on February 6, Napoleon was able to direct his troops toward the waiting Russians.

Bennigsen had 67,000 men and 460 guns under his command, while an additional 9,000 Prussians commanded by General Lestoq were marching south from Königsberg to join him. He drew his men up in a line to the northeast of the town, covering the road that led north for 20 miles to his supply base.

When Napoleon arrived at Eylau on February 7 he drew on Soult's IV Corps of 20,000 men, Augereau's VII Corps of 9,000 men, and 6,000 of the Imperial Guard. A further 14,000 from Ney's VI Corps lay to the northwest, while Davout's 15,000 troops of III Corps were beyond the southern extreme of the French line. Soult's men fought for control of Eylau into the early evening, a skirmish that cost both sides approximately 4,000 men. The opponents spent the night in the snow, waiting for the real battle to begin the following morning.

Napoleon had no contact with Ney and Davout, but at least the reserve cavalry had arrived; some 10,500 horsemen commanded by Murat. Soult was arrayed to the northwest of Eylau and Augereau to

the southeast, with the Imperial Guard and reserve cavalry massed behind the front line. Napoleon's plan was to pin the Russians on his center while Ney and Davout outflanked the two ends of the Russian line.

A hail of fire

Soon after 8am the Russian artillery opened up, prompting Napoleon to launch Soult's IV Corps forward through the snow showers to probe the Russian line. They were met by the powerful Russian divisions of Tutchkov and Essen, who threw the French back in disorder.

Davout's leading division appeared on the southern (left) flank of the Russian line, only to be repulsed by General Tolstoi's command. Both French wings were in trouble, so Napoleon ordered Augereau to advance in his center, to ease the pressure. His men were swallowed up by a blizzard as they crossed the plain, emerging in front of the main Russian battery of 70 guns. Augereau's command was disintegrated in a hail of artillery fire. Bennigsen launched his reserve (Doctorov's division) against Eylau and the Russians fought their way into the town, driving back the survivors of Soult's corps until they reached the Imperial Guard, which became embroiled in the hand-to-hand fighting.

Napoleon had one last force at his disposal. At 11.30am he launched Murat's reserve cavalry against the Russian center. They crashed into the two divisions that had pinned Soult and overran the grand battery that had destroyed Augereau's corps. The charge cost Murat 1,500 horsemen, but defeat had been averted, since the Russian center took over an hour to reorganize its shattered lines. The battle continued into the afternoon, as Davout's remaining divisions joined the battle in the south, and Lestocq's Prussians arrived from the north in time to prevent Ney from intervening in the center.

Bennigsen withdrew his army under cover of darkness, but although the Russians had abandoned the field, it was clear that French army had been shattered. About 20,000 French and 11,000 Russian soldiers lay where they fell, to be buried by the drifting snow. When Ney arrived on the battlefield the next morning, he exclaimed, "What a massacre… and with no result!"

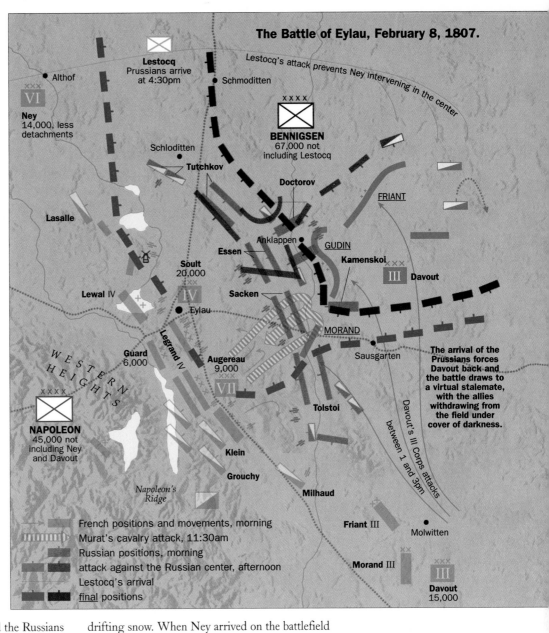

The Russian commanders whose forces shattered the French at Eylau: Levin August, Count Bennigsen (1745–1826), left, and Alexander Ivanovich Tolstoi (1770–1857).

Battle of Friedland

Napoleon realized that he could only force Russia to sue for peace by defeating General Bennigsen's Russian army. After the bloody slaughter at Eylau, both sides prepared for the decisive battle of the campaign.

After Eylau, both shattered armies went into winter quarters to regroup, re-equip, and draw on fresh reinforcements. The surrender of Danzig on May 27, 1807 eased Napoleon's supply problems and released another 20,000 Polish and Italian troops to join the Grande Armée, bringing its operational strength back over 200,000 men; the Russians could draw on less than 120,000.

Despite this disparity in numbers, Bennigsen struck first, clashing with French screening forces in East Prussia during early June before launching the main thrust of his attack across the Alle at Heilsberg. Soult's IV Corps was badly mauled in a battle fought on June 10, and the two sides withdrew after each had suffered 10,000 casualties.

Bennigsen planned to renew his offensive and marched north along the Alle to Friedland, 30 miles southeast of Königsberg. Sited in a bend of the river, Napoleon quickly realized that Bennigsen's position

was vulnerable. The Russians' only route to safety lay across the river, where three pontoon bridges were built alongside the town's main bridge.

Napoleon had already sent Lannes' V Corps to Friedland, while Soult (IV Corps) and Davout (III Corps) probed toward Königsberg. The bulk of the French army waited in reserve at Eylau. Once Napoleon discovered that the bulk of the Russian army was massing at Friedland he ordered Ney (VI Corps) and Mortier (VIII Corps) to join Lannes.

By 9am on June 14, Lannes' 17,000 men (including 8,000 French cavalry) faced over 45,000 Russians, and more were flooding west over the bridges. The potential for disaster was averted by Bennigsen's uncharacteristic reluctance to give battle and the timely arrival of Mortier. Napoleon arrived to take command of the French army at noon, accompanied by the Imperial Guard. Preparations were made for a full-scale attack, and when Marshal Victor's I Corps arrived around 4pm, the French ranks were swollen to 80,000 men, supported by 118 guns. When these reinforcements were in position an hour later, Napoleon gave the order to advance.

Bennigsen had 60,000 men and 120 guns at his disposal, deployed in a four-mile arc around the

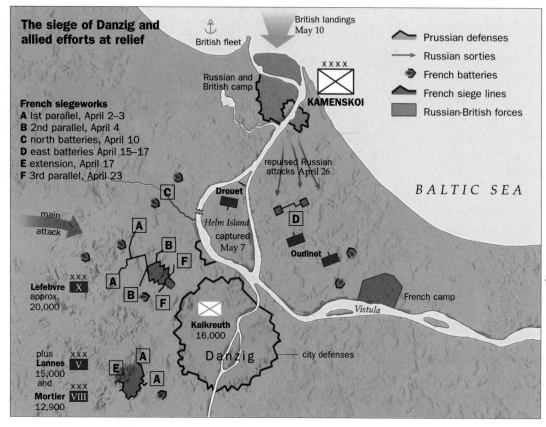

The siege of Danzig and allied efforts at relief

British landings
May 10

British fleet

Russian and
British camp

XXXX
KAMENSKOI

French siegeworks
A lst parallel, April 2–3
B 2nd parallel, April 4
C north batteries, April 10
D east batteries April 15–17
E extension, April 17
F 3rd parallel, April 23

repulsed Russian
attacks April 26

BALTIC SEA

main
attack

Drouet

*Helm Island
captured
May 7*

D

Oudinot

Lefebvre
approx.
20,000
XXX
X

French camp

Vistula

Kalkreuth
16,000

city defenses

plus
Lannes
15,000
and
XXX
V

E

D a n z i g

Mortier VIII
12,900
XXX

Prussian defenses
Russian sorties
French batteries
French siege lines
Russian-British forces

town. Two Russian divisions lay south of the mill stream that formed the northern border of Friedland, while four more were deployed to the north, supported by Cossacks. Napoleon ordered Ney to attack the southern two divisions, while Lannes and Mortier pinned the troops to the north. The Imperial Guard and Victor's corps remained in reserve.

Left to retreat

Bagration, commanding the two southernmost Russian divisions, fought back with tenacity, supported by massed Russian guns on the far bank of the river. For a time it looked as if the French attack would be halted, but at a critical moment Napoleon sent in Victor's corps, who deployed artillery immediately in front of Bagration's line. The Russian defenses crumbled.

Attempting to restore the situation, Bennigsen ordered General Gortschakov to advance with three of the four divisions to the north of the mill stream. Mortier and Lannes held their positions, driving back the attackers with the help of the Guard Cavalry. Ney had penetrated Friedland and Bennigsen was forced to commit the Russian Guard to protect the vital river crossings. A desperate battle ensued, but the elite Russian troops could do little than cover a disorderly retreat by the rest of the army.

By 8.30pm the Russian Guard had withdrawn over the river and the burning town of Friedland was in French hands. To the north, Bennigsen led the bulk of his army across a ford to the north of the town and retreated throughout the night toward the

Russian border. Inexplicably, Mortier, Lannes, and Grouchy (the wing cavalry commander) did nothing to prevent the withdrawal.

Friedland was a decisive victory. The French lost somewhere under 10,000 casualties, but the Russian losses exceeded 20,000, plus the bulk of their artillery. Czar Alexander had little option but to sue for peace.

Above: A French print of 1807 depicts the Battle of Friedland.
Facing: General Peter Ivanovich Bagration (1765–1812).

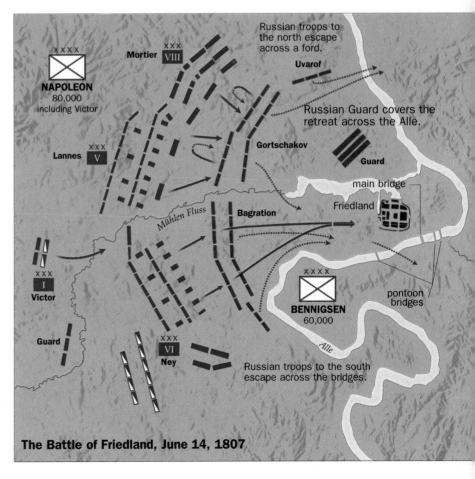

The Battle of Friedland, June 14, 1807

The Treaty of Tilsit

Friedland may have been decisive for the French, but the Polish campaign had been wasteful of life. It felt more like a draw. Less than two weeks after the battle Czar Alexander and Emperor Napoleon met and forged and alliance that created a new European order.

*T*he dramatic venue was an elaborate raft moored in the Niemen, a symbolic place of neutrality between the Russian and French armies. Napoleon realized that if the talks went badly, his

The meeting of Napoleon and Alexander on a purpose-built raft moored on the Niemen at Tilsit, in July 1807.

army was ill-prepared for an invasion of Russia. For his part, Alexander was aware that his defeated army was in no condition to fight and, after a decade of intervention in European affairs on behalf of her allies, there was little Russian willingness to continue the struggle. Peace benefitted both parties.

They came to the first of several parleys from opposite banks of the river, together with their advisers. Napoleon was first to arrive, where he waited for Alexander. The two then retired to the conference chamber on the raft and talked for 90 minutes. The client-king and queen of Prussia were excluded from the proceedings and frustratingly waited for a summons from either ruler.

Queen Louisa visited Napoleon on July 6 to persuade him to adopt a less than draconian stand regarding Prussia, but he remained unmoved. The czar had expressed his willingness to abandon Prussia to its fate in return for a favorable peace between Russia and France, and the two rulers had developed something of a close rapport after two weeks of discussions.

On July 7 Napoleon and Alexander signed a series of agreements, including a peace treaty, a provisional agreement to an alliance, and other diplomatic papers outlining a distribution of political and geographical power in Europe. These documents, known collectively as the Treaty of Tilsit, represented the emergence of a new order in Europe and the final humiliation of Prussia. A secondary treaty outlining the exact nature of the Prussian dismemberment was signed two days later, at which point King Frederick-Wilhelm III was summoned to the raft to learn his country's fate.

Carving up territory

Prussia lost all of her territory east of the Elbe, including East Prussia. Stripped of all but four provinces, Prussia would have to pay a large war indemnity before the French army withdrew from its soil. Part of Prussia's land in Poland was given to Russia, but the bulk was amalgamated into a new Grand Duchy of Warsaw, which would form part of the pro-French Confederation of the Rhine. French troops would remain to garrison the major Polish cities, while the King of Saxony would rule the new country. In Germany, the Kingdom of Westphalia was formed as a pro-French bulwark in northern Europe, while the Kingdom of Holland gained East Frisia from the Prussians.

Russia would annex Finland, then try to steer the Baltic countries into a pro-French alliance, while countering British influence in the region. A handful of Russian enclaves in the Mediterranean were turned over to France, and in return Napoleon offered to support Russia in any future struggle against Turkey. In fact, the French emperor had little intention of intervening in Turkish affairs, and would have been wary if the czar's troops had wrested control of Constantinople from its sultan.

It is a striking demonstration of the personal hold Napoleon had that the Russian ruler should agree to such unfavorable terms. His country had become a silent partner in the new continental system that Napoleon had created. Both rulers preferred to ignore the potentially damaging long-term effects of their solution for Poland. The Duchy of Warsaw amounted to a French enclave in eastern Europe, and gave Napoleon a secure base of operations against any future conflict with Austria, Prussia, or even Russia. Although the Treaty of Tilsit marked the zenith of Napoleonic achievement in terms of establishing a new political and military order, it contained a number of flaws that would create major diplomatic problems in the future.

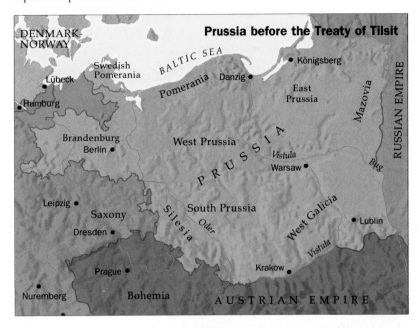

Prussia before the Treaty of Tilsit

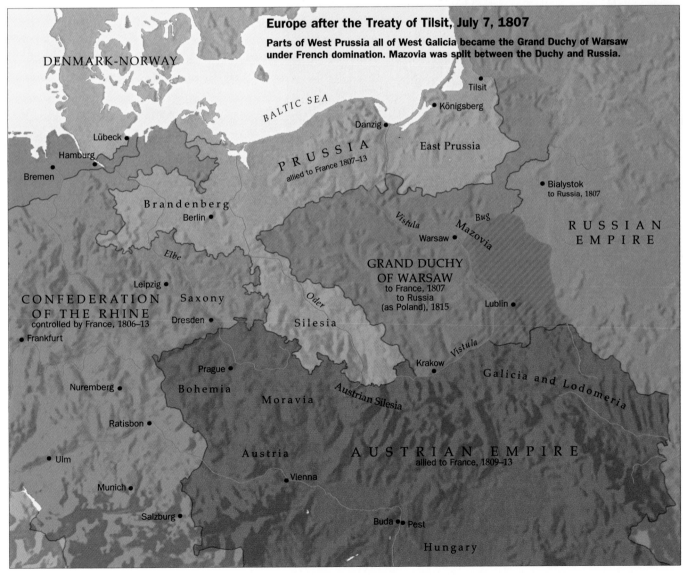

Europe after the Treaty of Tilsit, July 7, 1807

Parts of West Prussia all of West Galicia became the Grand Duchy of Warsaw under French domination. Mazovia was split between the Duchy and Russia.

The Code Napoleon

The civil legal code introduced by Napoleon in 1804 became his most enduring legacy. It remains the basis of the French legal system, and its ideas have been exported throughout the world.

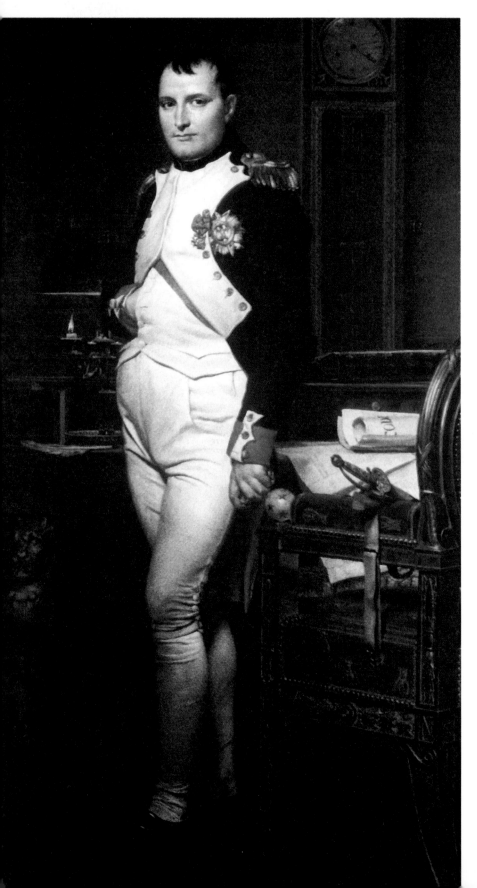

*B*efore the French Revolution, there was no unifying legal system in France, only a patchwork based on ancient Roman law, medieval custom (known as Teutonic law), and provincial dictats. Successive monarchs added laws as if by whim, a policy summarized by Louis XIV's phrase, "It is legal because I wish it." To the political idealists of the age of enlightenment, this was a deplorable state. Pre-revolutionary thinkers proposed the replacement of the old system with a unified legal code, based on logic, justice, and reason. This became a goal of the revolutionaries.

In 1791 the *Declaration of Rights of Man and the Citizen* included the article: "The exercise of the natural rights of each man has no limits other than those that ensure to other members of society enjoyment of those same rights. These limits can be determined only by statute." The search began for a legal system that could enshrine these rights, but reformers were daunted by the tangled complexity of existing statutes.

As First Consul, Napoleon founded a committee to work on the draft of a new legal code in 1800, 11 years after the start of the French Revolution. The committee's initial aim was to produce a brief but comprehensive and logical guide to French law that would be intelligible to the regular citizen. Napoleon insisted on brevity over complexity. The clarity of intent enshrined in the code would permit those charged with imposing the law with the freedom to interpret it in a way that suited the case before them. It was a work of simple legal genius, emphasizing the nature of the law, as opposed to its precise definition. It was for this reason that the French poet Paul Valery described the Civil Code as "the greatest book of French literature."

Ending feudalism

The Civil Code was introduced in draft form in 1800, then improved several times before its formal introduction in 1804, shortly before Napoleon's coronation. While it became known as the *Code Napoléon* in 1807 as an acknowledgment that he was its leading proponent, it represents the combined work of some of the greatest legal, moral, and social reformers of post-revolution France. This said, Napoleon presided over many discussions while the code was being drafted, and as First Consul he

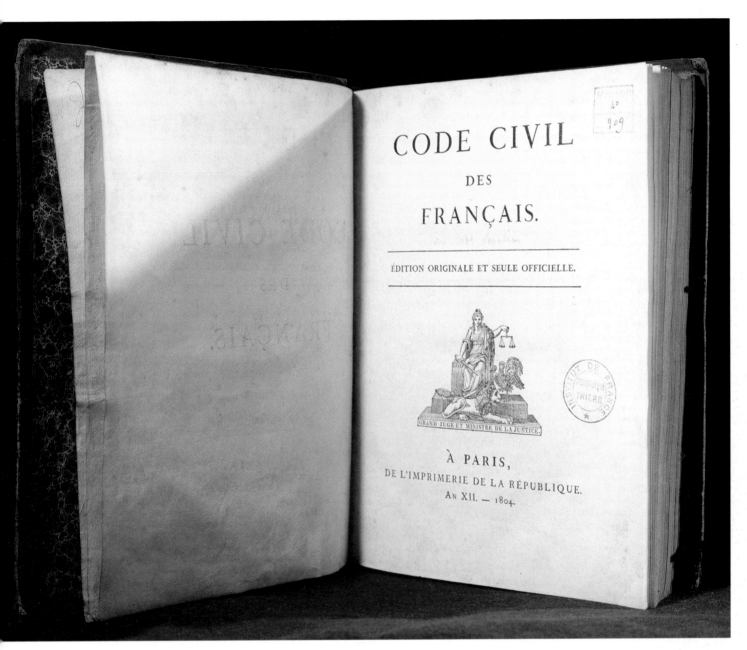

represented the executive authority responsible for the Civil Code's enforcement. Some of its content betrays Napoleon's moral views, such as its tough stance on divorce, the rights of women, and parental rights.

When Napoleon began to impose his military and political will across Europe, the influence of the *Code Napoléon* made itself felt abroad, particularly in regions where entire states became French client-states (such as in Italy, Belgium, Holland, and the Confederation of the Rhine).

The Code enshrined the civil rights of Frenchmen, an egalitarian concept that proved popular with other European liberal reformers, who embraced the opportunity for legal reform. Older European legal systems came under pressure to reform in order to counter the spread of pro-French libertarian ideas, creating a legal drive that effectively removed the last vestiges of organized feudalism in Europe, apart from in Russia. The old privileges enjoyed by the landed aristocracy came to an end in countries outside the French sphere, a final export of the French Revolution that altered the social fabric of contemporary society. For example, when Napoleon created the Duchy of Warsaw in Poland, he abolished the system of serfdom that had existed in Poland for over a thousand years.

The fall of Napoleon in 1814 did not lead to a collapse of the *Code Napoléon*. A legal system based on fairness, judicial logic, and civil rights was too important a cultural advance to abandon. In France, the Code remained unaltered for a century-and-a-half, and still forms the basis of French law today. It remained the core of the legal system for much of Europe for decades, making it the most enduring and widely exported legacy of the French Revolution.

A bound copy of the *Code Civil des Français* open at the title page, dated 1804. This was perhaps the greatest legacy Napoleon left the French people.

Facing: Napoleon in his study by Jacques Louis David. Painted in 1812, it shows a ruler who has comfortably outgrown the gaucheness that hindered his early years in power.

The Changing Face of Warfare

In 1805 and 1806, Napoleon had won sweeping victories partly through luck but mostly because of doctrinal superiority of the French army. The campaigns in Poland (1807) and Austria two years later marked a turning point—his enemies were learning.

"The Russian Veteran of 1812" by Piotr Zabolotsky (1836). The veterans of Napoleon's army were relatively young compared to those of Austria, Prussia, and Russia, which gave the French an added early advantage. However, as the Napoleonic Wars dragged on, better organized and trained soldiers began filling the allies' ranks, like the officer and infantryman of a mid-19th century Austrian batallion shown here.

As has been demonstrated, among other things, Napoleon was a gifted military reformer. The French Revolutionary Army he had inherited served him well during his early career. The troops were enthusiastic, fired by the fervor of having overthrown a despotic monarchy. Revolution had brought about a looser, more flexible approach and, as a result, the new French army was capable of moving faster, concentrating more troops, and attacking with more élan than its opponents. The French ability to outmaneuver more conventional armies played an important part in Napoleon's early victories, as did his men's willingness to live off the land without centralized depots. On the battlefield, the innovative tactics of using massed skirmishers, dense columns, and concentrated cavalry formations, which ran contrary to the established rules of warfare, proved to be battle-winning tactics in the hands of skilled French generals who thought as one with Napoleon.

Napoleon further improved on this military legacy by developing the corps that allowed the French army to operate at speed. Able to maintain the initiative on campaign and capable of moving further and faster than its enemies, the French could concentrate troops at a decisive point almost at will. The 1805 campaign was a prime example of this new-found strategic mobility, when Napoleon concentrated the bulk of his army behind the Austrians, severing their lines of communication and forcing their surrender. Similarly, during the Prussian campaign of 1806, he was able to outmaneuver the Prussians and place his corps between two enemy formations, allowing him to destroy both armies at will.

The staid tactics of the Russians, Austrians, and Prussians seemed to play into Napoleon's hands. This led increasingly to a tendency to underestimate his opponents, and the French paid the price for this over-confidence during the 1907 Polish campaign. The army commanded by Bennigsen in 1807 was far better handled than the Russian armies that fought at Austerlitz less than two years before. It all but defeated Napoleon's Grande Armée at Eylau, and continued to perform well until Bennigsen's defeat at Friedland that summer. The enemies of France were starting to learn from their mistakes.

Quantity over strategy

The truth was, the nature of warfare was evolving, and both the French and their adversaries were busy reforming their military structures. For the French, while the size of the Grande Armée increased steadily, the number of experienced revolutionary veterans diminished. Napoleon paid little attention to these losses, but the cumulative attrition of the period 1805–7 meant that his army included an increasing number of raw conscripts and non-French contingents to replace them. This drop in quality led to a rethinking of tactics, and increasingly Napoleon was forced to make use of large divisional-sized columns, massed artillery, and his experienced reserve, the Imperial Guard. In short, his army was becoming less capable of dramatic battlefield maneuvers. Bit by bit, Napoleon was forced into accepting less subtle and ultimately more costly tactics.

The other European armies were also improving. Under the guidance of Archduke Charles, the Austrians abandoned those linear tactics that cost them so dearly during the early years of the Napoleonic Wars, and instead adopted French-style column formations, skirmishing units, and large batteries of guns. A corps system was introduced, and the use of *landwehr* (militia) provided additional units to counter the growing French army.

After 1807 the Russian army underwent a series of changes under the guidance of Alexei Arakcheev and Barclay de Tolly. Within four years, the Russian troops and support regiments that faced the Grande Armée in battle were considerably more formidable than they had been in 1805 and 1807. These improvements meant that Napoleon's military advantages were being steadily eroded. The French were no longer going to win easy victories over their opponents. Increasingly, warfare would become a matter of attrition and sheer weight of numbers.

Crisis on the Danube

The Wagram Campaign of 1809

*F*ollowing the Treaty of Tilsit, Napoleon dominated continental Europe. His lightning campaigns of 1805 and 1806 defeated Austria and Prussia, and his hold on the remainder of Europe was consolidated through his creation of French client states such as the Confederation of the Rhine,

Kingdom of Italy, and Grand Duchy of Warsaw.

Only Britain continued to challenge Napoleon's mastery of Europe. For years the British government had provided financial incentives to other European powers in an attempt to entice war against France. Despite this continued opposition, a change in the British political climate, financial excess, and a general war-weariness combined to encourage peace. The British government was willing to negotiate a peace treaty if only France would restore the balance

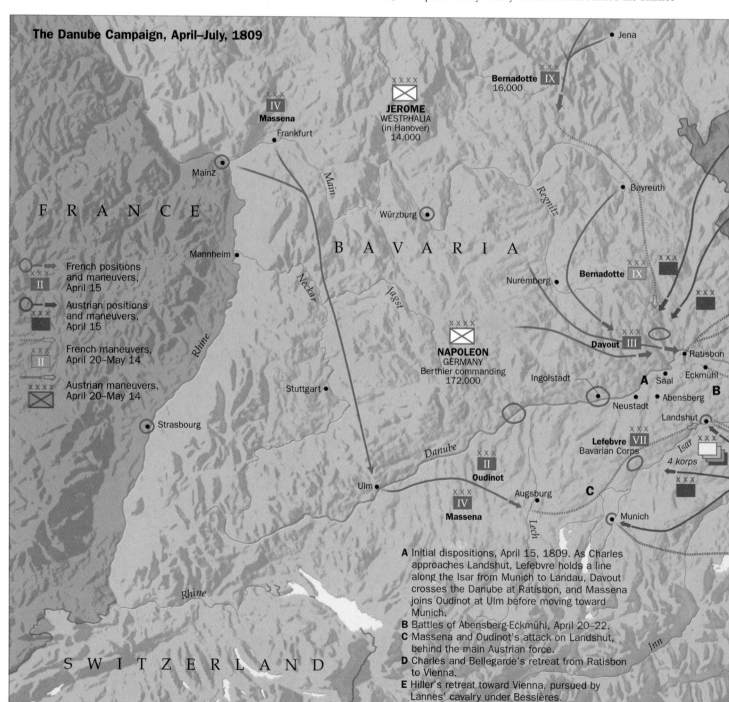

The Danube Campaign, April–July, 1809

French positions and maneuvers, April 15

Austrian positions and maneuvers, April 15

French maneuvers, April 20–May 14

Austrian maneuvers, April 20–May 14

F R A N C E

S W I T Z E R L A N D

B A V A R I A

Jena

Bernadotte IX
16,000

JEROME
WESTPHALIA
(in Hanover)
14,000

IV
Massena
Frankfurt

Mainz

Würzburg

Bayreuth

Mannheim

Nuremberg

Bernadotte IX

Davout III

Ratisbon
Eckmühl
Saal

Ingolstadt

Neustadt

Abensberg

Landshut

Lefebvre VII
Bavarian Corps

4 korps

NAPOLEON
GERMANY
Berthier commanding
172,000

Stuttgart

Strasbourg

Ulm

Danube

Oudinot II

Augsburg

Munich

IV
Massena

A
B
C

A Initial dispositions, April 15, 1809. As Charles approaches Landshut, Lefebvre holds a line along the Isar from Munich to Landau, Davout crosses the Danube at Ratisbon, and Massena joins Oudinot at Ulm before moving toward Munich.
B Battles of Abensberg-Eckmühl, April 20–22.
C Massena and Oudinot's attack on Landshut, behind the main Austrian force.
D Charles and Bellegarde's retreat from Ratisbon to Vienna.
E Hiller's retreat toward Vienna, pursued by Lannes' cavalry under Bessières.

of power in Europe by returning her annexed territories to Prussia, and permitting Austria to re-establish her traditional control over the southern German states. Napoleon refused to compromise or to undermine the political achievements won through military conquest. The war continued.

By 1809, the governments of Austria and Britain were aware that French involvement in Spain had turned sour (see *following chapter*), and while her armies were bogged down in the Iberian Peninsula, a renewed offensive in central Europe might place an unbearable strain on the Napoleonic empire.

When Austria began a fresh campaign, it became isolated even before it got properly under way.

Prussia secretly agreed to supply 80,000 troops, then repudiated the deal. Russia remained neutral at first, but when Napoleon learned of Austrian preparations, he struck his own secret deal, for Russian intervention on the French side in the event of war with Austria.

The war began early in April 1809, when an Austrian army of 90,000 under the command of Archduke Charles crossed the border into Bavaria, following the Danube. Despite an improvement in Austrian speed, Napoleon moved still faster, arriving in time to halt the invasion only two weeks after it had begun.

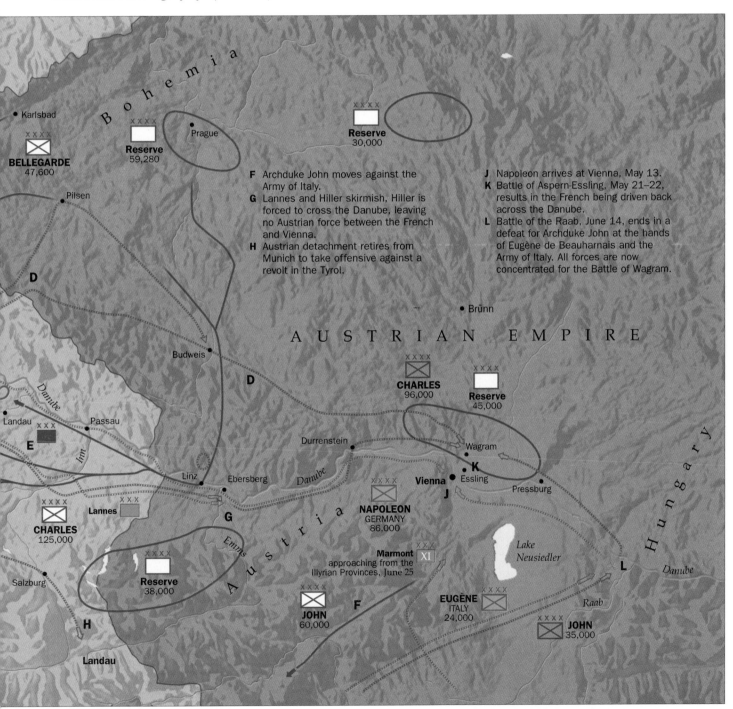

F Archduke John moves against the Army of Italy.
G Lannes and Hiller skirmish, Hiller is forced to cross the Danube, leaving no Austrian force between the French and Vienna.
H Austrian detachment retires from Munich to take offensive against a revolt in the Tyrol.

J Napoleon arrives at Vienna, May 13.
K Battle of Aspern-Essling, May 21–22, results in the French being driven back across the Danube.
L Battle of the Raab, June 14, ends in a defeat for Archduke John at the hands of Eugène de Beauharnais and the Army of Italy. All forces are now concentrated for the Battle of Wagram.

Campaigning on the Danube

In 1809 Austria needed to catch the French off-guard to have any real chance of success. This meant seizing Bavaria and then attacking individual French corps as they arrived in the region. Although the Austrians moved quickly, Napoleon reacted with greater alacrity.

The final battle for Ratisbon (today part of Regensberg), April 22–23, 1809. With the Austrian army safely across the Danube, only a small garrison defended the city, which came under intensive French bombardment before being taken.

*T*he decision to invade Bavaria was a political one, designed to weaken the Confederation of the Rhine and reclaim a traditionally Austrian sphere of influence. Austria still hoped that Prussia would intervene on the Austrian side, and this influenced the invasion plan. Although the direct route from Austria to Bavaria lay up the Danube valley, the main Austrian army was deployed in Bohemia, where it could link up with any Prussian forces that might, just might, appear. A more northerly invasion route was therefore chosen, striking west from Bohemia toward Nuremberg and Frankfurt-am-Main. Six

corps were earmarked for this task, supported by a further two to guard the Austrian border in the Danube valley.

Napoleon's immediate problem was that the majority of his forces were now engaged in the Spanish war, which had become the main theater after Austria's last defeat. He reacted rapidly to Austria's mobilization by ordering troops and leading marshals from Spain to Germany, then dispatching the 60,000 troops closest to the invasion in Germany and the Rhine to concentrate on Nuremberg and Ratisbon on the Danube. Berthier was placed in overall command. Napoleon also ordered his Confederation of the Rhine troops to mobilize and rendezvous in Bavaria.

Intelligence reports suggested the Austrian offensive would not begin until May, but Archduke Charles entered Bavaria in early April 1809, before French forces were able to concentrate. By this time,

any hope of a Prussian intervention had faded, so Charles moved his area of operations south, toward the Danube. His intention was to fight a short, sharp campaign in Bavaria to defeat the small, isolated French and Bavarian forces in the area before the massed regiments of the Grande Armée could arrive from Spain.

At the time of the invasion, Davout's III Corps was marching east along the Danube to Ratisbon, while Massena's IV Corps was at Frankfurt-am-Main. In the Austrians' path lay 30,000 Bavarian troops of Lefebvre's VII Corps. They would have to absorb the initial attack, buying time for Davout and Massena to intervene.

Running battle

On April 10 the Austrians entered Bavaria and within a week the archduke's columns had reached Landshut and were close to Ratisbon, which was held by Davout. While General Bellegarde, with two corps, threatened Ratisbon from the northeast, Archduke Charles tried to deploy his army between Davout and Lefebvre's corps. By April 17 he changed his line of attack, screening Landshut with one corps, then moving the bulk of the Austrian army toward Ratisbon, where it could join up with Bellegarde's army.

Napoleon pulled both his corps back to Ingolstadt to make a united front, while General Oudinot was ordered to form a provisional corps from reinforcements sent from France. Meanwhile, Massena marched toward Ingolstadt. Napoleon's resources were small but powerful and, with the enemy split into two forces in front, it was the perfect strategic situation for him.

Napoleon ordered Davout and Lefebvre to hold the line between Ingolstadt and Ratisbon, while he sent Oudinot and Massena in a sweep to the south to roll back the Austrian left wing. On April 21 the running fight known as the Battle of Abensberg resulted in the defeat of the Austrian left

and the advance of Massena and Oudinot to Landshut, where they turned north behind the main Austrian army. At the same time, Lefebvre and Davout pinned the Austrians to their front, preventing any sensible reaction to the developing crisis to their south.

By dawn on April 22, the 161,000-man Austrian army was strung out along the southern bank of the Danube, facing 113,000 French and Bavarians commanded by Davout and Lefebvre. Another 48,000 Austrians were massed north of the river outside Ratisbon. While Bellegarde spent the day securing the bridge at Ratisbon, Napoleon hurled Oudinot and Massena's 57,000 men against the rear of the Austrian army at Eckmühl.

The Austrians faced destruction, and only the skill of Archduke Charles allowed the army to escape the pincer movement and retreat in disorder through

Ratisbon to the safety of the north bank of the Danube. Massena and Oudinot had achieved the impossible, but their men were too exhausted to pursue the broken enemy. Bavaria was saved, but the Austrians were alive to fight another day.

Archduke Charles of Austria (1771–1847), who proved to be one of Napoleon's more successful opponents.

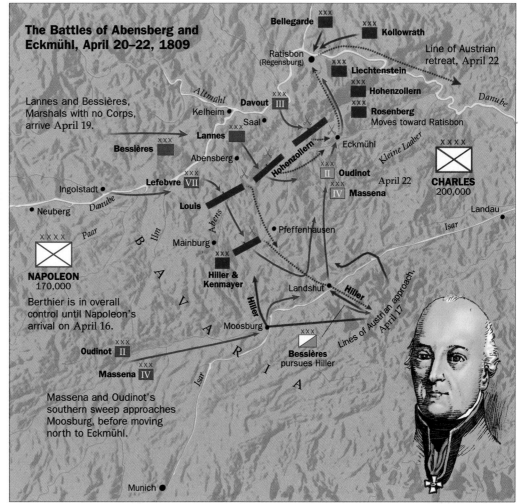

The Battles of Abensberg and Eckmühl, April 20–22, 1809

Bellegarde

Kollowrath

Ratisbon (Regensburg)

Line of Austrian retreat, April 22

Liechtenstein

Hohenzollern

Lannes and Bessières, Marshals with no Corps, arrive April 19.

Altmühl

Davout III

Kelheim

Danube

Rosenberg
Moves toward Ratisbon

Saal

Lannes

Eckmühl

Kleine Laaber

Abensberg

Hohenzollern

Bessières

Oudinot

CHARLES
200,000

Lefebvre VII

Louis

Massena

April 22

Ingolstadt

Landau

Neuberg

Danube

Paar

Isar

Pfeffenhausen

NAPOLEON
170,000

Berthier is in overall control until Napoleon's arrival on April 16.

Mainburg

B

I

L

M

A

Hiller & Kenmayer

Landshut

Hiller

Lines of Austrian approach, April 17

Oudinot II

Moosburg

R

Bessières
pursues Hiller

Massena IV

Massena and Oudinot's southern sweep approaches Moosburg, before moving north to Eckmühl.

Isar

A

Munich

Johann Freiherr von Hiller (1754–1819), commander of the VI Korps, remained south of the Danube.

The Drive on Vienna

The nature of the 1809 campaign had changed. The Austrians were now on the defensive and in full retreat toward Vienna. Napoleon gave pursuit in an effort to capture the capital and force Austria to make peace.

The Battle of Abensberg and Eckmühl had cleared the Austrians from Bavaria, and the army of Archduke Charles was in full retreat along the north bank of the Danube. The decision for Napoleon was whether to pursue the Austrians toward Vienna with the few troops he had, or wait for reinforcements from Spain. The latter course risked the chance that Austrian nerve might recover and give Charles the opportunity to entice either Prussia, Russia, or even both to join the Austrian cause. He opted for immediate pursuit and initiated a racing month-long campaign for Vienna.

Archduke Charles had lost about 15,000 men in Bavaria, but after joining with General Bellegarde the combined army numbered just under 160,000. In fact, Napoleon had about the same number, but because the two armies were on opposite banks of the Danube from each other, there was little immediate risk of an engagement.

In north Italy, The French commanded by Prince Eugène de Beauharnais pushed Archduke John back into Austria, but the nervous John was buoyed by news of the Austrian victory at Aspern-Essling (May 22) and turned to give Eugène battle on the banks of the Raab on June 14. Despite being outnumbered, Eugène's Army of Italy defeated the Austrians, who retired along the north bank of the Danube, while Eugène went to link up with his stepfather in time

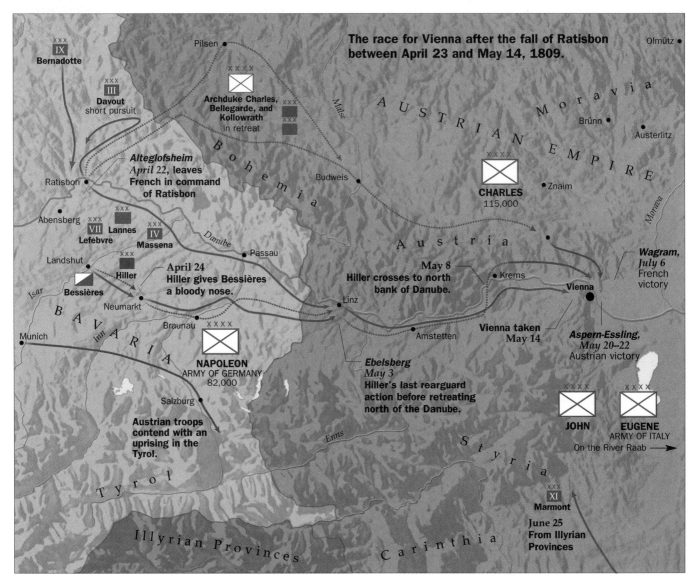

for the Battle of Deutsch-Wagram.

Emperor Francis I's attempt to widen the scope of the war by appealing to German nationalism had come to nothing. Apart from a rising in the Tyrol against the Bavarians and small-scale insurrections in Westphalia, the Confederation of the Rhine remained firmly allied to France. The situation was dangerous for Austria, but the emperor felt that his armies could defend the capital. The decisive battle of the war was likely to be fought close to Vienna, so while Archduke Charles marched down the Danube, the Austrian government mobilized the *landwehr* and prepared supplies and matériel for the inevitable battle.

Outpaced but not outsmarted

Napoleon also moved along the Danube in pursuit of a detached Austrian corps of 40,000 men on the south bank commanded by General Hiller, who had become isolated from the main army in Bavaria. A delaying action fought at Ebelsberg (May 3) failed to halt the French and Hiller was forced to slip across the Danube to the north on May 8, 1809. This meant there was no longer an Austrian force between the French and Vienna.

Napoleon was faced with another decision: continue on to Vienna or chase Archduke Charles across the Danube into Bohemia. Again, Napoleon

opted for Vienna on the grounds that capturing the Austrian capital would force a peace on Francis, while pursuit of Charles offered little but a risky campaign. With the pressure off him, Archduke Charles wheeled about and also force-marched toward Vienna in an attempt to reach it before Napoleon.

He did not win the race. The French were past-masters at outpacing their opponents. By May 10 the French were within 20 miles of Vienna, and three days later the heavily outnumbered garrison withdrew north across the Danube, destroying the bridges behind them and abandoning the city.

Napoleon entered the Austrian capital on May 14, two days before Archduke Charles appeared opposite Vienna on the north bank of the river. Both sides had been depleted by the need to leave garrisons to guard their communications; Napoleon commanded 82,000 men, while Charles mustered 115,000. It soon became clear that the Austrians had no intention of surrendering while the army remained intact.

Napoleon had to concentrate his army deep in enemy territory, then find a way to cross the river and defeat Archduke Charles before the Austrians could sever his tenuous line of supply along the southern bank of the Danube. Time was on the Austrians' side, and Napoleon needed a quick victory.

The pontoon bridges erected by Napoleon's engineers from the south bank of the Danube over Lobau Island to the north bank (*see following page*) allowed the French to gain a foothold on the northern bank. The event depicted in this French illustration of 1809 by Rugendas shows the victorious French recrossing toward Vienna on July 6 after the Battle of Deutsch-Wagram (*see pages 94–95*).

Aspern-Essling

Napoleon held Vienna, but the peace he had hoped to force on the emperor eluded him while the Austrian army sat on the far side of the Danube. To defeat the Austrians, Napoleon had to cross the river, establish a bridgehead, then bring the enemy to battle.

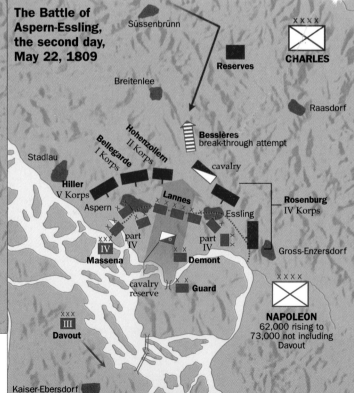

The Battle of Aspern-Essling resulted in the highest casualty list yet for the French. "Napoleon Honoring the Courageous Wounded," undated engraving by Lefevre.

A river crossing in the face of a waiting enemy is one of the most difficult military operations, and the Danube is a wide and treacherous river. While Napoleon concentrated his army on the south bank, he sent engineers to scout for a suitable crossing point. Lobau Island was suggested, which divided the river into two unequal channels about four miles downstream from Vienna.

The main channel was further divided by a number of smaller islands, close enough to each other to bridge. The channel on the north shore of Lobau was narrow enough for French artillery to cover the engineers and then a crossing, and it appeared to permit the establishment of a secure bridgehead from which the rest could deploy to attack the Austrians.

No plan is perfect, and for this one to work smoothly it required the Austrians to remain inactive during the crossing operation. But would the enemy sit back and let the French cross the river unopposed? Napoleon was confident that this was exactly what they would do, given their previous lack of initiative. He was wrong, however. The skirmishes to this point had not indicated any real changes in Austrian tactics. But the army facing Napoleon had

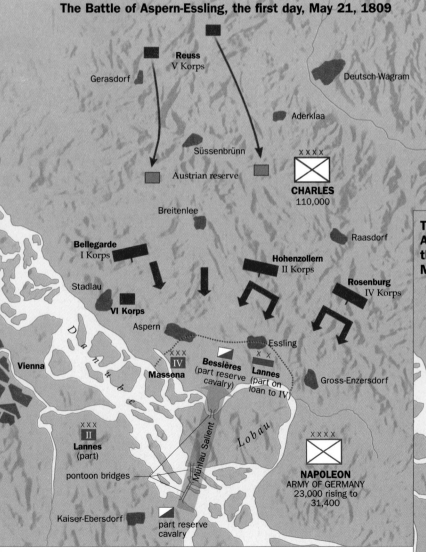

The Battle of Aspern-Essling, the first day, May 21, 1809

The Battle of Aspern-Essling, the second day, May 22, 1809

been reformed, and it was better motivated than during any previous campaign against the French.

French troops secured Lobau Island during the night of May 18–19, 1809. The next morning engineers began building a series of pontoon bridges spanning the main channel of the river to the south. A small island was chosen as a midway point, meaning that two sets of bridges were needed to reach Lobau, a total length of 2,475 feet. More pontoons were needed to cross the 375-foot stretch between Lobau and the north bank. These were in place by the following morning, and on May 20 Marshal Massena's IV Corps of 24,000 men and 60 guns crossed the river and established a bridgehead on the north bank of the Danube.

His men occupied a semi-circular line, centered on the two villages of Aspern and Essling. The Austrian army was nowhere to be seen. That evening, Austrian hulks floated down the river damaged the bridges and slowed the build-up of French troops. Worse still, the river level rose by three feet the following day, causing further delays.

Losing the foothold

At about noon on May 21, the Austrian army appeared from the north; 95,000 men divided into five large corps-sized columns commanded by Hiller, Bellegarde, Liechtenstein, Hohenzollern, and Rosenburg. The Austrians attacked throughout the afternoon, but Massena held onto the bridgehead with grim determination, aided by a lack of co-ordination between the Austrian columns.

During the afternoon, Lannes crossed the river to support Massena, followed by Bessières and the reserve cavalry. By nightfall the bridgehead contained 31,500 French troops, supported by 90 guns, but the Austrians kept releasing logs and rafts downriver onto the bridges, making them virtually useless. The French held on until dark, but in a tenuous position. Napoleon seethed with frustration on the southern bank while the engineers struggled to repair the pontoon crossing.

At dawn on May 22, in a renewed assault, the Austrians captured Aspern and threatened Essling. In response, Napoleon crossed the Danube himself with the Imperial Guard and forced the Austrians out of Aspern at bayonet point. Lannes commenced a second attack between the two villages, but Archduke Charles fed more soldiers into the center of the battlefield and the Austrian line held.

When Lannes was forced from Essling, it became clear that the bridgehead was no longer tenable. Napoleon ordered an evacuation to Lobau Island, sending Lannes' corps over first, screened by the Imperial Guard, who launched a counterattack against Essling. During the night the rest of the French army slipped away to safety. Lannes was mortally wounded and Napoleon wept for the loss of his old friend. He was also shocked by the casualty list— over 21,000 men, roughly two-thirds of the French force in the bridgehead. Charles' casualties were equally high, but Austria had won a crucial victory.

Count Heinrich Graf Bellegarde (1756–1845) fought the French in Italy, Germany, and Switzerland. Made field-marshal in 1806, he was president of the Imperial War Council 1809–13 and governor of Galicia.

Jean Lannes, Duc de Montebello at the Battle of Aspern-Essling, in which he lost his life, depicted in a French engraving of his heroic action.

Battle of Deutsch-Wagram

While the battered French army recovered, Napoleon and his staff planned a return across the Danube. There was no longer any room for mistakes. Six weeks preparation went into a battle to decide the war.

Facing below:

"Napoleon After the Battle of Wagram" by Francesco Hayez.

*I*n the weeks following the Battle of Aspern-Essling, Archduke Charles—unlike his enemy—did little to prepare for a new round of fighting. Napoleon used the time to concentrate his forces, including the recall of the French Army of Italy. By late June 1809 he had 188,000 men at his disposal, while the Austrian army remained at 155,000. Bonaparte fortified his forward base on Lobau Island, in preparation for the second crossing of the river. The pontoon bridges were strengthened and additional crossing points were prepared between Lobau and the north bank.

During the night of July 4–5 Napoleon moved his entire army onto the north bank of the Danube, which was only screened by General Klenau's VI Korps, who retired before the French advance. Napoleon deployed his army on the plain beyond (the Marchfeld), then led them north on a broad front until they encountered the forward line of Austrian positions, centered on the village of Deutsch-Wagram.

At Napoleon's disposal were Massena's IV Corps, IX Corps under Bernadotte, Oudinot's II Corps, and Davout commanding III Corps. Eugène's and Macdonald's two Italian corps, the Imperial Guard, and the reserve cavalry were kept behind the allied center. In all, Napoleon had 145,000 men on the battlefield, with a further 43,000 of Marmont's XI Corps guarding Vienna. The seven Austrian korps lined the high ground to the north of the Marchfeld, with 90,000 men to the left of the village of Deutsch-Wagram and 65,000 men to the right. Both sides prepared for battle the following morning.

Napoleon had planned to launch a co-ordinated series of attacks against the Austrian positions, but at dawn on July 6, 1809, the Austrians were first to attack. Charles planned to turn Napoleon's left flank, then work between the French army and the river, heading for the bridges to Lobau. By cutting off the French retreat, he would have them at his mercy.

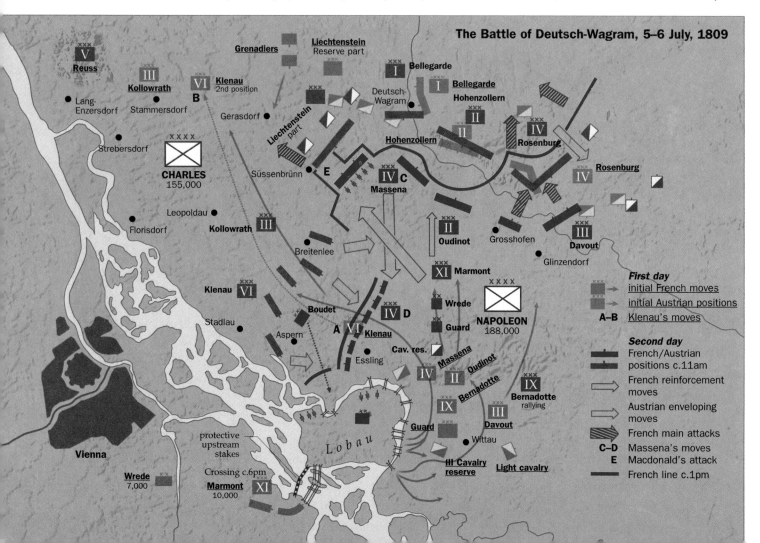

A bloody battle

Bernadotte's Saxon force fell back in the face of an attack by two Austrian korps, prompting Napoleon to summarily dismiss the marshal. He was ordered to "Leave my presence immediately, and quit the Grande Armée within 24 hours." Bernadotte's fall from favor was to have significant consequences for Napoleon four years later (*see page 135*).

Massena took charge of the French left wing, rallying the defenders to form a solid line in front of Aspern. Massena then counterattacked, supported by French artillery fire from Lobau, which pounded the Austrian right flank. Meanwhile, Davout and Oudinot had advanced to the attack, pounding the Austrian left wing and pinning it in place. The French advanced slowly, the Austrians counterattacking whenever they could. In this eastern sector of the battlefield the outcome hung in the balance until late afternoon, when Austrian resistance collapsed.

At about 2pm Napoleon exploited a flaw in the Austrian center. To support his flanking attack on Bernadotte and Massena, Archduke Charles had drawn troops from his own center. Napoleon ordered the two Italian corps forward to charge the weakened

position. He risked leaving a gap in the French line, but the Austrians were unable to take advantage of it, since it was plugged by a massed battery of over a hundred guns.

Macdonald attacked to the northwest and rolled up the Austrian center. He then formed his men into a giant column and advanced to split the Austrian army in two. A subsequent attack by Marmont's rearguard, supported by General Wrede's Bavarians, smashed into the Austrians to the right of Marmont, around Deutsch-Wagram. By mid-afternoon the Austrian left wing was falling back all along the line, while its right wing was being pushed back toward its starting position. By 4pm Archduke Charles conceded that the battle was lost and ordered his men to quit the field.

Napoleon's victory had been won at a terrible cost. In one of the bloodiest battles of the Napoleonic era, over 40,000 French and French allies were killed or captured—roughly one out of every four men who participated, including 40 generals. The Austrians suffered almost as badly, approximately 37,000 dead. In recognition of the crucial part he played, General Macdonald was awarded his marshal's baton on the battlefield.

Above: Jacques-Etienne Joseph-Alexandre Macdonald was the only one of Napoleon's marshals to be awarded his baton on the battlefield.

Affairs at Home

Victorious in Austria, Napoleon concluded a peace very favorable to France, then returned to Paris to attend to civil matters. Napoleon had to deal with his wife, who had long proved a thorn in the emperor's side.

*F*our days after his hard-won victory at Wagram, Napoleon was approached by ambassadors dispatched by Emperor Francis I, who proposed an armistice. The Armistice of Znaim was duly signed, and the peace talks that began resulted in the Peace of Schönbrunn and the Treaty of Vienna, concluded on October 19, 1809.

The peace terms were harsh. Austria was forced to cede the Inn valley and Salzburg to Bavaria, while Trieste and part of the Dalmatian coast were ceded to Italy. This effectively cut off Austria from the sea. The Duchy of Warsaw gained territory around Kracow, while other eastern regions were ceded to Russia. Finally, a large indemnity was paid to France before the treaty was ratified. In all, Austria ceded border territories containing over three million inhabitants; a major change of the political landscape.

In three years, Napoleon had humbled Prussia and Austria, and reduced the risk that either power would renew opposition toward France. The treaty left him free to concentrate on domestic political matters, such as the reform of the French civil administration, the reconstruction of Paris, and the growing problem in Spain. Above all, Napoleon could at last deal with his wife, Josephine.

Marie Rose Josephine Tascher de la Pagerie was a Creole, born in the French West Indies in 1763. When she was 16 she married Viscomte (Viscount) Alexandre de Beauharnais, and the couple bore two children, a son Eugène (1781) and a daughter Hortense (1783). Eugène later became a Prince of the Empire, while his sister married Napoleon's brother Louis, King of Holland.

Alexandre went to the guillotine in 1794 and his widow became the mistress of French Revolution leader Paul François-Jean Barras (1755–1829). She met Napoleon in 1795 and the Corsican was smitten, although Josephine was six years older. The couple married in March 1796, but his military duties kept him from Paris.

Despite their amorous correspondence, Josephine occupied herself by taking several lovers, most notably

An engraving by Jean Pierre Marie Jazet (1788–1871) from the painting by Henri-Frederic Schopin of "The Divorce of the Empress Josephine." The removal of Josephine left Napoleon free to marry Marie-Louise, daughter of his former enemy, Francis I, Emperor of Austria (below, seen with their son Napoleon II).

Captain Hippolyte Charles. Napoleon's friends and family advised him of Josephine's infidelities, which forced her to be more discreet in her relationships. Napoleon threatened to divorce her on grounds of infidelity in October 1799 but relented, and the couple remained married for reasons of protocol.

Finding an heir

When Napoleon became emperor in December 1804, Josephine was crowned Empress of France and her opportunity for secret liaisons vanished, due to her social and state commitments in Tuileries Palace. However, the relationship never fully recovered from

her earlier infidelities, and her failure to produce a male heir placed an unbearable strain on the marriage. Certainly the inability was not due to Napoleon—he sired two illegitimate children between 1802 and 1808, proving that in early 19th-century France a husband could be adulterous, but his wife could not.

When Napoleon returned from Paris in early November he confronted Josephine and demanded a divorce. The legal action took its course, and the couple officially separated on December 15, 1809. Josephine was given a chateau at Malmaison, where she continued to live until her death in May 1814.

Freed from his wife, Napoleon set about completing his grand social reorganization. As the leading political figure in Europe, he required a bride who could match his position. He chose Marie-Louise, the 19-year-old daughter of Austrian Emperor Francis I and the grand-niece of Marie-Antoinette. No doubt the initial arrangements had been made before Napoleon left Vienna in 1809.

The announcement of the betrothal was made in early 1810, and Marshal Berthier arranged a marriage by proxy on March 11, before escorting the young bride from Vienna to Paris. She was 22 years younger than Napoleon, but their relationship was a loving one, and on March 20, 1811 she gave birth to a son. Empress Marie-Louise provided a link between the ruling houses of Austria and France, and although the two countries resumed their war with each other in 1813, Marie-Louise remained loyal to her husband until his abdication, when she returned to Vienna with her son. Napoleon and his family were never reunited.

CHAPTER SEVEN

The Spanish Ulcer

War in the Peninsula, 1807–14

*F*rench involvement in Spain developed almost by accident. The Spanish proved to be fickle allies. The Habsburg monarchs of Spain had been ousted during the War of the Spanish Succession (1701–14) by the ruling French Bourbons. Over the century, an uneasy alliance had existed between the two Bourbon arms of Spain and France, but the country opted in 1793 to join the anti-revolutionary alliance. They then switched sides again in 1795. Meanwhile, Spain's neighbor Portugal retained its age-old links with Britain and rejected Napoleon's requests to join his continental federation of allies.

Following the loss of the Spanish fleet at the Battle of Trafalgar in 1805, Spanish enthusiasm for the French alliance waned. This coincided with the French victories of 1805–7 that culminated in the Treaty of Tilsit. With a secure peace in central Europe, Napoleon turned his attention on bolstering his continental alliances. From July 1807 onward, Charles Talleyrand, Napoleon's leading diplomat, issued a string of ultimatums in an attempt to coerce Portugal into the French sphere of influence, but without any result.

On October 17, 1807 Napoleon resorted to force, when General Junot entered Spain in transit for Portugal at the head of 24,000 French troops. A month later Junot crossed the border and captured Lisbon on November 30. Sir William Sidney Smith, the man who had helped halt Bonaparte at Acre, took the Portuguese royal family and its treasury to safety onboard a British warship just before the capital fell.

Under the terms of the Treaty of Fontainebleu, (October 1807), the Spanish government, represented by its leading minister Manuel de Godoy, agreed to support the French invasion in return for the favorable settlement of long-standing territorial claims with Portugal. Well aware that Godoy was more than likely to renege on his alliance, Napoleon determined to replace the Spanish royal house and government with one he could trust. So began the Peninsular War, a campaign that would slowly bleed the French of their best soldiers, destroy the reputation of its marshals, and erode the stability of Napoleon's Europe.

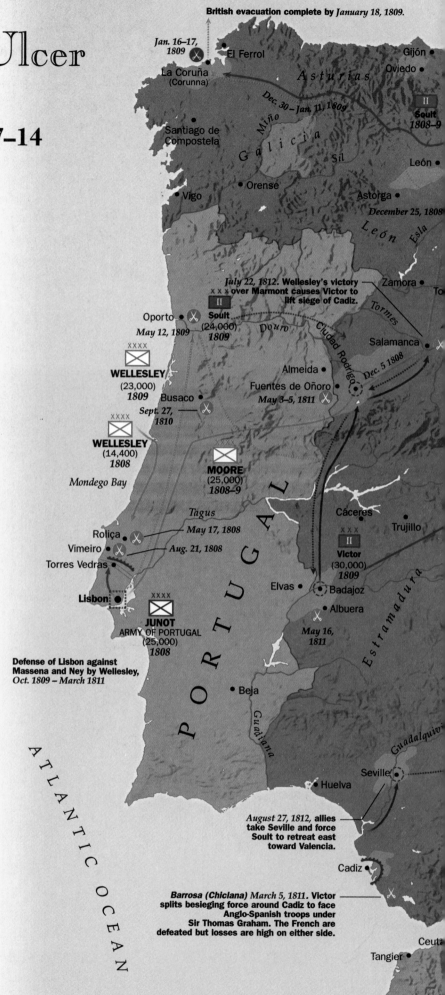

Siege July 7–Sept. 8, 1813

Charles IV of Spain is removed to Bayonne by Murat and forced to abdicate in favor of Napoleon's brother, Joesph Bonaparte, in 1808.

Santander

San Sebastián

Bayonne

Carcasonne

Narbonne

Bilbao

Lourdes

FRANCE

Roncesvalles

Perpignan

Vitoria

Pamplona

June 21, 1813. Allied soldiers become wealthy after looting 5.5 million francs of war chest.

Navarre

Arga

Logroño

Catalonia
to France 1812–13

Gerona

XXX
St. Cyr
10,000
1808

XXX
Bessières
17,150
1808–9

Sahagun

Burgos — Siege Sept. 19–Oct. 22, 1812 (failed);
Battle June 10–12, 1813

Ebro

June 1808

XXX
IV
Lefebrve
14,000

Lérida

Douro

Soria

Saragossa
Siege lifted
Aug. 14, 1808

Barcelona

Valladolid

Medina del Rio Seco July 14, 1808.
Bessières, outnumbered, defeats Spanish under Don Gregorio de la Cuesta.

S P A I N

Aragon

Tarragona

Ebro

Tortosa

August 12, 1812, Wellesley enters Madrid, but retires when Soult approaches.

Avila

JOSEPH
ARMY OF SPAIN
30,000 (1808) rising to over 300,000 (1811)

Valencia

Teruel

Madrid

June 1808

Castellón
de la Plana

Talavera

Toledo

Tagus

Cuenca

XX
de Moncey
8,800 1808

July 27–28, 1809

Valencia

Faced with collapse of his Spanish allies, Wellesley retires to defend Lisbon.

New Castile

August 11, 1812,
Joseph abandons Madrid and retreats to the southeast.

Júcar

July 23, 1808.
General Dupont surrenders his 13,000 men to a slightly larger Spanish force—Napoleon's biggest setback to date. Dupont is jailed for his failure, but later reistated by the Bourbons.

Ciudad Real

Guadiana

Albacete

Soult advances on Madrid, takes capital back on Nov. 1, 1812.

Soult meets Joseph,
October 2, 1812.

Hellin

Alicante

XXX
Dupont
13,000
1808

Córdoba

Bailén

Aug. 27 – Sept 2, 1812

Murcia

Murcia

Lorca

II
Soult
1812

Granada

Cartagena

Andalucia

Almería

ibraltar

Malaga

M E D I T E R R A N E A N   S E A

Oran

French advance, 1808–9

French retreat, 1808–9

Spanish movement, 1808–9

British/allied movement, 1808–9

area of local Spanish resistance

British Oporto–Talavera campaign, 1809

French advance, 1812

French retreat, 1812–13

British advance, 1812

British retreat, 1812

final Allied campaign in Spain from Valladolid to Roncesvalles, 1813

French victory

Spanish victory

British/allied victory

Lines of Torres Vedras

French stronghold 1808–9

French stronghold, 1812

British stronghold 1809

French siege

Allied siege

The major campaigns and battles of the Peninsular War, 1808–1813.

99

Spain in 1807

Once the richest and most powerful country in Europe, Spain had undergone two centuries of decline under the later Habsburgs and Bourbons. As corruption and political disputes reduced the effectiveness of the government, the Spanish army and navy were neglected.

*B*y 1807 Spain was widely regarded as one of the most backward, inefficient, and corrupt countries in Europe. When the Bourbon king Charles IV (r.1788–1819) came to the throne he inherited a government run by his father's principal advisor, Don Jose Moñino, Count of Floridablanca (1728–1808), who discouraged royal interference in politics. Since the king was described as "a benign imbecile," this was hardly surprising.

a Franco-Spanish alliance was ratified by the Treaty of San Ildefonso, a partnership that led to defeat at sea and isolation from Spain's extensive overseas colonies in the New World and Pacific Rim.

Despite his temporary removal from office and frequent allegations of corruption, Godoy remained in power and agreed to the transit of French troops through Spain in 1807 during Napoleon's invasion of Portugal. This allowed Napoleon to infiltrate even more troops into Spain, this time "to stabilize the country." Certainly the court was unstable, since the king's son Ferdinand (1784–1833) had plotted a palace coup, plans that were thwarted by Godoy. Spain had become the weak link in Napoleon's unified Europe. In 1808 he forced Charles IV to abdicate in favor of Joseph Bonaparte, Napoleon's

A 19th-century Spanish engraving of "The Incarceration of Manuel de Godoy." When Napoleon forced the abdication of Charles IV, the duplicitous Spanish minister was sent into exile.

While Floridablanca favored joining the European alliance against the French revolutionaries, Queen Maria Louisa of Parma opposed the war, and engineered the removal of the minister. After one failed principal, a replacement was found in Manuel de Godoy (1769–1851), the queen's lover. Despite his favored position, the Spanish declared war against France despite the queen's wishes, but the Spanish army was so inept that Godoy was forced to sign the Treaty of Basel in 1795. The following year

brother. Ferdinand was incarcerated in France until 1814 and Godoy was exiled.

When the Spanish populace rebelled against the imposed French monarch, political power devolved into the hands of local *juntas* (committees), since what remained of the administration in Madrid was regarded as a French puppet government. An attempt to form a central *junta* at Seville under Floridablanca was denied by the minister's death and the capture of the city by the French.

Struggling toward adolescence

It was only after the French tide receded in southern Spain that a new *cortes* (or government) was formed in Cadiz. A new Spanish constitution was passed in 1812, a liberal piece of legislation that hindered any future deal between the *cortes* and the exiled Ferdinand VII, who represented the popular Spanish alternative to Napoleonic rule.

With a corrupt and divided government before the French invasion and a lack of central control afterward, it is hardly surprising that the Spanish army was in a poor state. Years of neglect had left it ill-equipped to face Napoleon's troops, despite its paper strength of 100,000 men. In 1808 it consisted of a guard division, 36 foot regiments, and 24 regiments of cavalry, plus a sizeable artillery train. This regular army was supported by over 50 militia battalions and, as a cosequence of the French invasion, thousands flocked to the colors.

Despite a string of defeats, Spanish troops remained in the field in the extremities of the country throughout the war. Spanish armies represented little more than armed rabbles; a mixture of regular troops, militia, and peasant volunteers. They lacked equipment, supplies, and military experience. A string of inept commanders did little to improve their chances, although on rare occasions the Spanish did defeat the French in battle.

Wellington described the Spanish as children in the art of war, whose only ability was in running away. It was a typically harsh criticism from a man short on patience with troops, but it was also the impression French soldiers had of their Spanish counterparts. However great their patriotism and despite the encouragement of their priests, most Spanish soldiers lacked the hardened experience needed to survive the dangers of battle with any real chance of success. The Spanish navy was in an equally poor state, since a lack of royal support after its defeat at the Battle of Trafalgar led to its virtual abandonment. Its remaining warships were left to rot at anchor during the Peninsular War. However, with British logistical help and training, the Spanish army developed into a reasonably efficient force.

"The Declaration of the Constitution in Cadiz" by Salvador Viniegra. The painting celebrates the events of 1812, when members of the independent Spanish government formulated legislation to prevent the return of the Bourbon kings.

The French Invasion

French troops first entered Spain on the pretext of annexing Portugal, then as an army of peaceful occupation. The Spanish rebelled against what they regarded as a foreign invasion and, in spring 1808, the French launched a full-scale campaign of conquest.

At first, the Spanish government welcomed the appearance of French troops as they marched through the countryside to invade Portugal. Soon, Napoleon sent thousands of additional troops into Spain, ostensibly as reinforcements to the army in Portugal. These were no reinforcements, but garrison troops with orders to seize Spain.

On May 2, 1808 an anti-French uprising in Madrid was ruthlessly repressed by Murat, a rashness that spawned ever greater animosity. This act set the tone for the rest of the campaign; the regular armies fought each other according to accepted codes of military conduct, but retaliation to uprisings by the local population or attacks by guerrillas involved massacres and atrocities on both sides.

Regional *juntas* rose up against Joseph Bonaparte's authority and the rebellion spread across country. French detachments were attacked, vessels seized, and militiamen took arms against the French. Since the was no central authority, the Spanish army came under the control of local *juntas*, preventing any

A contemporary Spanish engraving shows the entrance of Napoleon into Madrid in 1808.

Napoleon sent Marshal Murat to Madrid to act as his representative. Murat was an exceptionally brave cavalry commander, but no diplomat. Murat arranged the transfer of the royal family from Madrid to Bayonne in France, where the king was forced to abdicate in favor of Joseph Bonaparte (r.1808–13). This was an extremely unpopular move, particularly because the crown prince had already been anointed Ferdinand IV during the coup against his father. Joseph assumed the throne with reluctance, protected by an increasingly powerful French military presence.

cohesive defense plan. Individual cities stood up to the French alone, while elsewhere existing armies were the nucleus for militiamen and volunteers, forming cumbersome field armies of dubious military value. Andalucia and Galicia formed the major centers of resistance.

A panicked Bonaparte

By the end of May there were 100,000 French troops in Spain. Apart from Lisbon and Madrid, they held the northern cities of Pamplona, Barcelona, and San

Sebastian. Napoleon ordered his troops to seize the Mediterranean ports and secure the road between Madrid and the French border. General Dupont was sent to secure the region of Andalucia with 13,000 men, while Marshal de Moncey was sent to capture Valencia. Marshal Lefebvre was ordered to take Saragossa, while other columns maintained the links between the various corps and expanded French control into Asturias.

Though unskilled in the art of war, the Spanish were tougher opponents than Napoleon had expected. The assaults on Saragossa and Valencia were bloodily repulsed, as was another French attack on the Catalan city of Girona. All three cities became symbols of popular resistance against the invader. Several French victories against Spanish armies (most notably at Medina del Rio Seco on July 14, 1808) were countered by a humiliating defeat at the Battle of Bailén (July 23), when Dupont was forced

to surrender his entire army.

The Bailén disaster sent shockwaves throughout Europe because it marked the first serious defeat of a French army since Napoleon's coronation. The victory also encouraged further resistance. By August the French were in a precarious situation. Their troops were concentrated in the center and north of Spain, plus Portugal. Napoleon planned to restore French control elsewhere by sending overwhelming numbers of reinforcements to Spain, but Joseph Bonaparte panicked and fled Madrid for the north on August 1, which prompted a general withdrawal of French troops to the line of the River Ebro.

It was at this critical moment that a small British expeditionary force landed on the coast of Portugal, to offer its support to Britain's Portuguese allies. It was commanded by Lieutenant-General Sir Arthur Wellesley, a man who became better known as the Duke of Wellington.

Lejune's painting of the Battle of Somosierra indicates the rugged terrain which dominated the way the campaign was fought.

Britain's Iron Duke

Sir Arthur Wellesley, Duke of Wellington (1769–1852) was not the British government's first choice for commander of the British army in the peninsula, but his string of victories made him indispensable. By 1815 he was regarded as the best general in Europe, bar one....

The Duke of Wellington, painted by Francisco de Goya. Wellington's concerns over the footwear of his staff officers and even the infantry led to the development of long boots with better protection against water seepage. They became known as "Wellington Boots," a term that lives on today in the English language to describe vulcanized waterproof boots.

The son of Garret Wesley, Earl of Mornington, Arthur was born in Dublin. His father later adopted an older form of the family name, Wellesley. After an education at Eton, 18-year-old Wellesley gained a commission in the 73rd Foot, and through the purchase scheme (by which officer commissions were bought by those who could afford to) he rose through the ranks with rapidity, becoming a lieutenant-colonel of the 33rd Foot in 1793. He campaigned with the regiment in the Netherlands where he saw his first action at Boxtel in 1794, and then fought again at Geldermalsen the following year. It was during this badly mismanaged campaign that, as he later recalled, he "learned how not to do it."

When his elder brother Richard became the new Governor-General of India in 1797, Wellesley took the 33rd Foot out there and founded a great reputation for himself as a brilliant but also painstaking commander. He won a spectacular victory over a Maratha Indian army at Assaye (September 23, 1803) and returned to Britain in 1805 as an experienced major-general, albeit a mere "sepoy-general" in the eyes of the British military establishment. Nevertheless, a grateful monarch awarded Wellesley a knighthood.

While pursuing a career in politics he married Kitty Packenham, the daughter of Lord Longford. Despite being a marriage made more for political reasons than for love, the union produced two sons. In 1807 Wellesley abandoned his post as Chief Secretary for Ireland to participate in a British expedition to Copenhagen, where he played a major role in the seizure of the Danish capital and the confiscation or destruction of its fleet.

His first real opportunity for independent command in Europe came in 1808, when he was placed in command of a small British force sent to Portugal. Wellesley defeated the French at the battles of Roliça and Vimeiro, driving the French from Portugal, but his command was withdrawn following the arrival of Wellesley's superior, Sir Hew Dalrymple. Dalrymple signed a shameful treaty with the French, and Wellesley was made the scapegoat on his return to Britain.

A notorious duke

A second British force sent to Spain was given to Sir John Moore, but following Moore's death at La Coruña (1809, *see page 109*) Wellesley was restored to temporary command in Portugal in April 1809. In July he defeated the French at Talavera in concert with Spanish allies, but his experience of Spanish military and political incompetence encouraged him to avoid further co-operation. Instead, he returned to Portugal to counter a series of French offensives aimed at recapturing Lisbon. Wellesley's victories at Busaco (1810) and Fuentes de Oñoro (1811) earned him the titles of Baron Douro and Viscount Wellington of Talavera.

Further successes followed. After securing the Spanish fortresses of Badajoz and Ciudad Rodrigo in 1812, Wellington was given the title *Generalissimo* of all Spanish forces. His defeat of the French at Salamanca (1812), Vitoria (1813), and his capture of San Sebastian later in the year ensured that the French were ejected from Spain. Shortly before Napoleon's abdication Wellington won his final victory of the Peninsular War at Toulouse (1814) and was awarded the title of duke. His final campaign was fought a year later, when he commanded the British and allied army that faced Napoleon at Waterloo (1815).

Wellesley was a difficult man to like. Nicknamed Hooky by his men, because of his angular nose, he remained cold, aloof, and even disdainful of the troops he commanded. But he was insistent in their proper provision, devoting considerable attention to their food and quality of equipment.

His post-war political career was a stormy one, and his popularity waxed and waned for three decades after Waterloo. He entered the British Cabinet in 1818, staying there as Master-General of Ordinance until 1827. The following year he became prime minister and in 1829, despite being a reactionary Tory, and against his private inclinations, he helped pass the Catholic Relief Act, with the aid of Sir Robert Peel. He resigned in 1830 when it became clear that he could not prevent parliamentary reform from being enacted. His Iron Duke

nickname was inspired not by his battlefield reputation but rather the shutters he had installed over the windows of his London home, to protect it against hostile mobs. While newspapermen labeled him the Great Duke, the soldiers whom he led across Spain continued to regard him somewhat affectionately as "that long-nosed bugger who licks the French."

The British Army

Despite its poor performance during the French Revolutionary Wars, the British Army of the Peninsular War was a highly trained force. In the hands of commanders such as Moore, Beresford, and Wellington, the British foot soldier was widely regarded as the best infantryman in the world.

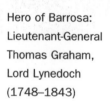

Hero of Barrosa: Lieutenant-General Thomas Graham, Lord Lynedoch (1748–1843)

A thousand men of the 33rd Foot Regiment take part in the funeral procession through London for Sir Arthur Wellesley, Duke of Wellington, in 1853.

*I*n the late 18th century, there was no love lost between the British people and their army. Years of press-gangs and "taking the king's shilling"—an easy lure for the young men of the unmonied class—had led to the view that service in the ranks was a poor alternative to prison. Even the Duke of Wellington vilified the British soldier, collectively calling them "the scum of the earth." These were the men who stood up to the French Imperial Guard and defeated the French in virtually every battle where the two armies clashed. Wellington's qualifying phrase is frequently omitted from the quote: "it is really wonderful that we should have made them the fine fellows they are."

Compared to other European forces, the British army was of moderate size. In 1805 it consisted of a guard of three cavalry and three foot regiments, and a line strength of 96 foot regiments and 32 dragoon regiments. Eight artillery battalions, two engineer battalions, and ten troops of horse artillery completed its establishment. Unlike most continental armies, British regiments rarely consisted of more than one battalion, averaging 600 men.

Only a small proportion of this force was available for service in Europe. Most was retained for the defense of the British Isles, while other troops were scattered around the globe, defending British interests in Canada, the West Indies, Africa, the Mediterranean, India, Australia, and the Far East. When the British first sent an expeditionary force to Portugal, it barely exceeded 14,000 men.

The core of the army was the infantry. Unlike the French and eventually most other European armies, the British infantry retained the linear tactics of the late 18th century, although fire tactics were greatly improved by military reformers. Deployed in a two-deep line, British regiments broke their opponents through pouring fire into the approaching enemy.

A determined barrage

Although heavy firepower was an essentially defensive tactic, the British used the tactic offensively as well, advancing toward an enemy formation, then breaking it through musketry. A well-trained British infantryman fired three rounds per minute. The big advantage of this "thin red line" tactic was that every man in the battalion was able to fire. By contrast, in the dense columns favored by the French, only the men in the front rank could use their muskets—the others behind risked hitting those in front of them.

The psychological impact of an approaching massed column demanded that the infantry that stood in its path have faith in their ability to beat the enemy before they came into close contact.

The British infantryman proved to be one of the steadiest soldiers in the world, with the nerve to stand his ground. After a string of victories, these tactics became second nature, and were only seriously modified after the killing fields of World War I.

While the majority of British line regiments were English, the army contained Scottish (highland and lowland), Irish, Welsh, German, and even French Royalist regiments. As the war progressed, additional battalions were raised in many regiments; by 1809, 61 regiments contained two battalions, and an additional five regiments contained three or more.

The elite were the light infantry regiments, created after experience in the American Revolutionary War showed the benefit of trained skirmishers. While each infantry regiment contained a light company, six regiments were exclusively light infantry formations, while a seventh regiment, the 95th, was trained as an elite unit of riflemen, later expanded to include three battalions.

The Royal Artillery and Royal Horse Artillery were also highly professional troops, but the weakest element in the British army during this period was the cavalry. British cavalry regiments developed a reputation for being impetuous, and during the Battle of Waterloo the dashing but ultimately wasteful charge of the Scots Greys typified the lack of control British commanders had over their horsemen. Despite this limitation, the British army proved highly successful in Spain, pushing the French out of the country before invading southern France. No other army achieved such a string of victories over the veterans of the Grande Armée.

The Battle of Barrosa (Chiclana), March 5, 1811. In an action to break Victor's siege of Cadiz, the garrison's commander, Lt.-Gen. Thomas Graham, landed a force of British and Spanish troops to the south of the city to outflank the French. In the battle, the Spanish withdrew, leaving Graham heavily outnumbered. It was the high-speed firepower of the British infantry that won the day, taking Barrosa hill from Victor's forces. Without allied support, Graham was obliged to withdraw to Cadiz, leaving Victor free to continue the siege.

Roliça to Talavera

Britain's first victories in Portugal were thrown away, and the army was almost annihilated by the French. A second expedition was more successful, but in an inauspicious start to the campaign, its battlefield victory in Spain was followed by another retreat.

General Sir John Moore, commander of the British land forces, killed in action at Coruña, is credited with creating the modern light infantry.

*I*n the summer of 1808, the Spanish *juntas* sent appeals to the British government for help. A small expeditionary force was sent to Portugal, 14,000 men commanded by Sir Arthur Wellesley. He landed at Mondego Bay, north of Lisbon, in early August. With his poor view of the senior British military command, Wellesley was eager to begin offensive operations before Sir John Moore (1761–1809) would arrive to assume command of all land forces, and Lieutenant-General Sir Hew Dalrymple (1750–1830), assisted by his deputy, Sir Harry Burrard, would become overall commander in Portugal.

On August 17 Wellesley attacked a French division of 14,400 men commanded by General Henri Delaborde (1764–1833) at Roliça, driving the enemy from the field at the cost of 500 men. Wellington was delayed from continuing the advance by Burrard's arrival on the coast to assume command. However, he stayed on his ship while the British army remained camped around Vimiero.

Then the French took affairs into their own hands. On August 21 General Jean Junot (1771–1813) attacked Wellesley, who still commanded the army in Burrard's continued absence. Three French assaults were driven off by musket fire. The completeness of the British victory was marred only by the impetuous behavior of the light cavalry. British losses amounted to about 750 men.

Burrard elected not to take advantage of the victory by marching on Lisbon, and when Dalrymple arrived he signed a treaty with Junot rather than finish driving him out of the country. The Treaty of Cintra (August 22) permitted Junot to escape back to France, transported by British ships, a concession that led to the court martial of all British senior officers, including Wellesley, who had consistently opposed any deal with the French.

When John Moore arrived in Lisbon he assumed control of the army and, on October 26, he marched east into Spain to link up with Britain's Spanish allies. Moore halted at Salamanca to rendezvous with reinforcements sent through northern Spain, then pressed on to Sahagun. On November 28 he discovered that the Spanish in the region had been defeated, and despite pleas for assistance from the *junta* in Madrid, the capital had surrendered to the French, who were pouring reinforcements into the country. The force closest to Moore was Marshal Soult's corps, and the cavalry of both armies clashed at Sahagun on December 25.

Ill-matched allies

It became clear that if the British remained in central Spain they would be overwhelmed, so Moore ordered a retreat toward the coast at La Coruña. It became a horrendous march through the snow-

Battle of Corunna, January 16, 1809

La Coruña

ATLANTIC OCEAN

Old City

Puerto Harbor
Fortress San Antón

British evacuation fleet

FRASER

Fane

Altos de Santa Margarita

Beresford

Santa Lucia

Fortress San Diego

French outflanking maneuver is foiled by sharpshooting riflemen of the 95th Foot.

PAGET

Anstruther

Moore is killed in the defensive action, but the evacuation is a success, saving thousands of British troops to fight another day.

Francesky

Disney

MOORE 19,000

San Christobal

Las Jublas

BAIRD

Eiris
Warde

HOPE

Lahoussaye

Bentick

Crawfurd

Altos de San Christobal

Manningham

Hill

Altos de Parillo

Mesoiro

Elvina

Leith

Piedralanga

River Mero

II SOULT 20,000

Mermet

Merle

Lorges

Delaborde

Altos de Peñasquedo

Altos de Pazalea

Soult targets the British defensive line at Elvina, but fails to break through.

covered mountains; a ten-day ordeal during which discipline was lost and stragglers were left in the snow to die or be captured.

On January 11 Moore entered La Coruña with 19,000 men. On the following day, while the wounded were being embarked first, Soult arrived at the head of 20,000 French soldiers. The Battle of Corunna (as it is spelt in English) was a defensive one, in which Moore fought off Soult's attacks, allowing the British to evacuate in peace, but Moore was mortally wounded in the action.

In April 1809 the British returned. Sir Arthur Wellesley landed near Lisbon with 23,000 men. Two French armies were operating in Portugal: Soult's 24,000 men at Oporto and Victor's 30,000 men at Badajoz. On May 12 Wellesley defeated Soult on the Douro near Oporto, driving him back across the border into Spain. He then turned on Victor, marching up the Tagus to rendezvous with the Spanish army of General Gregorio del la Cuesta (1740–1812).

The allies met Victor at Talavera on July 28; 21,000 British and 33,000 Spanish against 22,000 French troops. The untrained and ill-disciplined Spanish were virtually useless during the battle, but the British infantry repulsed several attacks, forcing the French to retreat. Losses on both sides exceeded 5,000 men. With his army reduced and faced with the incompetence of his Spanish ally, Wellesley retired to Lisbon.

The fruits of the British victory at Roliça (1808) were lost when Portugal was abandoned later that year.

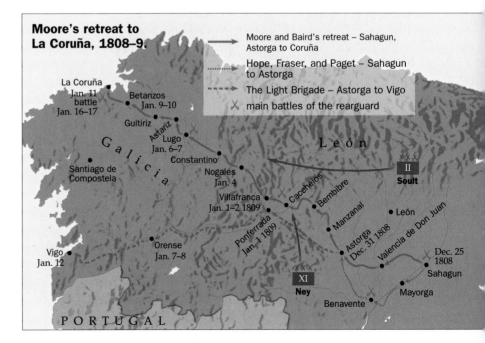

Defending Portugal

Having come to the conclusion that fighting alongside the Spanish was to court disaster, Wellesley withdrew the army to Portugal. There, he defended Lisbon while gathering strength for a counter-offensive.

André Massena, Duc du Rivoli and Prince d'Essling, fought a frustrating campaign against Wellington in Portugal, while his army starved outside the defenses of Lisbon.

While Wellesley led the British army back to Lisbon, the *juntas* developed ever-more grandiose plans for the liberation of Spain. General Cuesta was replaced by General Areizaga, who was decisively defeated by the French at the Battle of Ocaña on November 19. This justified Wellesley's concerns over his Spanish allies. From that point, the British strategy would be to operate independently, relying solely on Portuguese allies, who were trained and equipped in the British manner.

Lisbon was vital to British plans, since it provided a secure port to supply the army and bring in reinforcements. The supremacy of the Royal Navy ensured that Wellesley's sea communications were safe from attack, but it was up to the army to ensure that Lisbon remained in British hands. Consequently, in October 1809 Wellesley ordered the construction of fortified lines protecting the city from the north. The Lines of Torres Vedras turned the peninsula on which Lisbon sat into a virtually impregnable fortress. If threatened, the British army could retreat behind the lines, while the navy ensured it remained fully supplied.

By this stage the French had over 320,000 troops in Spain and, although the British army remained a threat, almost all regular Spanish armies had been defeated. King Joseph Bonaparte was free to deal with the British. He therefore sent Marshal Massena to Portugal with orders to defeat Wellesley's army and capture Lisbon. His Army of Portugal besieged the Spanish-held border fortress of Ciudad Rodrigo in June 1810, and the city fell within a month.

Another French column led by Marshal Ney captured the Portuguese city of Almeida, despite a setback on the River Coa when the British light division fought a skilled delaying action in defense of the city. Massena and Ney joined forces and advanced on Lisbon with 60,000 men. Wellesley placed his 52,000-strong army in the line of the French advance, selecting a long steep ridge at Busaco for his battlefield.

Divided but not conquered

The French attacked on September 27, 1810. Wellesley deployed his troops on the reverse of the slope, where they were protected from French fire until the last possible moment. The first French assault by General Reynier's corps was checked with musket fire. Ney's corps attacked next, meeting the same fate. Having suffered 4,500 casualties, Massena called off the attack. The British and Portuguese had lost 1,200 men.

Wellesley—now granted the title Viscount Wellington—withdrew his army to the safety of the Lines of Torres Vedras. Massena followed, but he could do little but camp his forces in front of the defensive lines and wait. An assault would have been

Henry William Paget (1768–1854), Lord Uxbridge and Marquess of Anglesey, distinguished himself in the Peninsular War. Originally an infantry colonel with the 80th Foot, Paget saw action in the Netherlands in 1794 before switching to the cavalry. Under his direction, the Seventh Light Dragoons became a highly respected unit and, in 1808, the now Lieutenant-General Paget led the British cavalry in the Peninsular War at Sahagun, Benavente, and La Coruña. At Sahagun, 400 of his 15th Hussars fought a much larger French cavalry force under General Debelle and scattered them for two dead, as against Debelle's loss of 120. In the delaying action at the River Coa, his light division fought skilfully in defense of Almeida. After an impressive military career Paget, as Lord Uxbridge, was Britain's second-in-command to Wellington at Waterloo.

suicidal, but waiting was even worse, since his army now lacked supplies. Conditions deteriorated through continual harassment of his communications by Spanish and Portuguese guerrillas, and Massena's army starved during the winter. By March 1811 the French Army of Portugal was reduced to 40,000 men, while Wellington's had been reinforced and numbered 43,000. Massena had little option but to retreat to Almeida. Lisbon had been spared, and the British were ready to extend their control over the rest of the country.

During the campaign that followed, Marshal Soult captured the fortress city of Badajoz on the Portuguese-Spanish border, while Massena reformed his army at Almeida. Wellington was forced to divide his army to protect Lisbon from the two forces. He won the Battle of Fuentes de Oñoro on May 3–5 and Massena abandoned Almeida, retreating to Spain.

Meanwhile, General Beresford threatened Badajoz, a move that brought Soult to battle at Albuera on May 16. It was a close-run affair, but ended in a marginal British victory. As Wellington observed, "Another such battle would ruin us." For the rest of the year, the British and French avoided further clashes, as Wellington prepared his army for a new campaign that would take the war to the the whole of the Iberian peninsula.

The Guerrilla War

While the campaigns between armies on the peninsula were fought according to contemporary codes of civilized behavior, the guerrilla war between French regulars and Spanish partisans was fought with the utmost savagery, with no mercy given on either side.

The series of sketches by Spanish artist Francisco de Goya called "Disasters of War" represents one of the most horrifying collections of war pictures ever created. **Above:** "The Same" depicts guerillas dealing out revenge.

Facing above: "Heroic feat! Against the Dead!" no longer distinguishes between Spanish and French.

Facing below: The masterly painting "Third of May, 1808" shows French troops executing guerillas.

The ferocity of the guerrilla struggle in the Peninsular War came as a surprise to the French. Ever since the first spontaneous uprising against French rule on May 2, 1808, Spanish partisans gathered into guerrilla bands to attack isolated French garrisons and harass supply lines. As the regular Spanish armies were defeated, experienced soldiers began to join the guerrillas, along with land-owners, peasants, priests, and brigands. By the end of 1808, guerrilla bands operated throughout the country, answerable to nobody but themselves.

The rising of May 2 was crushed with great savagery and hundreds of Spanish civilians were executed by French troops, captured by the artist Goya in his wartime sketches, "Disasters of War." This fed a spiral of violence, and Spanish atrocities against French prisoners were met with equal acts of barbarity by French punitive expeditions sent to root out guerrillas and destroy any villages that harbored them.

One French soldier wrote that "We fear to walk alone." Certainly the practice of sending individual

couriers with dispatches was soon halted, since individual French horsemen stood little chance of survival in areas controlled by guerrillas. While most bands, numbering anywhere from a dozen to over 200, were based in the high mountains of central Spain, guerrilla activity spread over the whole country, even to large cities.

It became commonplace for even the most routine courier missions or supply convoys to travel with escorts of 200 men or more in order to get them safely to their destination. Forage parties were vulnerable, as were French soldiers enjoying the hospitality of local wine shops and brothels in garrison towns. The situation became desperate, since to the French troops it seemed as if the whole population was hostile to their presence.

Drained by guerilla attacks

Mercy was not a consideration. Victims were often tortured or flayed alive, then left tied to a tree or a roadside post as a warning to others. Clearly these attacks had a detrimental effect on French morale in Spain. By 1810, when Napoleon resorted to widespread conscription to maintain the size of his armies, a posting to Spain was considered the most dangerous of all deployments. French troops regarded the Iberian Peninsula rather like a posting to the Russian Front came to be seen as a death sentence for German soldiers in World War II.

To counter the guerrillas, the French had to scatter their troops throughout the Spanish countryside, garrisoning and patrolling regions far from the main areas of conflict. Thousands of French troops were tied down in this manner, and therefore unavailable to the commanders who fought against Wellington.

The French were not the only victims of guerrillas. Any Spaniard who collaborated with the French became a target, as did the revolutionary liberals who had initially welcomed the arrival of the French in 1808. Guerrilla bands came to dominate the political climate, and—while some acted as little more than highwaymen and brigands—many became a rudimentary form of paramilitary local government, forcing the local population to follow their lead or risk summary execution.

The military value of these guerrilla bands was

immense. Well aware of the contribution that guerrillas played to the erosion of the French position in Spain, Wellington sent British liaison officers into the hills to locate and recruit them to gather military intelligence.

As Wellington advanced into Spain, fresh field armies could only be maintained by withdrawing French troops from garrison duties. This effectively ceded the country to the guerrillas. The combination of a powerful conventional offensive and a brutal guerrilla campaign ensured the final defeat of the French in the Peninsular War.

Salamanca to Vitoria

By December 1811 Wellington's army was ready to take the fight back across the border into Spain. The first actions of the capaign centered on the Portuguese-Spanish border, still in the hands of the French.

*B*efore Wellington could advance into Spain, he needed to capture the two fortress cities that guarded the Portuguese-Spanish border: Ciudad Rodrigo and Badajoz. The encirclement of Ciudad Rodrigo began in January 1812 and the bombardment commenced one week later. By January 19 two breaches were made in the fortress walls. Wellesley's light division stormed one breach, the third division assaulting the other. The city was taken after heavy fighting, which cost Wellington over 500 men.

A lack of co-operation between Marmont and Soult meant that Badajoz fortress was unprotected by one of the two French armies in western Spain. Wellington took advantage, investing the city on March 16. His batteries fired over 35,000 rounds against the walls. By April 6 three breaches had been made. The assault went in late that evening, the two sides fighting to the death in the rubble, amid fires lit by the defenders to screen the breaches. A participant described the scene at the main breach as "the mouth of hell."

Over 40 assaults were made on Badajoz before the British established a foothold inside. As dawn came the shattered city was in British hands. Widespread arson and looting continued until the afternoon before Wellington managed to impose order on his rampaging troops.

With the two fortresses in British hands, Wellington was free to march into Spain. The British army was at the peak of efficiency, and he felt confident that it could defeat the French in open battle. Marmont and Soult desperately needed reinforcements from France, but none was available because of Napoleon's invasion of Russia. The build-up for this new venture had been going on all spring of 1812, and began officially on June 24 (*see following chapter*). With Soult tied up in southern Spain at the siege of Cadiz, Marmont's force faced Wellington alone.

The British advanced to the east from Ciudad Rodrigo in mid-June and, after a brief campaign of maneuver around Salamanca, Wellington and Marmont's armies clashed on July 22, 1812. They were well matched in numbers: Marmont had 49,000 men, Wellington 52,000. The French marshal occupied the high ground of Los Arapiles some three miles south of Salamanca, while the rest of his army tried to march behind the Anglo-Portuguese positions. Wellesley sent General Packenham's third division to block the French advance, then launched two more divisions into the French flank. The French were scattered, and when the rest of the allied army seized Los Arapiles and pursued the broken enemy, Wellington's victory was assured.

Losing a kingdom

Marmont lost over 14,000 men, nearly three times the casualties suffered by the allies. With his army in ruins, he withdrew to the east. King Joseph Bonaparte abandoned Madrid, allowing Wellington to enter the city in triumph on August 12. However, the arrival of Soult's 80,000-strong army outside Burgos forced Wellington to withdraw to his forward base at Ciudad Rodrigo, and Joseph returned to his capital.

The surrender of Ciudad Rodrigo on January 19, 1812 marked the end of French dominance in the Iberian peninsula, as the British crossed back into Spain.

Wellington enters Salamanca at the head of a regiment of hussars in May 1812.

Joseph Bonaparte (1768–1844), reluctant king of Spain for a mere five years.

As the following summer started, Wellington was ready to renew his conquest. He had 52,500 British, 28,000 Portuguese, and 46,000 Spanish troops under his arms. During May the allies advanced to Madrid and recaptured the city on May 17 while the French retired beyond the Ebro. Spanish guerrillas reported that the French were concentrating three armies (South, Center, and Portugal) at Vitoria, with the king in command of the entire 63,000-man force. Wellington advanced on the town to discover the French dispositions scattered along a ten-mile front.

Sending a British and a Spanish division to screen the French Army of Portugal to the east of the French line, the rest of the British army concentrated on the French left. The Army of the South held La Puebla Heights, and the Army of the Center guarded the crossings over the Zadorra. On June 21, 1813 Wellington launched five British, one Spanish, and one Portuguese division into the attack, driving the French from the heights and throwing the Army of the Center back from the

river toward Vitoria.

Only the French Army of Portugal survived the onslaught and, as the rest of the French army fled the field, King Joseph abandoned his baggage train and treasury. The victory was complete. For the loss of 5,000 men, Wellington had deprived Joseph of his kingdom and was on the verge of liberating the entire country.

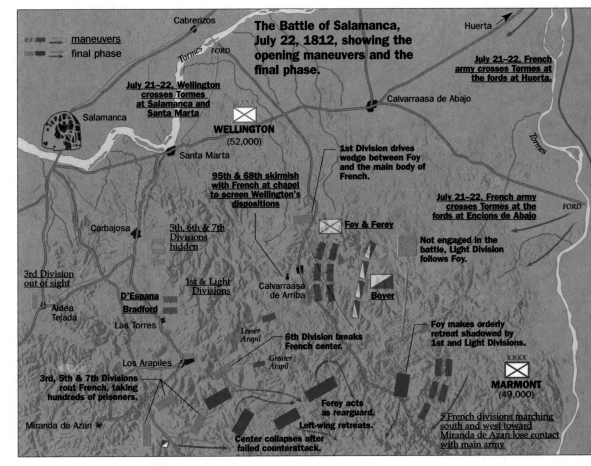

The Battle of Salamanca, July 22, 1812, showing the opening maneuvers and the final phase.

maneuvers
final phase

July 21–22, Wellington crosses Tormes at Salamanca and Santa Marta

July 21–22, French army crosses Tormes at the fords at Huerta.

Cabrerizos

Huerta

Tormes FORD

Salamanca

WELLINGTON (52,000)

Santa Marta

Calvarraasa de Abajo

1st Division drives wedge between Foy and the main body of French.

95th & 68th skirmish with French at chapel to screen Wellington's dispositions

July 21–22, French army crosses Tormes at the fords at Encions de Abajo

Tormes

FORD

Carbajosa

5th, 6th & 7th Divisions hidden

Foy & Ferey

3rd Division out of sight

1st & Light Divisions

Calvarraasa de Arriba

Not engaged in the battle, Light Division follows Foy.

D'Espana
Bradford

Boyer

Aldea Tejada

Las Torres

Lesser Arapil

6th Division breaks French center.

Foy makes orderly retreat shadowed by 1st and Light Divisions.

Los Arapiles

Greater Arapil

3rd, 5th & 7th Divisions rout French, taking hundreds of prisoners.

MARMONT (49,000)

Miranda de Azan

Ferey acts as rearguard. Left-wing retreats.

Center collapses after failed counterattack.

5 French divisions marching south and west toward Miranda de Azan lose contact with main army

Over the Pyrenees

While his Spanish allies dealt with the last remaining French outposts in central Spain, Wellington's army embarked on the last phase of its peninsular campaign, driving his enemies over the Pyrenees mountains to France itself.

Napoleon blamed his brother Joseph for the French failure in Spain and stripped him of his army, appointing Marshal Soult as overall French commander in Spain. Soult still had 80,000 men at his disposal; not enough to reconquer Spain, but sufficient to prevent any attempt by the allies to cross the Pyrenees into southern France. This Army of Spain used the mountains as a natural barrier, protected on its coastal extremities by fortified ports and cities such as San Sebastian, Gerona, and Pamplona.

The extent of the British advance was now giving Wellington supply problems, due to his long lines of communication. He moved his supply base to Bilbao, but to protect the port he needed to prevent the French from using San Sebastian as a base. He laid siege in June 1813 and massed his army near the coast, in the hope that Soult would fight to save the city. Instead, the French attacked the British forces screening the mountain pass of Roncesvalles, hoping to relieve the besieged French garrison at Pamplona. Although the French attack was repulsed, casualties were heavy on both sides.

San Sebastian was assaulted and captured on August 31, costing Wellington another 2,000 men. A belated French attempt to relieve the city was repulsed by a Spanish corps at San Marcial on the same day. The garrison of Pamplona surrendered on October 30, allowing Wellington to prepare for a winter assault on the mountains.

By this stage Soult had realized that any attempt to maintain garrisons in Spain would be a waste of resources, so he concentrated his efforts on defensive fighting in the mountains. On the Mediterranean coast, Marshal Suchet maintained a foothold in Catalonia around Girona, but otherwise the French were spread in a defensive line along the mountainous border. Soult ordered his engineers to fortify every pass through the Pyrenees, and the coastal city of Bayonne was turned into a fortress.

Duped and outmaneuvered

By early November Wellington was ready to begin. He launched a diversionary attack near the Atlantic coast, which forced Soult to concentrate his troops in the area. Wellington then directed his main assault further to the west, breaking through the French defensive positions near Roncesvalles and Maya,

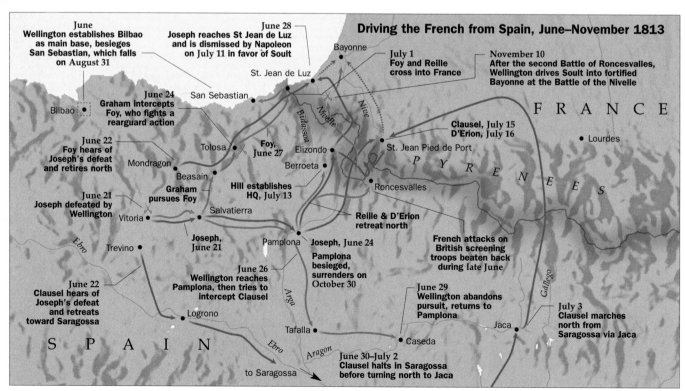

Driving the French from Spain, June–November 1813

then striking north toward the rivers Nivelle and Nive. Outmaneuvered, Soult fell back on Bayonne.

This small offensive placed the British on the north side of the Pyrenees, and both armies spent the winter facing each other on the far west of the mountain chain. Soult counterattacked British positions along the Nive on December 10, but by December 14 he was forced to call off the engagement, which cost at least 2,000 more casualties on each side. Severe weather prevented further action for two months, but both commanders prepared for what would be the final operation of the long-fought campaign.

Wellington feared that his Spanish allies would cause excessive damage in France in retaliation for the suffering the French had inflicted in Spain. And for this reason he sent almost all of his Spanish allies home. The final battle would be fought using the veteran Anglo-Portuguese army. During the winter lull, Soult recalled Suchet's forces from Catalonia, and the last French troops left Spanish soil in mid-February.

In early February 1814 moderate weather permitted Wellington to begin his long-awaited offensive. He advanced on Bayonne, outflanking Soult's army by building a pontoon bridge over the tidal estuary of the Adour. Soult fell back to Orthez and Wellington attacked him on February 27, driving him northward. Bordeaux fell on March 12, the allies having been assisted by a minor anti-Napoleonic rebellion in the region. Soult withdrew into Toulouse, and Wellington's army caught up with him there in early April.

News of Napoleon's abdication on April 6 did not reach southern France before the final battle of the Peninsular War was fought on April 10. After some of the most bitter fighting of the conflict, Soult abandoned Toulouse, which fell to the allies on April 11. The following day news of the abdication reached Wellington, and he and Soult concluded their own armistice a week later. The conflict that had cost France 300,000 men was finally over.

Fighting in the narrow valleys and inhospitable terrain of the Pyrenees around Roncesvalles was difficult for both sides. Undated painting.

CHAPTER EIGHT

Disaster in the Snow

The Russian Campaign, 1812

The alliance forged between Emperor Napoleon and Czar Alexander I by the Treaty of Tilsit was an uneasy partnership; neither really trusted the other. The greatest source of discord was caused by the Continental System, which first came into effect in December 1807 and in which Russia was expected to participate. The system was an economic boycott designed to exclude Britain from European trade.

However, the ban on the import or transit of goods owned or manufactured by Britain was a double-edged sword. While British trade with Europe was blocked, the overwhelming superiority of the Royal Navy effectively blockaded Europe, not only from overseas and colonial trade, but also from inter-continental trade between European ports.

The Russian merchant fleet had expanded in the late 18th century. Her merchants dominated Baltic trade, and were increasingly involved with the Mediterranean and Black Sea ports. Participation in the Continental System crippled and Russian resentment against Napoleon grew.

Further, the Grand Duchy of Warsaw in Poland, a pro-French state on the Russian border created out of the Treaty of Tilsit, remained a source of friction between France and Russia. The czar was also concerned about French involvement in Germany and the Balkans, both areas where Russian political influence had been effectively curtailed. While Prussia remained isolated and cowed, Napoleon was free to strengthen his hold over the smaller German states, and could demand that both Prussia and Austria furnish contingents for his army. The Russians viewed this domination of Germany with suspicion.

Alexander sat on the fence when Napoleon requested Russian support for the 1809 campaign against Austria, which did a lot to sour the relationship between the two. Only France's involvement in Spain prevented Napoleon from trying to force the Russians to dance to his diplomatic tune.

In 1806 Russia went to war with the Ottoman empire, following Russian support for a Slavic revolt in the Balkans. This created further tension, since Napoleon still harbored ambitions in the Middle East. The war dragged on until 1813, during which

the Russians became involved in another conflict, this time against Sweden (1808–9).

While these wars resulted in a geographical expansion of Russia's borders and encouraged the reform of the army, they did nothing to ease the distrust between France and Russia. Following Alexander's dismissal of the pro-French minister Speranski in March 1812, the alliance plummeted into outright hostility, and by April war appeared inevitable. Alexander prepared by settling peace terms with Sweden and the Ottoman empire to secure his northern and southern borders.

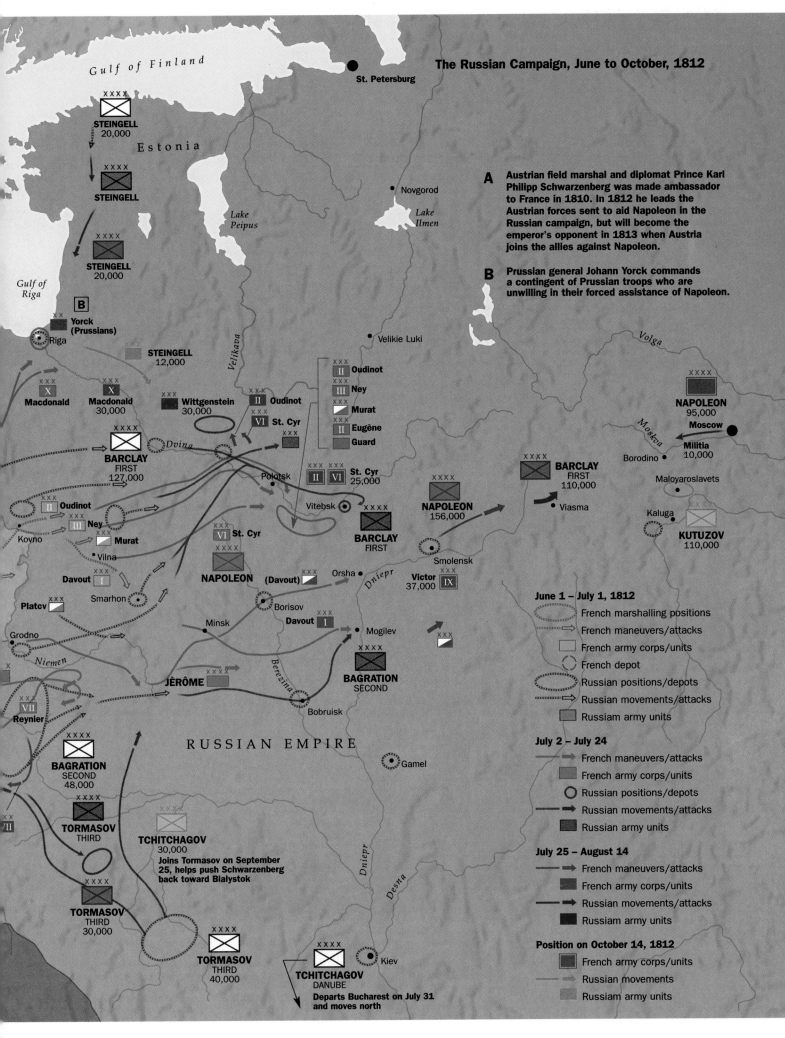

The Russian Campaign, June to October, 1812

Gulf of Finland

St. Petersburg

STEINGELL
20,000

Estonia

STEINGELL

Novgorod

Lake
Ilmen

STEINGELL
20,000

Lake
Peipus

Velikava

A Austrian field marshal and diplomat Prince Karl
Philipp Schwarzenberg was made ambassador
to France in 1810. In 1812 he leads the
Austrian forces sent to aid Napoleon in the
Russian campaign, but will become the
emperor's opponent in 1813 when Austria
joins the allies against Napoleon.

B Prussian general Johann Yorck commands
a contingent of Prussian troops who are
unwilling in their forced assistance of Napoleon.

Gulf of
Riga

B Yorck
(Prussians)

Riga

STEINGELL
12,000

Velikie Luki

Volga

X
Macdonald

X
Macdonald
30,000

Wittgenstein
30,000

II Oudinot
VI St. Cyr

II Oudinot
III Ney
Murat
II Eugène
Guard

NAPOLEON
95,000

BARCLAY
FIRST
127,000

Dvina

Polotsk

II VI St. Cyr
25,000

Moscow

BARCLAY
FIRST
110,000

Militia
10,000

Borodino

II Oudinot
III Ney
Murat

St. Cyr

Vitebsk

BARCLAY
FIRST

NAPOLEON
156,000

Viasma

Maloyaroslavets

Kovno

VI St. Cyr

Kaluga

KUTUZOV
110,000

Davout I

NAPOLEON

(Davout) Orsha

Dniepr

Smolensk

June 1 – July 1, 1812

Platov

Smarhon

Borisov

Victor
37,000 IX

French marshalling positions

French maneuvers/attacks

Vilna

Minsk

Davout I

Mogilev

French army corps/units

Grodno

Niemen

Berezina

BAGRATION
SECOND

French depot

Russian positions/depots

Russian movements/attacks

JÈRÔME

Russiam army units

VII
Reynier

Bobruisk

July 2 – July 24

BAGRATION
SECOND
48,000

RUSSIAN EMPIRE

Gamel

French maneuvers/attacks

French army corps/units

Russian positions/depots

VII

TORMASOV
THIRD

TCHITCHAGOV
30,000
Joins Tormasov on September
25, helps push Schwarzenberg
back toward Bialystok

Russian movements/attacks

Russian army units

July 25 – August 14

TORMASOV
THIRD
30,000

French maneuvers/attacks

French army corps/units

Russian movements/attacks

Russiam army units

Dniepr

Desna

TORMASOV
THIRD
40,000

TCHITCHAGOV
DANUBE
Departs Bucharest on July 31
and moves north

Kiev

Position on October 14, 1812

French army corps/units

Russian movements

Russiam army units

119

Invasion of Russia

In the spring of 1812 the Grande Armée had 650,000 men under arms, including contingents from almost every European country. Napoleon predicted a lightning campaign, designed to force the czar to make peace.

Napoleon and Czar Alexander I studying the map of Europe at Tilsit on July 7, 1807. The two rulers divided Europe between them, but it was a partnership doomed to failure. Undated engraving from the painting by P. Grolleron.

*I*n preparation for the invasion of Russia, Napoleon ordered the concentration of troops and resources in the Grand Duchy of Warsaw and in eastern Prussia. His Army of Twenty Nations included corps-sized contingents from Prussia, Austria, Poland, Bavaria, Saxony, and Westphalia, while smaller contingents were gathered from as far afield as Italy and the Netherlands. Despite high confidence in the outcome, Napoleon had the foresight to gather and distribute supplies for the army, but not in any quantity that might anticipate a worse-case scenario.

Napoleon's main force of 250,000 men consisted of two cavalry corps, the Imperial Guard, and the forces

Bonaparte with 70,000 advanced on the southern wing of the main Russian army. In their path near Pinsk lay 48,000 Russian troops under Prince Bagration (1765–1812). With hostilities on the Ottoman border at an end, a third force of 48,000 under General Tormasov was marshaling in southern Russia.

An Austrian corps of 34,000 men under General Schwarzenberg protected the Grande Armée's southern flank, while a 34,000-strong Prussian force commanded by Marshal Macdonald advanced along the Baltic coast. A further 225,000 men remained in reserve in central Europe.

Napoleon intended to march his main force between the armies of Barclay and Bagration, so he could defeat both in detail. Barclay's retreat from Kovno forced the French to advance deeper into Russia to deny the Russians the chance to combine the two main forces. Napoleon ordered his columns to march on Vilna in a last-ditch attempt to interpose themselves

of Davout, Ney, and Oudinot. This army crossed the Niemen on June 24, 1812, prompting the retreat of General Barclay de Tolly (1761–1818) and his main Russian army of 128,000 men. Further to the south, Eugène de Beauharnais with 80,000 men and Jérôme

between the retreating Russian armies. Barclay continued to retreat and Napoleon halted at Vilna, awaiting news from the south. Bagration's army evaded Davout and Jérôme, giving Murat's cavalry a chance to probe Barclay's dispositions behind the Dvina.

Louis Nicolas Davout, Duc d'Auerstadt and Prince d'Eckmühl, became one of Napoleon's most able marshals. He remained loyal to the emperor to the end.

Veteran General Kutuzov replaced Barclay de Tolly (below) as commander of the Russian armies after the latter had failed to repel the French invaders.

A psychological target

In mid-July the thrust resumed, but hopes of a decisive battle dwindled as Barclay frustratingly continued to drop back eastward to evade the French advance. Vitebsk was captured on July 28, but the summer heat and lack of food for the men and fodder for the horses obliged Napoleon to call a temporary halt. The Russians had laid waste to the countryside behind them, making further demands on Napoleon's dimishing supplies.

The two Russian armies joined forces at Smolensk on August 4, and Napoleon's attempt to encircle the enemy failed when they escaped to the east, after a clash with French advanced troops at Krasnoe on August 14. The French were being lured deeper into the vast country, and the Russian fall was beginning. About 100,000 men had already been lost through attrition, and the further east they marched, the worse the situation became.

A decisive victory was desperately needed to end the campaign. On August 24 Napoleon gave the order to march directly toward Moscow, hoping to force the Russians to stand and fight in defense of the city. He became convinced that the fall of Moscow would force Czar Alexander to sue for peace. Consequently he concentrated his forces, then advanced up the Smolensk–Moscow road.

Indeed, the czar was not prepared to surrender Moscow without a fight, and Alexander had no intention of making peace, since the French invasion had awakened a patriotic fervor in Russia that he intended to harness. He appointed veteran general Prince Mikhail Kutuzov (1745–1813) to be commander of the joint Russian army of 120,000 men and ordered the troops to make a stand at Borodino, less than 70 miles from Moscow. It suddenly seemed Napoleon would get his decisive battle after all.

The Russian Army

The Imperial Army of Russia participated in the French Revolutionary War, and fought Napoleon's troops in 1805, 1807, and 1812–14. Reformed shortly before the French invasion in 1812, it became one of the largest and most feared military forces of the era.

Russian cavalrymen of the Guard-Cuirassier.

The Russian Empire loomed on the sidelines of European affairs throughout the 18th century. In 1793 Czarina Catherine II the Great (r.1762–96) waged war against revolutionary France. While Russians fought in the Netherlands and Switzerland, it was in Italy that Russian troops achieved their

greatest success of the period. Under the leadership of General Alexander Suvarov (r.1729–1800) the French were driven out of Italy in 1799, but Czar Paul (r.1796–1801) was unwilling to prosecute the

war and his troops were withdrawn.

Under Czar Alexander I (r.1801–25) the army was reformed, first in 1801, then in 1810. By the time of the Battle of Austerlitz in late 1805, it consisted of 83 line infantry, 13 grenadier regiments, and 26 *jäger* (light infantry) regiments, each of three battalions. The cavalry arm contained 49 regiments, 30 of dragoons, six of *cuirassiers*, nine of hussars and four of *ulhans* (lancers), while artillery support was provided by 11 well-equipped artillery regiments, each with over 300 guns.

The Russian Guard comprised another four infantry regiments (one a guard *jäger* regiment), five cavalry regiments, and an artillery battalion. In addition, a further 101 garrison battalions protected Russia's extensive frontiers, and there was a substantial pool of Cossack cavalry to be drawn on. The total force approached half a million men, making it the largest standing army in Europe.

In 1806 a permanent system of grouping regiments into brigades and divisions was instituted and, by 1809, 25 of these three-brigade divisions existed. The appointment of General Barclay de Tolly as war minister in 1810 prompted another series of reforms. He introduced a new type of infantry musket with the aim of standardizing the weapon throughout the army. Although this had not been fully adopted by 1812, the majority of regiments were using it. The great advantage of this was that almost every soldier in the Russian army now used the same size musket ball, greatly easing the previous logistic nightmare of ensuring that the right supply of the correctly sized missile reached disparate troops in the field to suit the wide array of earlier muskets.

A vast revamped force

Improvements were also made to army personnel, logistical organization, and the practicality of the uniforms. A korps system was introduced in place of the older mixed divisions of cavalry and infantry shortly before the French invasion in 1812.

To meet the French, Barclay de Tolly's First Army of the West contained four korps (commanded by generals Baggavout, Tutschkov, Tolstoi, and Doctorov), plus the Russian Guard under Grand Duke Constantine, three reserve cavalry corps, and a large force of Cossacks. The Second Army of the West, commanded by Prince Bagration, contained the korps of Raevski and Borosdin, one cavalry corps, and more Cossacks. Combined, these two forces would become the army of General Kutuzov at the Battle of Borodino. General Tormasov commanded a third Army of the West, but its three korps had not fully assembled when Napoleon began his invasion, while the Army of the Danube and Army of Finland protected the northern and southern flanks of Russian armies in the west.

In July 1812 an *opoltchenie* (militia) was raised, a force that consisted mostly of poorly armed and equipped horse and foot Cossack regiments. Some of these levies would see action at Borodino, but most were held back until after the French retreat from Moscow.

Just before the 1812 campaign began, the main Russian field army had expanded to almost 400,000 men, and the number of line regiments was increased to 160 infantry and 60 cavalry formations. A further 30,000 Cossacks provided a horde of irregular light cavalry. Although the level of training was basic and the army remained incapable of anything other than the most straightforward of maneuvers, the Russian infantry were renowned for doggedness and ability to hold their ground, irrespective of casualties. Napoleon would find the Russians of 1812 to be a far more formidable opponent than the army he had defeated at Friedland in 1807.

"Summer Quarters of the Nizhegorodsky Dargoons" by Grigory Gagarin c.1840. Troops guarding Russia's extensive border with the Ottoman empire were freed to move north in 1812, but the respite was short-lived. With the final removal of Napoleon, hostilities with the Ottomans were renewed, culminating in the Crimean War in 1853.

Battle of Borodino

On September 5, French advance troops clashed with the main Russian army, arrayed in a series of defensive positions around Borodino, 70 miles from Moscow. The battle that was meant to decide the fate of Russia became a bloody stalemate.

*C*zar Alexander abandoned his policy of retreat from the Niemen. It had sucked the French deep inside the country and desperately extended their supply lines. Now patriotic fervor in Russia necessitated that a battle be fought before the invaders reached Moscow.

Alexander and Kutuzov, the czar's commander in chief of the Russian army, together selected Borodino as the ideal place to make a stand. The army built a series of fortified redoubts to anchor its center's defense, then drew into position to await the arrival of the French.

Kutuzov had somewhere under 100,000 men at Borodino: 72,000 infantry, 10,000 militia, and 24,000 cavalry, including approximately 7,000 Cossacks. The army was supported by a concentration of 640 guns. Barclay de Tolly's First Army of the West was deployed on the right of the line, while Prince Bagration's Second Army formed up on its left. The Russian Guard formed up behind the center, protected by an earthwork known as the grand redoubt.

Campaign losses had reduced Napoleon's Grande Armée to just under 135,000 men, giving the Russians the advantage in numbers. These included approximately 28,000 cavalry and 580 guns. A forward Russian redoubt at Shevardino was captured on September 5, and Napoleon planned an assault two days later. While diversionary attacks were launched on the Russian flanks, the main attack was to be on the grand redoubt. The plan lacked subtlety, but Napoleon hoped his veteran troops would be able to split the two armies, then his reserves could defeat each wing at their leisure.

Soon after dawn on September 7 Prince Eugène de Beauharnais assaulted the village of Borodino on the Russian right wing, while Prince Poniatowski's

Prince Eugène de Beauharnais (1781–1824), Napoleon's stepson through Josephine and Viceroy of Italy, was staunchly loyal and acquitted himself well at Borodino.

In the widespread fighting at Borodino, the French cavalry was used to launch costly frontal assaults against fortified Russian positions, during one of the bloodiest battles of the era.

Polish corps attacked the Russian left wing at Utitsa. The central attack was led by Davout, who threw the Russians out of a series of *flèches* (small arrow-shaped redoubts) in front of the grand redoubt.

Frenzy around the redoubt

After clearing Borodino on the French left, Beauharnais sent two divisions across the Kalatscha stream to hit the grand redoubt in the flank, while Napoleon sent in Ney and Junot's corps to take over the attack from Davout, whose men were pinned down in front of it. All the French reserves had now been committed to the battle, with the exception of the Imperial Guard. Kutuzov moved troops from the ends of his line into the center in preparation for the French assault.

The grand redoubt was captured then recaptured in hand-to-hand fighting that sucked in thousands of troops. By noon Poniatowski was forced to abandon his assault near Utitsa, so Napoleon committed his Young Guard to the fighting in the center to regain the initiative. To the left of the Russian center, Bagration held his ground behind a line of ravines

until he was mortally wounded. His men continued fighting to prevent the Young Guard from making any headway and so buy time for reinforcements to arrive. These came in the form of Tolstoi's corps taken from the Russian right wing. They were immediately thrown into the bitter fighting around the redoubt, having arrived in time for Beauharnais' flanking attack which smashed into the Russian line.

All available French cavalry was formed up, and when the redoubt was captured again the horsemen swept around it, only to meet the massed Russian cavalry on the far side. The Russian line held, and a fleeting chance for a French breakthrough had passed.

By late afternoon survivors on both sides withdrew as exhaustion set in. The fighting fizzled out by early evening, and Kutuzov withdrew his battered army during the night. The French were in no condition to pursue. Both sides had lost over 40,000 men. The Russians could replace their losses, given time. For the French, the loss of so many veterans was a disaster.

Prince Mikhail Kutuzov, commander of the Russian army, is depicted in an ivory panel leading a unit of Dragoon Guards and Guard Lancers at Borodino.

Napoleon in Moscow

Napoleon occupied Moscow a week after the Battle of Borodino, still hoping to force the czar to make peace. The longer he remained, the worse his supply situation became, and winter was fast approaching.

*T*he day after the Battle of Borodino, the French held the corpse-strewn field, while the Russian army withdrew toward Moscow. Neither side was in a condition to fight, so when Napoleon was offered free entry to Moscow in return for letting the Russian army escape unhindered, he accepted.

Napoleon's 100,000 weary and half-starved soldiers entered the city on September 14, 1812 to find it virtually deserted of its 300,000 people and stripped of almost all supplies. The capture of the city failed to produce a peace overture from the czar. His government camped with their army to the southeast of Moscow. Napoleon set up his headquarters in the Kremlin and awaited developments.

The following night Count Rostopchin, the city's departing Russian governor, ordered Moscow to be burned to deny the enemy shelter. Incendiary parties set fires throughout the city, and the French troops found themselves hemmed into the area around the Kremlin, the only part of Moscow to avoid destruction. The fires burned for two days, during which Napoleon moved his headquarters to safety outside the city. French troops looted the Kremlin, taking what little was left of Moscow's remaining provisions.

Napoleon thought that the fires were the work of isolated fanatics, not the act of the Russian authorities. The few surviving Russian inhabitants were deemed to be arsonists, and were rounded up and shot. His troops continued to garrison the smoking ruins while the emperor waited in vain for word from Alexander.

When no message was forthcoming, Napoleon sent two groups of envoys to the Russian camp, but both were turned away without being granted an audience. As the weeks passed, Napoleon remained convinced that peace was at hand. His marshals pleaded with him, but it was not until the return of the second French delegation on October 17 that he bowed to the inevitable.

Abandoning the city

Napoleon's army had virtually no food or fodder, their numbers were dwindling, and Cossacks and partisans were already threatening his long supply lines back to Prussia and Poland. The following day, the Russians launched a surprise attack on Murat's cavalry outposts at Vinkovo, destroying a French cavalry corps in the engagement. The appalling Russian winter was approaching, and with every day that passed Napoleon's army was wasting away while the Russians were getting stronger. He gave the order to abandon Moscow.

The 95,000 survivors of the Grande Armée began the retreat from Moscow on October 19, heading to the southwest along an indirect road that ran through largely undamaged countryside toward Smolensk. It was hoped that forage could be gathered in the city, but first they had to fight their way past Kutuzov, who moved his army into a position to intercept the French retreat.

On October 24 Napoleon won a minor but hard-fought victory over the Russians at Maloyaroslavets, some 70 miles southwest of Moscow. In an attempt to avoid another clash he turned northwest, rejoining the main Moscow–Smolensk road near Borodino. It was a decision that invited the starvation of his army, because the region had already been stripped bare of provisions, first by the retreating Russians and then the advancing French.

The French struggled into Viasma on October 31, where Napoleon ordered a temporary halt to take stock of the situation and allow stragglers to catch up. He was still deep in enemy territory, his army was starving and falling apart, and his enemies were closing in from the east and south. The illusion of an enforced peace in Moscow had cost the French a vital month, and now they faced the full force of the ferocious winter. Thoughts of victory had vanished. As the retreat resumed, Napoleon's main aim was to prevent the complete destruction of his army.

Count Fedor Vasilievich Rostopchin (1765–1826), governor of Moscow, who late in life denied having set fire to the city on Napoleon's arrival.

"The First Sight of Moscow" by Laslett John Pott. The French did not so much win the Battle of Borodino as the Russians gave it away. It left Moscow open to Napoleon, but the capture of the city turned out to be a poisoned chalice.

The Retreat from Moscow

Napoleon headed west, aiming for the safety of the Prussian border at the River Niemen. As the first heavy snows fell, his ragged army began to fall apart. Only Napoleon's determination and the skill of his marshals could avert disaster.

Russian generals Tormasov and Wittgenstein, whose forces harried the retreating French.

While he was at Viasma, Napoleon reviewed the strategic situation. The Austrian corps of General Schwarzenberg that guarded his southern flank was already retreating toward Warsaw. This left General Tormasov's army free to march north to block Napoleon's retreat. Marshal St. Cyr held the French line of communications from Smolensk to the Berezina river, but he was threatened by Tormasov from the south and another corps-sized force commanded by General Wittgenstein, advancing south from Riga. Napoleon had to move quickly or risk getting caught between these outflanking forces and Kutuzov's main Russian army.

On November 3 Marshal Davout's rearguard was defeated at Fiodoroivskoy and, while his corps was extricated by Beauharnais, it was no longer capable of fighting. Marshal Ney assumed responsibility for the rearguard. Victor's corps guarded the northern flank of the retreating French army, and together with Oudinot and St. Cyr, he attacked Wittgenstein's force near Polotsk (November 14).

This small French victory prevented any union between Wittgenstein and Tormasov, reducing the risk of isolation on the wrong side of the Berezina, the point where the Russian pincer movement was expected to meet. The battle involved around 40,000 French troops, mostly formations that had been left behind to guard the lines of communication as Napoleon thrust on toward Moscow.

On November 9 Napoleon entered Smolensk, where a small supply depot was able to issue food to the army. The troops consumed their rations within three days, and the retreat continued. By this stage the main army had withered to a mere 42,000 men, with stragglers and the malnourished falling by the roadside in their thousands.

Behind them, Ney's rearguard (approximately 20,000 strong) tried to protect the disintegrating army from increasingly heavy Russian attacks.

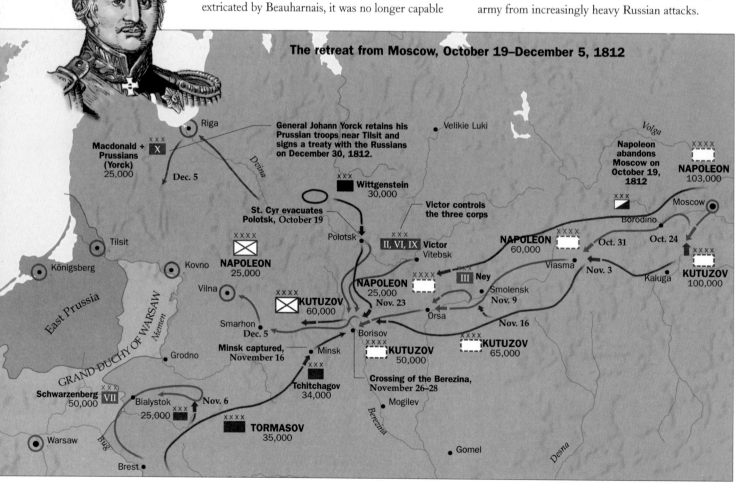

The retreat from Moscow, October 19–December 5, 1812

The first heavy snows had come on November 11, a week before Ney's rearguard abandoned Smolensk. The freezing weather killed the army's malnourished horses *en masse*, forcing artillerymen to abandon their guns and the cavalry to march alongside the infantry.

Losing combat ability

This march from Smolensk to the Berezina was the most critical part of what was now a full rout, since

The survivors of the army had now all safely crossed the Dneipr. Tchitchagov's corps of Tormasov's army captured the French depot at Minsk, prompting Napoleon's decision to force-march part of his army in an effort to rescue the city's isolated French garrison, which had retreated to Borisov, where another set of bridges crosses the Berezina. Napoleon discovered that these bridges were in Russian hands, and although the troops in Borisov had been rescued,

the army lacked provisions of any kind save horsemeat, and while Cossacks picked off stragglers, Kutuzov's troops continued to try to encircle the French. On November 17 Napoleon turned on one of these forces at Krasnoe, sending in the Imperial Guard to drive off the Russians. The guard and Ney's corps were the only combat-effective units in the main army, although Victor, Oudinot, and Beauharnais's forces maintained some semblance of order to the north.

At one point Ney was given up for lost, until his rearguard straggled into Orsha on November 20.

the Russians were in control of the west bank of the river, directly in the path of the retreating army.

In order to reach safety, the French had to fight their way across the Berezina before Kutuzov caught up with them. While Napoleon prepared for the operation, his men were collapsing from exhaustion and hunger all around him. Time was not on the emperor's side. The horrors of the campaign had brought the Grande Armée to its knees. Only a spark of Napoleonic genius or extreme good fortune could save the remnants of this once-proud army.

Lancers of the Guard escort Napoleon's sled through the Russian snows during the retreat from Moscow.

Over the Berezina

Trapped on the wrong side of a half-frozen river, Napoleon had to extricate his army before it was destroyed. At the crucial moment he temporarily recovered his old flair and saved what was left of the Grande Armée.

*T*he presence of a Russian corps on the far bank of the River Berezina was part of Czar Alexander's personal strategy to trap the French, now reduced to 50,000 men. The idea was to delay the French near Borisov until Kutuzov's army could catch up with them. But Kutuzov's men were also in poor shape, and the Russian commander remained unwilling to risk a battle with about the same number of men as Napoleon until his army was resupplied. This tardiness gave the French time to escape.

When a ford was found north of Borisov at Studienka, Napoleon decided to cross the river, relying on surprise and the valor of his few good units. An advanced column crossed the ford on November 25 and drove off the Russians guarding

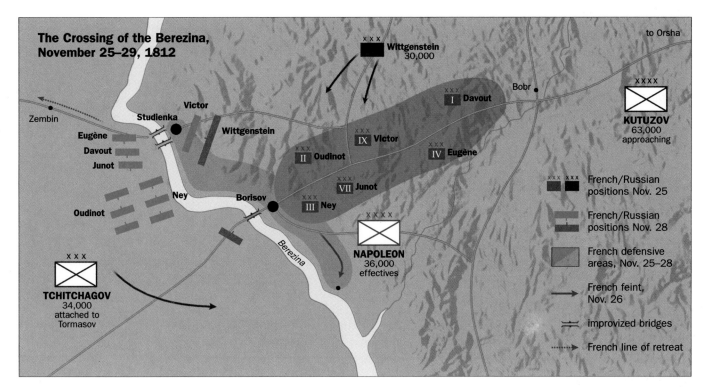

The Crossing of the Berezina, November 25–29, 1812

the far bank. Engineers dismantled a nearby village and used the timbers to construct two makeshift bridges, working all the while in the freezing water. Napoleon sent the Imperial Guard and Oudinot's corps over to the west bank to secure a bridgehead. While Oudinot held off Russian counterattacks, the rest of the army made its way to safety, protected on the east bank by Victor and Davout's corps.

The Russians attacked Oudinot the following morning, driving the outnumbered French back toward the river. On the eastern bank, Wittgenstein arrived near Borisov and attacked Victor's corps, trying to pin the French until Kutuzov arrived. The two attacks failed to prevent the rest of the French army reaching the relative safety of the west bank.

The collapse of one of the bridges during the afternoon of November 27 prompted a mass panic. The 20,000 civilian camp followers marching with the army tried to scramble over the bridge, causing pandemonium for several hours before order was restored. Somehow, over 25,000 French soldiers made the crossing, and by nightfall only Victor's corps remained as a rearguard on the eastern bank.

Finally reaching safety

Tchitchagov's force attacked Oudinot a second time on November 28 and almost broke through into the mass of disorganized French on the riverbank before Ney drove the Russians back with a cavalry charge. A simultaneous attack on Victor's position also looked like it would break through, but somehow the line held, supported by artillery fire from the west

bank, the guns positioned by Napoleon himself. When Wittgenstein called off his assault that evening, Victor began withdrawing his troops over the river. Numerous stragglers and civilians were milling around on the eastern bank when the bridges were burned early the following morning.

Napoleon had achieved a minor miracle, fighting enemies on two fronts while undertaking a hazardous river crossing; but the cost had been high. French losses during the four-day operation probably exceeded 20,000 men, while the Russians lost 10,000. Civilian losses have been put at 25,000.

With the main Russian army stranded on the wrong side of the river and the corps on the west bank defeated, Napoleon was free to continue his march to Vilna and safety. The Grande Armée had shrunk to about only one-tenth of its original size, and probably numbered no more than 25,000 men by early December, 1812.

On December 5 Napoleon left everything in the hands of Murat and returned to Paris ahead of his troops. He needed to restore order in his empire and raise another army. Murat stumbled into Vilna three days later, then reached the Niemen on December 14. By this stage all order had been lost; the treasury was abandoned, along with the last of the artillery, and the wounded were abandoned to their fate. Just over 20,000 tattered men struggled over the Prussian border, while other contingents straggled in from the flanking columns over the next month. The nightmare was over, but everyone knew the spring would bring a fresh campaign.

Ernest Meissonier's famous painting of 1864 is one of grim reality as the Russian debacle comes toward its end. The winter weather was often the bitterest of the two enemies the French faced. The mood is superbly caught, as the stony-faced emperor leads his army back toward the west.

Napoleon at Bay

The Campaigns of National Liberation, 1813–14

When Napoleon reached Paris shortly before Christmas 1812, he addressed his ministers: "I have made a great error, but I have the means of repairing it." The error was certainly great—the Grande Armée had been destroyed, Prussia was about to switch sides, and the pan-European empire Napoleon had created was being torn apart by the defections of several states.

The Russian army had also suffered heavy losses and needed time to return to strength for a campaign in Germany. However, that campaign appeared inevitable—the battle lines were already being drawn. While Prince Eugène de Beauharnais and Marshal Macdonald prepared the remains of the old army along the banks of the Elbe, Napoleon issued his government an edict to raise a new army for service in Germany.

In Russia, opinions were divided over the war, but Czar Alexander remained adamant that the campaign should continue. He saw himself as the arbiter of victory in Europe and actively courted allies from among Napoleon's former allies. The Austrian Empire had broken its alliance with France but preferred to remain neutral.

The Prussian General Yorck had already signed a neutrality agreement with the Russians, but French troops still occupied Berlin, and Frederick-Wilhelm continued to vacillate. While assuring Napoleon of his loyalty, he proposed a secret alliance with the czar, which was duly signed on February 27. A month later Prussia declared war on France. The stakes were high. Napoleon wanted revenge for the Prussian defection, and already he was gathering a new Grande Armée of 145,000 men, drawn from recruiting depots and from the ruins of Spain.

The Russians were on the move in early February 1813 with 68,000 men, planning to link up with a Prussian army that had been inspired by the growing tide of German nationalism. The new war would be as much a battle of political aspirations and national liberation as it would be a fight between European rulers. Napoleon had helped create the notion of the modern state, and finally the rest of Europe seemed to be awakening to the political possibilities of true populist nationhood.

UNITED KINGDOM

British defense forces comprised of 62,000 regulars and 77,000 militia

Château-Thierry February 12, 1814

Paris March 30, 1814

La Fère-Champenoise March 25, 1814

Some 400,000 recruits mobilzing in France

Nivelle, November 10, 1813

Roncesvalles, November 5, 1813

Vitoria, June 21, 1813

Toulouse, April 10, 1814

40,000 French troops on garrison duty

JOSEPH 100,000

SUCHET 35,000

Spanish regulars operating south of Madrid

WELLINGTON 88,000

The Leipzig Campaign and the Fall of France, March 1813 to March 1814. The general strategic situation at March 17, 1813 and the major battles of the year.

SWEDEN

NORTH SEA

Copenhagen

BALTIC SEA

Riga

Dvina

20,000 French troops trapped in Danzig

BERNADOTTE
SWEDEN
30,000 assembling

Swedish Pomerania

Pomerania

Danzig

Tilsit

Kovno

Königsberg

Vilna

Prussian army consists of 131,000 men, some engaged in siege duty and garrisoning

Niemen

150,000 conscripts mobilizing in Russia

Hamburg

Bremen

Mecklenburg Schwerin

Stettin

Vistula

RUSSIAN EMPIRE

Amsterdam

Holland

HANOVER

Brandenburg

PRUSSIA

Davout

Elbe

Berlin

35,000

Warsaw

Bug

Brussels

WESTPHALIA

Rhine

EUGÈNE
ELBE
58,000

SAXONY

40,000

Dennewitz
Sep. 6, 1813

KUTUZOV
30,000

Poland

Laôn
March 9–10, 1814

**Montmirail Feb. 11, 1814
& Vauchamps**
Feb. 14, 1814, 1814

Champaubert
Feb. 10, 1814

Hesse

Frankfurt

Leipzig
Oct. 14–19, 1813

Lützen
May 2, 1813

Main

Dresden
Aug. 22–25, 1813

Bautzen
May 20, 1813

Oder

Silesia

Vistula

Galicia and Lodomeria

Palatinate

Baden

MAIN
(forming)

BAVARIA

Ratisbon

Danube

Prague

Bohemia

Moravia

Mobilizing

Austria remains neutral while secretly mobilizing

Bukovina

Basel

HELVETIA

BAVARIA
30,000

Salzburg

Tyrol

Austria

Vienna

Danube

Buda Pest

Styria

Hungary

Transylvania

Moldavia

Savoy

Milan

Turin

Venice

Carinthia

Sava

Banat

Danube

Wallachia

Genoa

Illyrian Provinces

Herzegovina

OTTOMAN EMPIRE

Marseilles

LIGURIAN SEA

Florence

Tuscany

100,000 scattered French garrison troops in the Illyrian Provinces, Italy, and Naples

Bosnia

Corsica

KINGDOM OF ITALY

Papal States

Rome

ADRIATIC SEA

MONTENEGRO

Albania

NAPLES

Sardinia

TYRRHENIAN SEA

Naples

NEAN SEA

SICILY

Europe at the start of 1813

- France and territory under direct French rule
- State under French domination
- French ally
- Prussia
- Austrian empire
- Russian empire
- Ottoman empire

Opening positions and maneuvers

➤ French

➤ Allies

DENMARK - NORWAY

133

Notions of National Unity

Eager to avenge the humiliation inflicted on Prussia in 1807, its people were determined to bring about the liberation of their country. This surge of patriotism encouraged a notion of German brotherhood, under the protective shield of a reformed Prussian army.

Facing bottom: The Czar of Russia, King of Prussia, and Emperor of Austria give thanks (at last) for the victory at Leipzig, from a lampoon of 1813.

On December 30, 1812, General Johann Yorck (1759–1830) signed the Convention of Tauroggen with the Russians, effectively declaring his Prussian corps to be neutral after its withdrawal from Russia. The declaration brought an immediate upsurge of anti-French feeling in Prussia. Although Frederick-Wilhelm III had to distance himself from Yorck's actions (French troops still occupied Berlin), he secretly approved of the affair, although he formally dismissed Yorck for his presumption to involve himself in diplomatic matters. More than

anything else, Tauroggen encouraged nationalist elements in Prussia and other German states.

The carefully constructed network of French alliances that formed the foundation of Napoleon's empire in Germany began to fall apart. The smaller states of the Confederation of the Rhine remained reluctant to commit themselves against him, but Frederick-Wilhelm ensured that Prussia would become the new champion of Germany. While Czar Alexander saw himself as the "Deliverer of Europe," Frederick-Wilhelm elected to tie himself to the rising tide of popular national sentiment in Prussia.

Some historians have argued that the king's decision was encouraged by the advance of Russian troops on Berlin, but it is more likely that he realized the incredible political advantage he would achieve by establishing himself as Germany's liberator. An enhanced notion of German unity, with Prussia rather than Austria at the head of this confederation, would create a sphere of Prussian influence far exceeding the state's geographical borders. He also considered that during any peace negotiations that followed, Prussia could reclaim much of the territories stripped by Napoleon after the campaign of 1806–7.

In mid-February 1813, Frederick-Wilhelm left his palace in Berlin for Breslau, which was not occupied by French troops. Although he wrote to assure Napoleon of his loyalty, he was simply making time for his army to mobilize. He also initiated a secret pact with Russia, an alliance that came to fruition in the secret Treaty of Kalisch on February 27.

A unified force

Although Czar Alexander rejected most Prussian territorial demands (including the re-establishment of its pre-Tilsit borders and the seizure of Austrian Galicia), he agreed to discuss the redefining of Germany's borders following the end of the war. Alexander was also prepared to strip the French client-state of Saxony of its power in order to appease the Prussian king.

As the retreating French took up positions behind the Elbe early in March, the French garrison in Hamburg was withdrawn. This encouraged the spread of pro-German sentiments throughout northern Germany and the Baltic coast, as did an alliance between Britain and Sweden. In this case

Fruits of success—the growth of Prussia, 1813–66

Prussia in 1813

DENMARK-NORWAY · Swedish Pomerania · Tilsit · Königsberg · Danzig · Pomerania · East Prussia · Bremen · Hamburg · Stettin · Amsterdam · Brandenburg · Berlin · PRUSSIA · Holland · WESTPHALIA · Warsaw · SAXONY · Silesia · Poland · Frankfurt · Prague · BAVARIA · Bohemia · FRANCE · AUSTRIAN EMPIRE

Prussia in 1815

gains by 1866

DENMARK · Schleswig · Tilsit · Danzig · Königsberg · Pomerania · East Prussia · Bremen · Hamburg · Stettin · Amsterdam · Hanover · Brandenburg · Berlin · PRUSSIA · NETHERLANDS · Westphalia · Warsaw · Silesia · Poland · SAXONY · Frankfurt · Prague · BAVARIA · Bohemia · FRANCE · AUSTRIAN EMPIRE

former Marshal Bernadotte—never the staunchest of Napoleon's commanders—elected to switch sides and join the anti-French alliance. Following the death of Sweden's king in 1809, Bernadotte had accepted an offer to become Crown Prince and rule as regent. In 1813, he formally allied Sweden to Britain and offered an army to confront his former master.

The rise of national sentiment resulted in the formation of numerous volunteer units in the Prussian army, and a state militia (more accurately a national volunteer reserve, or *landwehr*) was created to augment the regular army. The phrase "national liberation" was widely touted by Prussian recruiting officers while they raised the strength of the regular army and created a new military force in East Prussia. The Prussian army would become the true winner in the coming war, earning a position within German society that it would retain until 1945. Prussia formally declared war on France on March 13, ending all remaining speculation.

The true benefit of Prussia's new political position was reaped in the Congress of Vienna (1815). Much of her lost territories were restored, increasing her population to over ten million. Prussia had finally become what Frederick-Wilhelm had intended:

the leading player in a revitalized German confederation of states and the rock on which the concept of German nationalism was founded.

Above: Prussia's Frederick-Willhelm III goes to war.

Battles of Lützen and Bautzen

Napoleon was on the strategic defensive in the spring of 1813, fighting Russian and Prussian armies for control of Germany. Against all the odds, he won two spectacular victories at Lützen and Bautzen, and for a time it seemed he had stemmed the tide of defeat.

With Britain, Spain, and Portugal presenting a united front in the Iberian Peninsula and Prussia allied with Russia, it seemed the French had too few resources and insufficient manpower to prevent the complete collapse of the Napoleonic dream. Somehow, Napoleon scraped together a new field army of 120,000 men, although they lacked the skill and experience of the old Grande Armée, and there was no cavalry.

This Army of the Main consisted of the Imperial Guard, plus four corps. In addition, Marshal

Davout commanded 20,000 men stationed west of Hamburg, supported by General Sebastiani's cavalry corps of 14,000. Prince Eugène de Beauharnais commanded the 58,000 remnants of the old Grande Armée, which had withdrawn to the River Saale in Saxony, while another 20,000 French troops were besieged in the port of Danzig. Napoleon intended to expand his army to 500,000 under arms, and fresh troops were raised throughout Europe.

For the time being he could still count on the Confederation of the Rhine for support, although the loyalty of its contingents was suspect. When the Prussians declared war on France in mid-March, Napoleon was as ready as he could be.

By April the allies had approximately 110,000 Russian and Prussian troops under arms, but reinforcements were marching west from Russia or were being raised across Prussia. In addition, the

Napoleon's counter-offensive, spring 1813, leading to the battles of Lützen and Bautzen.

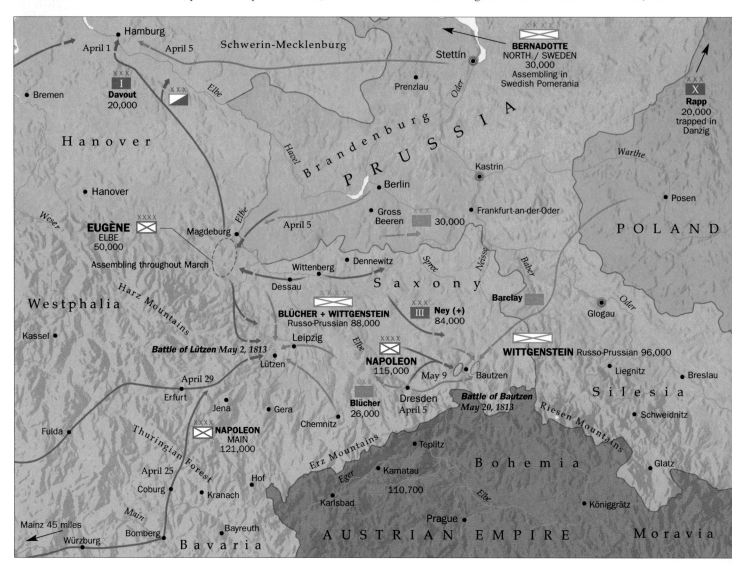

28,000-strong Swedish army commanded by Bernadotte was mobilizing in Pomerania.

Napoleon intended to march across Prussia to relieve Danzig, then turn and defeat the scattered allied contingents in Germany. His plans were altered when the main allied force advanced west from Dresden in late April, threatening Prince Eugène de Beauharnais' army. Napoleon reacted by marching into Saxony, crossing the Saale to the south of Beauharnais, in an attempt to cut the enemy's line of communications.

guns to disrupt the allied line, then sending in the Young Guard to break allied resistance on May 2. By nightfall the allies were in full retreat, leaving 20,000 casualties on the field.

Napoleon's shortage of cavalry prevented any real pursuit, but he had regained the initiative in Germany and followed the retreating allies through Saxony. The 96,000-strong allied army made a stand at Bautzen on the banks of the Spree, and Napoleon caught up with them on May 20 with 150,000 men. In a two-day battle Napoleon sent Ney to attack

Restoring Napoleon's reputation

Meanwhile, General Wittgenstein's 56,000 Russians and 37,000 Prussians concentrated on the Saale opposite Lützen. Ney and Marmont's corps marched to confront the allies, and the two armies clashed on May 1. Napoleon arrived with the Imperial Guard and reinforcements during the day, pitting 78,000 French against a similar number of allies. Both armies failed to concentrate all available forces, with the bulk of Beauharnais' army being the most serious omission.

The young French conscripts proved their worth. Ney's III Corps held off the allies with the help of Marshal Bessières and his cavalry, although the latter was killed during the action. Napoleon displayed a flair for improvization, massing a grand battery of 70

Wittgenstein's position from the north, while Oudinot attacked from the south. Ney failed to appear until May 21, when Napoleon launched a frontal attack on the allied line using Marmont, Soult, and Macdonald's corps, supported by a massed artillery battery. The Prussian-held fortifications in the center of the battlefield were captured but the advance stalled in the killing ground behind them. In the late afternoon Napoleon sent in the Imperial Guard and the allies withdrew. Casualties on both sides exceeded 20,000 men.

The battles of Lützen and Bautzen had gone some way to restoring the French strategic position, and while Napoleon advanced to occupy the line of the Elbe, the allies requested a six-week armistice, which was duly agreed on June 4, 1813.

Contemporary engraving of the Battle of Lützen, May 2, 1813, the first of two critical encounters that proved Napoleon had lost none of his flair for improvisation.

Armistice

The Armistice of June 1813 gave both sides time to prepare for the next phase of the campaign. It also allowed allied diplomats to exert pressure on the German states to declare their allegiance, most notably on the neutral Austrian Empire.

After the Battle of Bautzen a 36-hour suspension of hostilities was arranged, allowing talks to be held at Plaswitz. Both sides had suffered heavy casualties during the spring. While Napoleon needed time to train his new army and reinforce it, the allies also had to reform an army that had lost two major battles in three weeks. Above all, Napoleon realized that victories were not enough, since without cavalry he would be unable to exploit his success on the battlefield.

An armistice was declared until July 20. Neither side expected the peace to be anything other than temporary while they built up their forces. Napoleon consolidated his position along the Elbe, re-occupying Hamburg at the western end of the river and Dresden at the other.

While military efforts continued apace, the real benefit of the armistice was the opportunity it gave to launch a diplomatic initiative to isolate the enemy. Britain was a key player in this process, sending war subsidies in excess of £2 million ($3.2 million) to both Prussia and Russia to keep them in the war. British and Russian diplomats had already been working on the Swedes, whose troops occupied Pomerania, their German enclave on the Baltic coast. Following an initial agreement with the czar in April, Crown Prince Bernadotte officially joined the allied camp on July 7, adding 30,000 troops to the allied ranks. While the Confederation of the Rhine remained loyal to Napoleon, the states' future allegiance depended on the success of French arms.

The real diplomatic battle centered around the Austrians, who had only reluctantly supported Napoleon during the Russian campaign of 1812.

Prince Klemens Wenzel Lothar von Metternich was the archetype of the new order of European diplomats. He became minister of Austrian foreign affairs in 1809 and made a new constitution for Germany in 1815. That constitution created the German Confederation, composed of 39 states and four free cities.

The key player in Austria was Prince Klemens Lothar von Metternich (1773–1859), Emperor Francis's Foreign Minister. He had rejected calls to join the allies in early 1813, since he judged the timing to be inopportune. After Wagram (1809) he became the emperor's chief adviser, and encouraged Archduke Charles's reforms of the Austrian army. He helped arrange the marriage of Napoleon to Marie-Louise, daughter of Emperor Francis, and signed a formal alliance with France in 1812.

The pieces fall

While an Austrian corps participated with the French in the Russian campaign, Metternich was careful to assure Czar Alexander that its involvement was a token presence and that the Austrians harbored no

A meeting between Czar Alexander, Emperor Francis of Austria, King Frederick-Wilhelm of Prussia, and Crown Prince Bernadotte of Sweden takes place before the Battle of Dresden (1813), from a painting of the time.

ill-will toward Russia. Following the retreat from Moscow, he kept Austria out of the first campaign of 1813, hoping to use a weakened France to balance the rising power of Prussia within Germany.

This diplomatic game lasted until July, by which time the diplomatic stakes for Austrian involvement in the war had reached a peak. It was a superb piece of diplomatic brinkmanship, and Metternich was determined to broker the best deal he could for Austria. Secret meetings were held with allied representatives and, on July 19, the Convention of Reichenbach was signed, in which Austria agreed to join the Sixth Coalition against France if Napoleon rejected a peace deal proposed by Metternich.

This deal involved the removal of all French troops east of the Rhine and the partition of the states comprising the Confederation of the Rhine between Austria and Prussia. Napoleon rejected Metternich's proposal, but agreed to the Austrian diplomat's request to extend the armistice until August 16.

Metternich claimed the extension was needed to examine further peace proposals, but it also left him free to arrange Austria's membership of the Sixth Coalition at the Treaty of Teplitz, confirming the arrangements he made at Reichenbach in July. On August 12 Austria declared war on France, prompting the resumption of the campaign. The allies had a new and powerful ally, and Metternich had ensured that Austria would be the dominant player in the anti-French alliance for the remainder of the war.

Battle for Dresden

When the campaign resumed in August, the allies had a co-ordinated campaign plan. It was agreed to avoid battle against Napoleon's main army and instead concentrate on defeating isolated French forces.

*I*t was Austrian General Schwarzenberg who established the Trachenberg Plan. The strategy—which could have come from Napoleon's own manual—was to split the allied armies and, with superiority of numbers, tackle the widely scattered French forces commanded by Napoleon's marshals, while avoiding battle with the emperor's main army. If an allied army was to become trapped by Napoleon, allied forces would concentrate and march to its rescue. While admirable on paper, the scheme rashly assumed that Bonaparte would allow the allies to strike where they wanted.

The campaign began on August 14, 1813, two days before the end of the armistice, when Field Marshal Gebhard Leberecht von Blücher, Prince of Wahlstadt, who was nicknamed "Marshal Forward," advanced his 95,000-strong Prussian Army of Silesia

Karl Philipp von
Schwarzenberg
(1771–1826)

from Breslau toward the Elbe. To the south the Austrian Army of Bohemia consisted of 230,000 men under the command of General Schwarzenberg. The Army of the North, consisting of 110,000 Prussian and Swedish troops, began advancing from the north, under the command of Crown Prince Bernadotte. Finally, Prince Bennigsen's 60,000-strong Army of Poland remained in reserve, occupying the former Grand Duchy of Warsaw.

Napoleon had 440,000 troops in Germany, scattered from Hamburg to Dresden, with covering forces on the east bank of the Elbe in western Prussia and Silesia. Another 225,000 men guarded against an Austrian attack through Bavaria and protected Napoleon's lines of communication in western Germany. The bulk of his Army of the Main—some 250,000 men—was concentrated around Dresden, while Marshal Oudinot commanded 120,000 men, poised to protect the main army against an attack from the north.

At first the plan to attack isolated French detachments proved successful. Bernadotte defeated his old colleague Oudinot at the Battle of Gross-

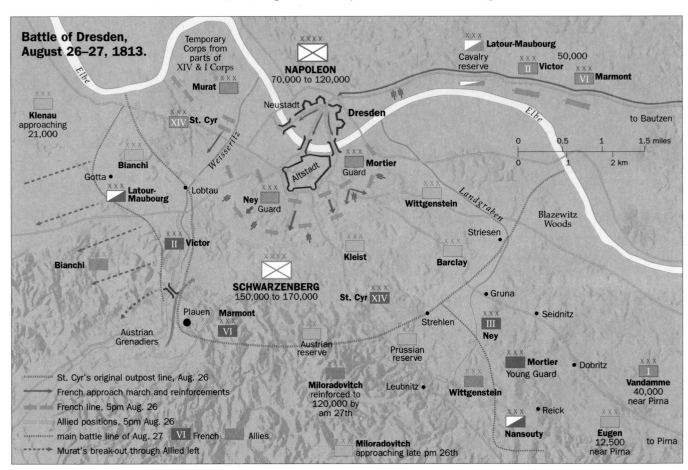

Beeren (August 23) south of Berlin, while Blücher defeated Macdonald at the Battle of the Katsbach, to the west of Breslau. In the south, the Austrians were emerging from the mountains of Bohemia and threatened to attack Dresden. The division of Napoleon's strength proved an uncharacteristic error, since it allowed the piecemeal destruction of a sizeable portion of the French army.

A spirited defense

True to the Trachenberg Plan, when Napoleon led the Army of the Main east to confront Blücher, the Prussians withdrew, while Schwarzenberg worked behind the main French army to strike at Dresden. The city was held by Marshal Gouvion St. Cyr with the 20,000 men of XIV Corps, and he repulsed a series of Austrian attacks launched over three days (August 22–25). This bought time for Napoleon to come to his rescue, arriving in the city on the evening of August 26 with 50,000 reinforcements.

The Austrian attack went ahead as planned, but—after driving the French from their first line of redoubts and some heavy house-to-house fighting—the allied attack faltered. A counterattack by the Imperial Guard drove the Austrians from the city. As night fell Napoleon had regained the old French front line. Victor and Marmont's corps reached Dresden during the night, which brought the French force to 120,000 men. Both sides prepared for an assault in the morning. Napoleon planned to hold in the center and send the rest of his men to the south in a double envelopment of Schwarzenberg's army.

The following morning (August 27) the French attacked first, the flanking forces cutting through the Austrian lines by noon and isolating a portion of the Austrian army against the banks of the small Weisseritz river. When rescue proved impossible, 13,000 Austrian troops surrendered. Meanwhile the French center held, despite repeated Austrian assaults. By evening it became clear that the outnumbered French had won a surprising victory.

The Austrian army withdrew during the night, pursued by Vandamme. The battle cost the lives of 10,000 French soldiers, but the Austrians lost 38,000, killed and captured, and their morale plummeted. Only a defeat of Vandamme at Kulm (August 30) prevented their continued retreat to Bohemia. While the battle prevented a union between the Austrian army and its allies, the reverses inflicted upon Macdonald and Oudinot meant that the strategic situation remained as volatile as ever.

After bitter fighting that claimed the lives of more than 30,000, the outnumbered French were the victors. "Battle Before Dresden," a painting by J.A. Atkinson of 1813.

General Dominique Vandamme (1770–1830) pursued the defeated Austrians to Kulm.

Routed at Leipzig

After a string of defeats the allies were ready in September 1813 to concentrate against Napoleon's main army. The Battle of Leipzig was the single most decisive battle of the Napoleonic Wars, when half a million men in five armies decided the fate of Germany.

Francis I of Austria, Frederick-Wilhelm III, and Czar Alexander of Russia meet on the battlefield after Napoleon's great defeat at Leipzig.

Following the French victory at Dresden, Napoleon's uncharacteristic inactivity gave the allies a second chance and the Trachenberg strategy began working. General Vandamme's 13,000 men surrendered to the Austrians on August 30. A week later, Marshal Ney was defeated during an abortive French drive on Berlin by Bernadotte at the Battle of Dennewitz (September 6). The two reverses prompted Napoleon to withdraw his army to the

Elster, concentrating his forces at Leipzig to prevent any more of his commanders from falling victim to the strategy. He concentrated a force of 195,000 men and 700 guns, divided into two armies, ten infantry, and four cavalry corps.

Politically, time was not on Napoleon's side. Bavaria switched sides in early October, and other members of the Confederation of the Rhine looked certain to join the defectors. Napoleon needed a crushing victory to restore his credibility. His plan was to await the advance of the allies, then use his central position around Leipzig to crush each army in turn, before it could be reinforced.

General Schwarzenberg's Army of Bohemia was approaching the city from the south with 115,000 men and 388 guns. Bernadotte's Army of the North

The death of Prince Josef Anton Poniatowksi at Leipzig. The Pole commanded a division of V Corps during the Russian campaign. After the retreat from Moscow, many Poles wavered in their allegiance to Napoleon, but Poniatowski remained faithful. He was rewarded by being made a Marshal of France. Entrusted with covering the French retreat from Leipzig, he and his remaining force of VIII Corps were trapped on the wrong side of the Elster. Pursued by the allies, Poniatowski refused to surrender and, covered with wounds, plunged into the river, where he died fighting to the last.

comprised 65,000 Russian, Prussian, and Swedish troops, while Blücher's Army of Silesia contained 52,000 Prussians and Russians, supported by 310 guns. The reserve of Wittgenstein's corps and a combined Prussian and Russian guard corps amounted to another 95,000 men and 480 guns.

The first clash came on October 14, when the largest cavalry battle in history was fought at Liebertwolkwitz between Prince Murat and Wittgenstein, but the result was inconclusive. The real "Battle of the Nations" began two days later, as the allies launched attacks on Leipzig from the south, supported by secondary attacks to the north and east.

The French evacuate

The battle south of the city was fought between Schwarzenberg's Army of Bohemia and three French corps, reinforced by Prince Poniatowski's Polish corps. Once Napoleon was convinced that the attacks in other sectors were feints, he committed his Imperial Guard in the south, throwing the allies back. Allied pressure in the north intensified as Blücher attacked Marmont's corps around the town of Mockern, but the French line held. Schwarzenberg tried to encircle Leipzig to the west, but his advance was halted by General Bertrand's corps. The first day's fighting cost 25,000 casualties on each side, but although the French had held their positions, Napoleon had been unable to crush any of his opponents.

The allies spent October 17 preparing for another co-ordinated attack, while the French improved their defenses. The arrival of Bernadotte gave the allies a significant numerical advantage. Napoleon made plans to withdraw, but little could be achieved before fighting resumed on October 18. An initial French withdrawal under cover of darkness and torrential rain only served to constrict the French perimeter, making it harder to defend.

While the French withdrew their supply wagons and artillery to the west, Schwarzenberg, Blücher, and Bernadotte launched simultaneous attacks on three sides of the city. The pressure was almost too great for the French. On its eastern side Macdonald was driven back by Bennigsen, while Bernadotte closed in on the town from the northeast. Somehow the defensive perimeter held, despite the defection of two Saxon divisions.

The evacuation began in earnest that evening. By dawn on October 19 only Oudinot's rearguard of 30,000 remained east of the Elster. The premature destruction of the bridges over the river sealed their fate. While the bulk of the army escaped, Oudinot's troops surrendered.

The battle was a disaster for Napoleon, who lost over 70,000 men, killed or captured. He had lost military control of Germany and, as remains of his army fled west toward the safety of the Rhine, his German allies switched sides. Although the allied pursuit was temporarily halted, both sides realized that the next campaign would be fought in France.

On the Brink of Disaster

Napoleon's strategic situation was bleak. An allied army of 300,000 was approaching the borders of France. In Spain, only a handful of troops and a chain of mountains prevented the British, Spanish, and Portuguese from invading southern France.

Print after the painting "Napoleon's Flight Across the Rhine, Near the City of Metz, Pursued by the Allies," engraved by John Heaviside Clark.

Karl Philipp von Wrede (1767–1838), commanding general of the Austro-Bavarian troops.

Technically, Napoleon escaped defeat at Leipzig, although his withdrawal was a bungled affair that cost him two marshals and a corps. Defections by various German contingents reduced his force to around 70,000 men, less than a quarter of allied strength in Saxony. The abandonment of Germany was inevitable, and consequently the remaining French army withdrew west along its line of supply toward Frankfurt-am-Main and the Rhine, crossing at Mainz. He reached Erfurt on October 23 without interference, but Schwarzenberg had sent General Wrede's Bavarian corps and an Austrian force on a parallel route to the south, and it swung north to intercept Napoleon's retreat at Hanau, near Frankfurt.

The last battle of the German campaign was fought on October 30, 1813, on the north bank of the Main as Napoleon forced his way past the Austrian and Bavarian blocking force. Macdonald's corps was in the front of the French column and launched a frontal attack at the allied line, supported by General Sebastiani's cavalry. Marshal Victor came up behind him, outflanking the Bavarian left wing and driving

Wrede's troops from the field. Frankfurt lay open to the French, and Napoleon's army reached the safety of its principal German depot the following day.

The French still had 100,000 men in Germany, including Davout's corps of 20,000 men at Hamburg and garrisons along the line of the Elbe, at Dresden, and in northeastern Germany. The defection of the Confederation of the Rhine had left these troops isolated and, despite Napoleon's orders to concentrate and pull back to the east, the majority were forced to surrender before they could reach the French border. There was no sensible alternative. With little hope of their being relieved, the allies refused to discuss terms other than a complete surrender. Davout was the exception. While Prussian troops and their German allies mopped up the north of Germany, he pulled whatever men he could find into Hamburg and refused to capitulate. Hamburg was still in French hands when Napoleon abdicated in April 1814.

The faith of one

The loss of the garrison troops accentuated the French plight, who had lost almost half a million men during the campaigns in Russia and Germany of 1812–13. The depleted army crossed over the Rhine at Mainz in early December and Napoleon prepared for the defense of France. Peace overtures in 1812–13 had suggested that the French empire should be constricted to the natural frontiers of France. Napoleon had rejected the proposals, and now these same natural frontiers were crossed by up to 300,000 allied troops.

While the allies temporarily halted on the east bank of the Rhine, Napoleon set about raising whatever soldiers he could find for the coming campaign. Since he had almost no manpower reserves, he was reduced to conscripting teenagers into the army during the winter of 1813–14. Such raw troops, nicknamed the Marie-Louises, after Napoleon's empress, formed the backbone of his latest army.

For the first time since 1799, a foreign army prepared to enter France. Times had changed and there was no widespread nationalist uprising against the invader. The majority of the French population were war-weary. The huge loss of life had led to a general apathy, even hostility to a new round of imperial decrees regarding conscription and national defense.

Although some 80,000 youths, bitter veterans, National Guard, militia, and old men were formed into a new army to defend *la patrie*, only one man had any faith in their chances of success. Despite his appalling losses, Napoleon refused to be disheartened, writing to Marshal Marmont that although his army was ill-prepared for the coming campaign, by late January "we shall be in a position to achieve a great deal." It would be the last roll of the die in a desperate game of survival.

After Leipzig, the forces massed against Napoleon proved too much for both the emperor and his remaining troops, and ultimate defeat seemed inevitable. Oil painting by Ernest Crofts.

The 1814 Campaign

Fought with little hope of success, the campaign directed by Napoleon in defense of France is regarded as one of his finest; a test of his skill as a military commander against the overwhelming numbers of his adversaries.

"The Battle of Montmirail" by Horace Vernet, painted in 1827. The encounter was the climax of a six-day French offensive which almost turned the tide of the campaign.

The first allied troops crossed the Rhine into France in late December 1813, and four weeks later Napoleon left Paris to join his army on the Marne. This small force of 80,000 men was all that stood between him and disaster. Even before the campaign began, the defections continued. The Dutch revolted, Westphalia was overrun, and Denmark abandoned the French alliance. Perhaps the worst blow was the defection to the allies of his

shivered in the snow. Allied armies advanced into northern France.

By the time Napoleon reached his army, Blücher's force was crossing the Meuse (also Maas) and approaching the Marne with 75,000 men, split into two columns. While the bulk of Schwarzenberg's 210,000-strong army was still on the Rhine, his advance guard was approaching the Marne's headwaters. Bernadotte's 60,000 men were occupied reducing the cities of the Netherlands.

As usual, Napoleon planned to isolate each allied army, then defeat them in turn. On January 29 he attacked one of Blücher's columns at Brienne on the Aube with 30,000 French conscripts, forcing the Prussians to retire to the south. The small French

trusted marshal, Murat, the king of Naples. Napoleon and France stood alone against the invader.

Austrian armies were sweeping through northern Italy, and Wellington's troops were poised to enter southern France. While the French press raised the specter of foreign invasion, Napoleon's troops

army was attacked by Blücher's second column two days later at La Rothière. Napoleon was outnumbered by almost four to one, since Blücher had been reinforced by Schwarzenberg. After a fierce battle in the snow, the French were forced to withdraw with 6,000 casualties. The advance on Paris continued.

A chance for peace

Even at this late stage, the possibility of a negotiated peace remained. Talks were held at Châtillon-sur-Seine while Napoleon reformed his army 30 miles up the river near Troyes. He also reinforced his army, which now consisted of the Imperial Guard (jointly commanded by Mortier and Ney), Victor's II Corps, Macdonald's XI Corps, and reserve cavalry (General St. Germain). Marmont's VII Corps occupied Arcis-sur-Aube on his left flank, and General Grouchy's I Cavalry Corps protected the gap between the two French commands. Oudinot was raising a fresh corps to the rear of the army. Because Schwarzenberg was still slow to appear in force in the area, Napoleon advanced his reorganized army of 70,000 men against Blücher, who was maneuvering around the north of the French front.

While Macdonald was left to screen General Yorck's Prussian corps and Ney watched Schwarzenberg, Napoleon launched the rest of his army in a lightning offensive (known as the Six Days campaign). First General Olsuviev's Russian IX Corps was overrun at Champaubert (February 10), then General Yorck's army of two Russian and one Prussian corps was defeated at Montmirail the following day. Yorck's defeated army was attacked again at Château-Thierry (February 12) and virtually destroyed.

Blücher counterattacked with three corps at Vauchamps (Etoges) on February 14, but the Imperial Guard commanded by Mortier and Ney repulsed the allies with relative ease. In five days the allies had suffered over 20,000 casualties, while French losses were under 4,000 men. This short campaign revealed Napoleon at his best; an incisive commander with a genius for outmaneuvering and outguessing his more pedestrian opponents.

While the Six Days campaign stopped Blücher's advance, its effect was nullified by the arrival of

Baron Winzingerode with 30,000 Russian reinforcements. The French success also prompted the allies to resume their old Trachenberg strategy, concentrating their attacks on forces not directly commanded by Napoleon.

The peace talks were broken off on February 21, but an optimistic Napoleon offered the Austrians a separate deal. While allied pressure on the Austrian emperor led to the proposal's rejection, Napoleon was clearly holding his own in France—further victories could cause a split in the anti-French coalition.

	Battle	Date	Victory	Opponents
1	Valjouan (Mormant)	Jan. 14	French	Grouchy v Wrede
2	Brienne	Jan. 21	French	Napoleon v Blücher
3	La Rothière	Jan. 23	Allied	Napoleon v Blücher
4	southern skirmishes	Jan. 24–Feb. 12	mixed	
5	Bar-sur-Aube	Jan. 27	Allied	Oudinot v Wittgenstein/Wrede
6	Château-Thierry	Feb. 12	French	Napoleon v Blücher
7	Vauchamps	Feb. 14	French	Napoleon v Blücher
8	Montereau	Feb. 18	French	Napoleon v Schwarzenberg
9	Champaubert	Feb. 20	French	Napoleon v Blücher
10	Montmirail	Feb. 21	French	Napoleon v Sacken/Yorck
11	Reims	March 3	French	Napoleon v St. Priest
12	Craonne	March 7	draw	Napoleon v Blücher
13	Laôn	March 9–10	draw	Napoleon v Blücher
14	Reims	March 12	Allied	city captured
15	Fismes	March 17	French	Marmont v Blücher
16	Arcis-sur-Aube	March 20	French	Napoleon v Schwarzenberg
17	Arcis-sur-Aube	March 21	Allied	Napoleon v Schwarzenberg
18	La Fère-Champenoise	March 25	Allied	Marmont/Mortier v Schwarzenberg
19	Paris (Montmartre)	March 30–31	Allied	Marmont/Mortier v Schwarzenberg

General Yorck

Inset area shows the major battles in France before the capture of Paris.

DENMARK-NORWAY break alliance with France

Hamburg
Bremen
Brussels
30,000
30,000
BERNADOTTE NORTH / SWEDEN 80,000
Frankfurt
BLÜCHER SILESIA 80,000
GERMAN STATES
Paris NAPOLEON 100,000
Basel
SCHWARZENBERG BOHEMIA 150,000
SWITZERLAND
Geneva
FRANCE
Bordeaux
SOULT 50,000
Lyon
Augereau
Milan
Turin
Bayonne
WELLINGTON 70,000
Toulouse
BELLEGARDE 50,000
Genoa
SPAIN
SOUCHET 30,000
EUGÈNE ITALY 40,000
Marseilles
Florence

The fall of France, January–March, 1814

13
12
11, 14
15
6 7
19
10 9
Montmartre
Paris
18
16, 17
1
5
2
Moret 8 Troyes
Nemours Pont-sur-Yonne 4 3
4 Sens 4
4

A Gamble Outside Paris

Napoleon was holding the allies at bay in northern France in early March 1814, but allied resolve stiffened. Although Blücher and Schwarzenberg were outclassed by Napoleon, the French emperor could not be in two places at once.

The allied rulers confer with their staff before the final assault on Paris (March 29, 1814). The attack, which took place the following day, was launched against the hill of Montmartre (seen in the background).

*P*lagued by defeat and dissension, the allied leaders met at Chaumont-sur-Marne to discuss strategy. By March 9 an agreement had been reached between Czar Alexander together with Metternich, Emperor Francis, King Frederick-Wilhelm, and British Foreign Secretary Viscount Castlereagh (1769–1822). The Treaty of Chaumont stipulated that a peace deal would be offered, based on the pre-French Revolution frontier, otherwise war would continue until Napoleon had been utterly defeated. The offer was rejected the following day.

The conference gave the allied commanders the chance to discuss strategy. Rather than combine forces, the principles of the Trachenberg strategy were again adopted, resulting in the decision to keep the Armies of Silesia and Bohemia apart. Facing a commander of Napoleon's abilities, this may have seemed rash, but Schwarzenberg and Blücher

thought the risk was worth taking on the grounds that Napoleon could not prevent the advance of two separate forces at the same time, so one was bound to succeed while Napoleon was distracted fighting the other.

The allied advance resumed on March 5, with Blücher advancing up the bank of the Aisne with 85,000 men and Schwarzenberg marching up the Seine. Napoleon turned on the Army of Silesia, and in the Battle of Craonne (March 7) he pinned Blücher's front while Marshal Ney attacked the Prussian flank using the Young Guard. The attack failed, resulting in a draw that cost both sides 5,000 dead.

Blücher withdrew ten miles north to Lâon, where he concentrated his army. Napoleon had less than 50,000 men under his command, but he attacked nevertheless. The Battle of Lâon (March 9–10) was another draw, but this time the French were forced to retire, having lost another 6,000, including most of Marmont's corps.

Napoleon led his battered army southwest to Soissons, where he learned that the Russians and Prussians had stormed and captured Reims on March 12. Napoleon force-marched east, retaking the city the following day and destroying an isolated

Russian corps in the process. This placed him firmly between and behind the two allied armies. While he considered threatening Schwarzenberg's lines of communication to force the Army of Bohemia to retreat, the two allied armies ignored Napoleon and continued toward Paris.

Fall of an empire

With his army "melting like snow" from attrition, combat losses, and desertion, Napoleon raced south to intercept Schwarzenberg. He caught up with the Army of Bohemia's advance guard at Arcis-sur-Aube on March 20 and drove them back to the west. By this time he was reduced to a mere 28,000 men, while Schwarzenberg gathered in his forces, counterattacking with 80,000 the next day. Napoleon withdrew back over the Aube, protected by Oudinot's rearguard.

Although the offensive had temporarily halted Schwarzenberg's advance, Napoleon was running out of space, options, and soldiers. The two-pronged advance on Paris continued, forcing the French to screen Schwarzenberg while Napoleon tried to sever the allies' lines of communications across the Marne. On March 25 Mortier and Marmont's 20,000-man screening force was destroyed by Schwarzenberg at

Robert Stewart, Viscount Castlereagh (1769–1822), formerly His Britannic Majesty's Secretary for Ireland, then War Secretary between 1805 and 1809, was now Foreign Secretary. He would play a major role at the Congress of Vienna (1814–15).

La Fère-Champenoise, effectively ending Napoleon's campaign of maneuver.

The emperor withdrew toward Paris, which was already being evacuated by the empress and the government. Joseph Bonaparte tried to hold the city, but 50,000 allied troops stormed the outer defenses of Paris at Montmartre on March 30. By the following morning the capital of France was securely in allied hands. The gamble had paid off.

Weary of the long-drawn out war, Parisians welcomed the Allies as they entered the city on March 31, 1814.

Abdication of an Emperor

On the day of the assault on Paris, Napoleon left his reduced army at Troyes and raced to the capital in an attempt to get there before the allies. But for once, the man who moved too quickly for others was too late.

*J*oseph Bonaparte was in command of Paris when the allies appeared in the suburbs. General Schwarzenberg launch an immediate attack before Napoleon could reinforce the city. Although there

were units of the Imperial Guard and survivors of Marmont and Mortier's commands, most of the 25,000 defenders were raw recruits. With 150,000 allied troops facing them, the outcome was never in doubt. Parisians came out onto the streets to welcome the allies and celebrate the end of the war.

At 2am on the morning of March 31, Marshal Marmont signed an armistice, handing Paris over to the allies at the insistence of Joseph Bonaparte. In return his men were allowed to withdraw without being attacked. A provisional government headed by Talleyrand declared that Emperor Napoleon had been deposed.

Napoleon reached Essones, 20 miles south, when he learned of the fall of Paris. He turned south to Fontainebleau, sending orders for the army to march from Troyes to meet him. On hearing of Talleyrand's defection, he declared that Orléans would become the center of government and issued orders for a call-up of every eligible French citizen. Napoleon's closest marshals knew he was deluding himself.

On April 3 the remaining army arrived from Troyes. With troops gathered from Paris and other outlying areas, his strength rose to 60,000 men, including 10,000 under Marmont's command. Worn out and faced with a continuation of the war, the men refused to fight. Torn between his allegiance to France, his men, or Napoleon, Marmont defected and his men laid down their arms. This betrayal was the final blow for Napoleon, a personal slight by a soldier he "drew out of obscurity."

An end, at last

The marshals tried to persuade the emperor that further bloodshed was not an option. He retorted, "The army will obey me," to which Ney replied, "The army will obey its chiefs." Resigned to the inevitable, on April 4 he sent Ney, Macdonald, and foreign minister Armand-Augustin Caulincourt (1773–1827) to Paris. They offered the three allied rulers Napoleon's abdication in favor of his and Marie-Louise's son. The allies rejected the offer, demanding Napoleon's unconditional abdication in return for peace. The delegation returned on April 5 without Ney, who was unable to face his chief with the news. It was left to Marshal Macdonald to break the news and convince Napoleon that his only recourse was to abdicate.

During the night Napoleon drafted a letter of abdication, renouncing all state powers and rights for himself and his heirs. The abdication was formally signed on April 6, 1814.

Ten days later the Treaty of Fontainebleau was ratified; Napoleon would retain the title of Emperor and be given full sovereignty over the Mediterranean island of Elba. A condition was that his heir would be controlled by an allied power, so Empress Marie-Louise returned to her father in Vienna with her son. Napoleon was allowed a guard of 600 soldiers and an income of 2 million francs per annum.

Charles Maurice de Talleyrand-Périgord, Prince de Bénévent (1754–1838), Napoleon's foreign minister since 1799, had resigned in 1807 in opposition to the wars against Austria, Prussia, and Russia. Having deposed Napoleon, he went on to favorably represent France at the Congress of Vienna, and continued to serve its governments, ending his long career as ambassador to Great Britain (1832–34).

On April 20, Napoleon's Old Guard paraded in the courtyard of Fontainebleau Palace for the last time. It was an emotional moment. As the emperor bid his tearful veterans farewell, a long and bloody chapter of European history drew to a close. Oil painting by Horace Vernet.

CHAPTER TEN

The Eagle and the Lion

The War of 1812

*D*espite its name, fighting between the United Kingdom of Great Britain and the young United States of America in one of the most needless conflicts in history continued until 1815. There was still much bitterness lingering on either side from the conclusion of the American War of Independence (1775–83), in which the French had played a decisive role in aiding the revolutionary American colonists in contesting imperial rule.

The defeat of a Royal Navy fleet by a French fleet off the Chesapeake Capes in 1781 forced the surrender of the besieged British troops at Yorktown. Britain managed to beat off a French invasion of the West Indies in the following year, protecting the Caribbean, but it was clear that the American colonies were lost. Humiliatingly for Britain, the Treaty of Paris of 1783 confirmed the independence of the United States of America.

British policy toward the new nation ranged from unco-operative to downright hostile. A state of affairs hardly improved when at one stroke President Thomas Jefferson (p.1801–9) more than doubled the area of the U.S.A.'s territory through what was known as the Louisiana Purchase. This vast tract of land belonged to France (who had taken it from Spain), and when the U.S.A. purchased it from Napoleon, it was a snub to the British and also a useful means of financing Napoleon's war effort against Britain.

British retaliation showed itself through the harassment of American mercantile shipping by Royal Navy vessels. America began to spoil for a war. The excuse came at a moment when almost all of Britain's military and capital naval resources were engaged in the Napoleonic Wars.

It began with a free-trade dispute when Royal Navy frigates stepped up their stop-and-search campaign, ostensibly to look for British deserters. Having been locked in conflict with France since 1793, naval desertions were increasingly common among the press-ganged crews—but the pretext did not wash with Americans. They understood that there was a deep-seated fear in Britain at the rapid growth of American trade that threatened British interests, especially when American ships tried to run supplies to France. With what was beginning to look like a blockade, President Madison (p.1809–17) declared war in June 1812.

Napoleonic war in the Caribbean

The French West Indian island of Martinique, which lies between the islands of Dominica and St. Lucia—both British colonies at the time—had been seized by Admiral Rodney in 1762. The British only stayed for a year but, taking advantage of the French Revolution, retook it in 1793. When the Peace of Amiens was signed in 1802, Martinique was handed back to the French. With the resumption of hostilities in 1804, Britain established a fort on Diamond Rock, a 600-foot tooth of basalt off the Martinique coast. The French did nothing to impede the landing of guns and remained helpless until Vice-Admiral Villeneuve arrived in May 1805. His attack on the seemingly impregnable fortress was successful. The British returned in February 1809 and seized Martinique, to hold it until Napoleon's defeat in 1815.

The island was strategically important for both nations, but its significance to the French went further; Martinique was the birthplace of the Creole Empress Josephine, who married Napoleon after her husband, Viscomte de Beauharnais, was guillotined in 1794. Her son by her first marriage, Prince Eugène de Beauharnais, became one of Napoleon's most important generals.

Black hero of the revolution

Born c.1743 an African house slave in French St. Dominique (later Haiti), Toussaint l'Ouverture was fortunate in being allowed by his liberal master to learn reading and writing. In 1798, French Revolutionaries granted new rights to black slaves, but furious plantation owners forced them to retract. A slave revolt followed in 1791, led by Toussaint, who fought a successful campaign against the French. In 1793, the Directory recognized Toussaint as governor-general and freed the slaves in Haiti. However, in 1801, Napoleon reinstated slavery and sent French troops to the island in 1802. Forced to make terms, Toussaint was treacherously taken prisoner during negotiations. Shipped to France, he died in prison. A few months later, in 1803, Napoleon rid himself of his New World possessions, abandoning Haiti and selling off French Louisiana territory to the Americans (the Louisiana Purchase).

THE
LOUISIANA
PURCHASE

GULF OF MEXICO

ATLANTIC OCEAN

Bahamas

Cuba

Havana

New Orleans

Arkansas

Mississippi

Jackson

Mississippi
1817

Montgomery

Alabama
1819

Alabama

Tallahassee

Atlanta

Georgia
1788

Savannah

Jacksonville

Florida
1848

Columbia

South
Carolina
1788

Raleigh

North
Carolina
1789

Nashville

Tennessee
1792

Kentucky
1792

Cumberland

Illinois
1818

Springfield

Indiana
1816

Dayton

Ohio
1803

Ft. Wayne

Tippecanoe
1811

Ft. Dearborn

Ft. St. Joseph

Ft. Stephenson

West
Virginia
1863

Charleston

Richmond

Virginia
1788

Baltimore

Washington
(US capital from 1800)

Chesapeake Bay

Delaware
1787

Maryland
1788

Pennsylvania
1787

Philadelphia
(US capital 1790–1800)

New Jersey
1787

New York
(US capital 1785–90)

Connecticut
1788

Rhode Island
1790

Massachusetts
1788

Boston

Portsmouth

New Hampshire
1788

Maine
1820

to United
States
1842

New Brunswick

Wisconsin
1848

Mississippi

Michigan
1818

Detroit

Lake Michigan

Ft. Mackinac

Lake Superior

Lake Huron

Georgian Bay

York

Hamilton

Niagra

Lake Erie

Lake Ontario

Oswego

Albany

Kingston

New York
1788

Ontario
(Upper Canada)

Kingston

Ottawa

Montreal

French
Mills

Plattsburg

Sorel

Vermont
1791

Quebec
(Lower Canada)

St. Lawrence

the original Thirteen Colonies
and date of formation

1783 Native cessions and
date of formation

Louisiana Purchase, 1803

Canadian British colonies

Spanish colonies

region of conflict, 1812–15

American War in Canada

The war along the Canadian frontier was the most important theater, for political and military reasons. James Madison claimed the conquest of Canada would be "a mere matter of marching." He was proved wrong.

James Madison
(1751–1836), fourth
U.S. president.

*I*n 1812, Canada was a British colony of 300,000 people. Its long land frontier with the U.S. and lack of garrisons or substantial forts made it vulnerable to attack. Given that the U.S. population exceeded eight million and its army outnumbered British garrisons in Canada by over eight to one, Madison's prediction seemed appropriate.

Despite the border's extent, the interruptions of the Great Lakes and the St. Lawrence river left comparatively small gaps, a series of bottlenecks any invading force would have to use. When the war began, the British garrison in Canada consisted of just six battalions and some garrison artillery companies—hardly sufficient to guard the 1,600-mile frontier. However, Canadian militia rallied to the defense of their country and moved into position alongside the British troops.

American strategists favored a four-pronged invasion: across the St. Lawrence at Montreal, across the river further west toward Kingston on the eastern shores of Lake Ontario, against Queenston between Lake Ontario and Lake Erie, and finally toward Amherstberg, on the western end of Lake Erie near Fort Ralden. In the west, the first success went to the British, who repulsed a half-hearted American invasion across the Detroit river in July 1812.

The British pursued the Americans and took their base at Fort Dearborn (now the site of Chicago). Their efforts were supported by Native American leader Tecumseh, who proved himself a capable commander, and his men caused widespread terror along the frontier. General William Hull surrendered his small American army of 2,500 men at Detroit without a fight when approached by Major-General Isaac Brock and his small force. Amherstberg was safe for the moment.

Massed amphibious assaults

A second American invasion force led by Major-General Stephen van Rensselaer crossed the Niagara river between Lake Ontario and Lake Erie with 3,000 men, establishing a bridgehead near Queenstown on the Canadian shore. Brock marched east to deal with the invasion and defeated Rensselaer at the Battle of Queenstown Heights (October 13). The death of Brock in the closing moments deprived the British of their most capable leader. The final American offensive toward the St. Lawrence ground to a halt when the American militia refused to cross the border.

Although British reinforcements were sent to Canada, Governor Henry A. Proctor faced a series of attacks throughout 1813, from the Detroit to the Niagara rivers. Both sides launched amphibious raids across Lake Erie, the British attacking Sackets Harbor and the Americans burning York (now Toronto). This ended on September 10, 1813, when Captain Oliver H. Perry defeated the British naval force at the Battle of Lake Erie, ensuring American control of the lake for the remainder of the war.

General Wade Hampton crossed the Niagara but was defeated at the Battle of Chateaugay (October 25), and another force under General James Wilkinson met with disaster two weeks later at

Tecumseh and the Battle of Tippecanoe

Tippecanoe, seven miles north of Lafayette, Indiana was founded in 1808, when two Shawnee brothers, Tecumseh and Tenskwatawa, were permitted to settle there by local tribes. The brothers planned to unite many tribes into a union against the growing number of western settlers. In 1811, the territory's governor, General William Henry Harrison, organized a small army of a thousand men, hoping to destroy the town while Tecumseh was on a southern recruitment drive.

Harrison's troops camped on a hill about a mile west of Tippecanoe after agreeing with Tenskwatawa that there would be no hostilities until after a meeting on the following morning.

But Tenskwatawa led his men near the army campsite before daybreak and gave the order to attack. However, Harrison had anticipated treachery, and his men were ready and bloodily fought off the reckless, determined Indian attack. The battle lasted two hours and left 62 soldiers dead and 126 wounded. Indian casualties were unknown, but their spirit was crushed after Harrison ordered the town burned to the ground.

On his return three months later, Tecumseh found his dreams in ashes. Believing the chance of Indian survival under the U.S. government to be slim, he gathered his remaining followers and allied himself with the British forces in the War of 1812.

Chrysler's Farm. The British and Canadians had managed to hold their own on the Niagara front.

To the west General William Harrison recaptured Detroit in September 1813, then crossed into Canada with 7,000 men. In the Battle of the Thames, Proctor and Tecumseh were heavily outnumbered and defeated, and Tecumseh was slain on the battlefield. Although the Americans had gained the initiative in the west by defeating the "Indian Confederacy," the war department ordered "Old Tippecanoe" Harrison's militia home, and all benefits of the victory were lost.

By 1814 the war had lost much of its momentum, and although a new invasion of Canada was attempted in July, after two months and three battles both sides were back where they started. A potentially dangerous British advance down Lake Champlain ground to a halt at Plattsburg in September, with no tangible result.

The real victors were the Canadians, who maintained their independence from the U.S. through tenacious defense of their frontiers. In the peace treaty which followed the war, the U.S. renounced any further territorial ambitions in Canada, ensuring a peace that has endured ever since.

Oliver Hazard Perry became a national hero when he defeated a British squadron in the Battle of Lake Erie (1813).

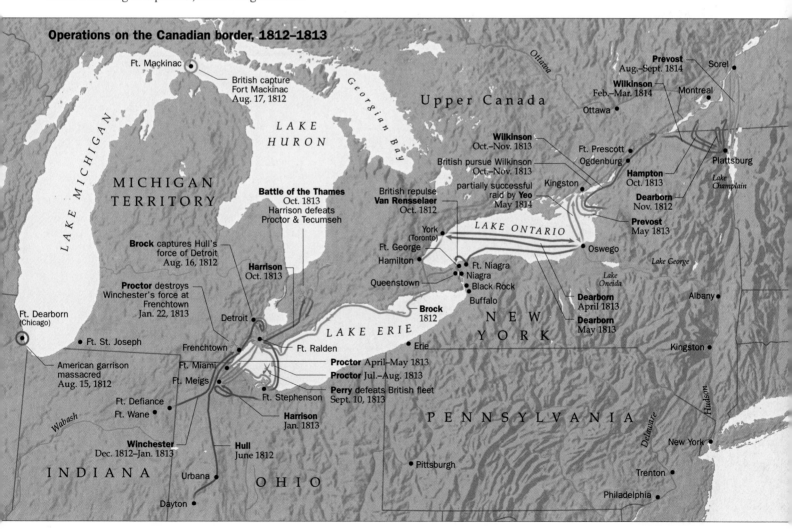

Operations on the Canadian border, 1812–1813

The War at Sea

**The Royal Navy enjoyed supremacy around the world.
The notion that any enemy could defeat her frigates in
single-ship action was considered preposterous.
This arrogance was shaken during the War of 1812.**

The incident that sent
shockwaves around
the world: in under
half an hour, the USS
Constitution captured
HMS *Guerrière* on
August 19, 1812, an
act that shook the
bedrock of British
naval supremacy.
Painting by
Thomas Birch.

While the performance of its army can best be
described as dismal, the American navy
achieved remarkable success against a much more
powerful British fleet. In 1812, the American navy
was a small outfit, but its three largest warships were
very heavy frigates of 44 guns. These were the
Constitution, *President*, and *United States*. In addition
the fleet contained three 36-gun frigates (*Congress*,
Chesapeake, and *Constellation*), the 32-gun *Essex*, and
several smaller vessels. With all the British capital
ships-of-the-line involved in blockading the European
theater, the smaller American fleet outgunned the
Royal Navy's frigates on a one-to-one basis.

On August 19, 1812, Captain Isaac Hull in the

USS *Constitution* evaded a British blockading
squadron, then attacked the 32-gun British frigate
HMS *Guerrière* off Nova Scotia. In an action lasting
just under 30 minutes, the British vessel was
dismasted and captured. The encounter sent
shockwaves around the world. This was a challenge
to the accepted naval order.

Two months later, on October 18, the 18-gun brig
USS *Wasp* fought a duel with the similarly sized
HMS *Frolic*. Although both ships were battered,
British reinforcements ensured that it was the
Americans who were taken prisoner. The loss of the
sloop was more than avenged a week later, when
Captain Stephen Decatur in the USS *United States*
captured HMS *Macedonian* off Madeira in a long-
range fight that lasted 90 minutes. The British
frigate was towed into Newport, Rhode Island, as a
prize. The last action of the year took place off the
coast of Brazil when the *Constitution*, now
commanded by Captain William Bainbridge, met the

frigate HMS *Java*. "Old Ironsides" took two hours to turn her British opponent into a battered wreck.

For years the British had enjoyed a qualitative superiority over their opponents. These actions demonstrated that ship for ship and crew for crew, the American navy was superior in gunnery, tactical handling, and ship design. By 1813, the Royal Navy was baying for revenge and, while its own heavy frigates were ordered from British shipyards, reinforcements were sent to join the blockade of the American Atlantic seaboard. By the end of the year the Britain had over a hundred warships on patrol in American waters. Although U.S. privateers had inflicted heavy losses to British merchant shipping during the first year of the war, the blockade prevented them from operating, and all but terminated American mercantile trade.

A labored British victory

On February 24, 1813 the USS *Hornet* sank another sloop, HMS *Peacock*, off Brazil after only 11 minutes of close-range gunnery. It would be over three months before the British were able to take revenge. HMS *Shannon*, commanded by Captain Sir Philip Broke, formed part of the blockade off Boston, Massachusetts. He challenged Captain James

Lawrence of the *Chesapeake* to single-ship action and, on June 1, the American frigate sailed out to give battle. The two opponents were well-matched, but the British frigate emerged victorious. Despite Lawrence's dying words of "Don't give up the ship," the *Chesapeake* was captured and towed into Halifax, Nova Scotia, as a prize.

Other British victories followed. On August 14 the sloop HMS *Pelican* captured the sloop USS *Argus* in the Irish Sea. On March 21, 1814, the commerce-raiding cruise of the *Essex* came to an end when she was captured off Valparaiso in Chile by the frigate HMS *Phoebe*, supported by an 18-gun sloop.

The British blockade had virtually brought American naval operations to a halt on the high seas. In the Great Lakes, American victories on Lake Erie (September 10, 1813) and Lake Champlain (September 11, 1814) ended all possibility of a British invasion of the U.S. from Canada, but did little to alter the strategic situation.

Overall, the reputation of the British navy was tarnished by its performance during the War of 1812, an outcome some have ascribed to complacency. After a string of victories against the French or Spanish, the U. S. Navy had taught the Royal Navy a sharp lesson in humility.

British revenge: The boarding and taking of USS *Chesapeake* by the officers and crew of HMS *Shannon* on June 1, 1812. Aquatint engraving by Matthew Duborg of 1816.

Sacking Washington and Baltimore

Royal Naval supremacy in American waters ensured that the British could land troops almost anywhere. While Baltimore's defenses proved too tough, the new national capital of Washington was an easy target.

Facing: American forces held off a British attack during the War of 1812 at Fort McHenry, now a National Monument. The engagement led to the writing of the American national anthem.

*T*he abdication of Napoleon in April 1814 meant an end to the war in Europe. The peace freed the British to divert highly experienced troops across the Atlnatic in troopships during the summer of 1814. Many went to the British garrison in Canada, but others were held in reserve and their commanders began looking for suitable ways to employ them. British naval control offered one obvious solution: amphibious assaults of small forces on selected points of the American coast to pin down troops that would otherwise reinforce U.S. forces on the Canadian border.

Admiral Sir James Cockburn had already been harassing settlements of the middle seaboard states, so a plan was devised to scale up this operation,

using newly arrived troops to launch an amphibious attack on Chesapeake Bay. A division of 5,400 British veterans was earmarked for the operation under the command of Major-General Robert Ross.

Admiral Cockburn's squadron entered Chesapeake Bay in mid-August, sealing off the maritime approaches to a large portion of Virginia, Delaware, and Maryland. The soldiers were landed at Benedict on the Patuxent river, Maryland, on August 19. An American gunboat flotilla retreated upriver and, after being forced to destroy their craft, the sailors led by Commodore Joshua Barney marched inland to help defend Washington. Ross advanced north up the river until he had secured the destruction of Barney's flotilla, then marched west toward Washington.

The British advance was blocked at the Anacostia river outside Washington by a mixed force of American regulars, Maryland militia, and sailors; 6,500 men commanded by Major-General William H. Winder. A political appointment, Winder proved completely unsuited to the task.

The burning of Washington DC by the British in 1812. In this undated wash drawing, the White House can be seen blazing in the background.

National anthem born

The British crossed the river at the hamlet of Bladensburg on August 24 and attacked American defenses on the far side, supported by fire from a Congreve rocket battery, an array of tripod-mounted tubes from which large firework-like missiles were launched. While most of the militia fled, the rest of Winder's small army held their ground as long as they could, pouring fire into the advancing redcoats. The British secured the battlefield, but the cost had been high. While a hundred Americans were killed, wounded, or captured, the British lost almost 300.

The American defeat at Bladensburg meant that Washington lay defenseless. The city was occupied later that day, and remained in British hands for 24 hours. Cockburn and Ross ordered the burning of the White House, the Capitol, and most of the other civic buildings in the newly built capital, in retaliation for the Americans burning of York in Canada. While Cockburn's flotilla advanced up the Potomac as far as Alexandria, the British soldiers returned to their ships on the Patuxent.

Two weeks later, Ross's men were landed again, 16 miles east of Baltimore, Maryland. This time the local militia were more willing to defend their city, and Major-General Ross was mortally wounded during a skirmish in Godly Wood (September 12). In the words of one observer, the expedition was like "a watch without a mainspring." The assault on Baltimore was called off and the troops embarked.

The withdrawal was covered by a naval bombardment of Fort McHenry overlooking the Patapsco river, guarding the approaches to Baltimore. The fort's defenders remained defiant, despite 25 hours of naval bombardment, an event which prompted Francis Scott Keys to compose *The Star Spangled Banner*. The reference to "rockets' red glare" and "bombs bursting in air" in the anthem reflected the use of Congreve rockets and bomb vessels by Cockburn's flotilla.

The Chesapeake Bay raids achieved little, apart from the death of a Peninsular War hero and the composition of a national anthem. The British departed on October 14 without altering the strategic situation or breaking the American will. It was economic ruin caused by the naval blockade that brought the U.S. to the peace table in December 1814, not the threat of military force.

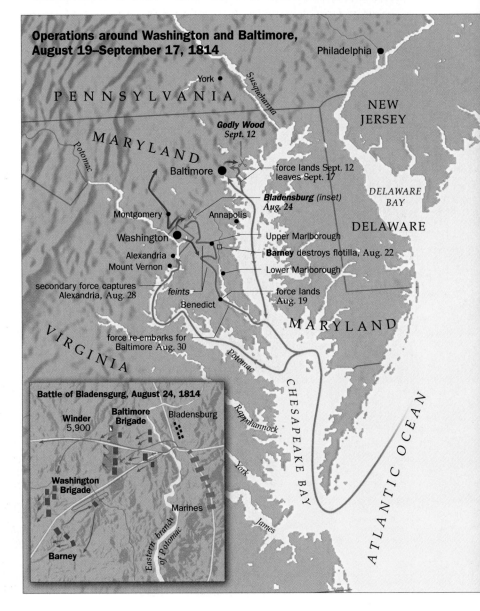

Operations around Washington and Baltimore, August 19–September 17, 1814

Philadelphia

York

PENNSYLVANIA

Susquehanna

NEW JERSEY

Godly Wood *Sept. 12*

MARYLAND

Potomac

Baltimore

force lands Sept. 12 leaves Sept. 17

DELAWARE BAY

DELAWARE

Bladensburg *(inset) Aug. 24*

Montgomery

Annapolis

Washington

Upper Marlborough

Alexandria
Mount Vernon

Barney destroys flotilla, Aug. 22

Lower Marlborough

secondary force captures Alexandria, Aug. 28

feints

force lands Aug. 19

MARYLAND

Benedict

VIRGINIA

force re-embarks for Baltimore Aug. 30

Potomac

Rappahannock

CHESAPEAKE BAY

Battle of Bladensgurg, August 24, 1814

Winder 5,900

Baltimore Brigade

Bladensburg

York

Washington Brigade

Marines

Barney

Eastern branch of Potomac

James

ATLANTIC OCEAN

Battle of New Orleans

The battle between a British and an American army at New Orleans was fought two weeks after the end of the War of 1812. The final bloodletting resulted in a victory that helped propel the American commander into the White House.

A scheme was developed in London to seize control of New Orleans and accordingly a force of some 7,500 Peninsular War veterans was gathered in Jamaica, under the command of Major-General

Sir Edward Packenham for the operation. New Orleans had been the gateway to the French-owned hinterland prior to the Louisiana Purchase, and was still very much a "French colony" in flavor. It was also the richest city in America. With the lower Mississippi in British hands and the coastline closed to shipping, America would be forced to acknowledge defeat—that was the planned outcome.

Despite the imminence of peace talks to be held in Ghent, plans for the amphibious attack continued throughout 1814. On November 26 the British expedition sailed from Jamaica. The Americans were watching. While the possibility remained that the force might land somewhere else on the coast of the Gulf of Mexico, New Orleans was widely acknowledged as the most likely target.

Consequently, Major-General Andrew Jackson (1767–1845) was sent to take command of the city's defenses. A veteran of the war against the Creek Indians of Florida and Georgia, he was a gifted but quarrelsome soldier. On his arrival on December 1, he noted the poor state of the city's defenses and organized a fortified line around Baton Rouge. This was to provide a secure base of operations should New Orleans fall to the British.

Jackson called for the mustering of militia from

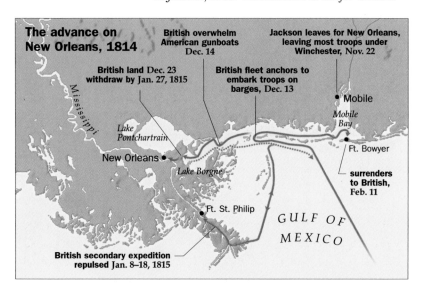

The advance on New Orleans, 1814

- British overwhelm American gunboats Dec. 14
- Jackson leaves for New Orleans, leaving most troops under Winchester, Nov. 22
- British land Dec. 23 withdraw by Jan. 27, 1815
- British fleet anchors to embark troops on barges, Dec. 13
- Mobile
- *Mobile Bay*
- Ft. Bowyer surrenders to British, Feb. 11
- *Mississippi*
- *Lake Pontchartrain*
- New Orleans
- *Lake Borgne*
- Ft. St. Philip
- GULF OF MEXICO
- British secondary expedition repulsed Jan. 8–18, 1815

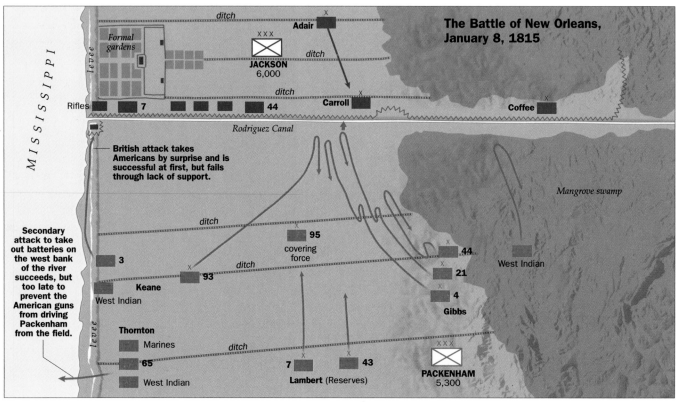

The Battle of New Orleans, January 8, 1815

- ditch
- Adair
- *Formal gardens*
- XXX
- ditch
- JACKSON 6,000
- *levee*
- ditch
- Rifles
- 7
- 44
- Carroll
- Coffee
- *MISSISSIPPI*
- Rodriguez Canal
- British attack takes Americans by surprise and is successful at first, but fails through lack of support.
- *Mangrove swamp*
- Secondary attack to take out batteries on the west bank of the river succeeds, but too late to prevent the American guns from driving Packenham from the field.
- ditch
- 3
- 95 covering force
- ditch
- 44 West Indian
- 93
- 21
- Keane
- West Indian
- 4
- Gibbs
- *levee*
- Thornton
- Marines
- ditch
- 65
- 7
- 43
- XXX
- West Indian
- Lambert (Reserves)
- PACKENHAM 5,300

Louisiana, Mississippi, Kentucky, and Tennessee to augment his small force of U.S. Army regulars and local volunteers. The latter included a contingent of former pirates, granted an amnesty to fight for the city. The French pirate Jean Laffitte, who commanded these brigands—and much of the lawless territory surrounding New Orleans—had rejected British approaches and sided with the Americans. For Lafitte, it would prove to be a poor decision, since it ultimately led to the establishment of military law over the Mississippi Delta and the eradication of piracy in the Gulf of Mexico.

Ill-advised assaults

After clearing the islands off the Mississippi coast, the British expeditionary force landed on the western side of Lake Bourgne, ten miles southeast of New Orleans, on December 13. Packenham's advance guard got within five miles of the city, where they discovered the defensive positions Jackson had constructed, blocking any further advance. This line ran along an abandoned irrigation ditch known as the Rodriguez Canal, with its left flank ending in a dense Cypress swamp and its right anchored on the Mississippi.

Jackson had 3,100 men under his command, including a small core of regulars. While other contingents were arriving daily, it would be some time before he had sufficient troops to take on the British. During the night of December 23–24

Jackson launched a moonlit raid on British forward positions, but most of his force became lost in the darkness and were captured.

For the next week Jackson improved his defenses, while the British brought up artillery to support their offensive. Finally, on January 8, Packenham launched his assault, 5,300 men against 6,000 entrenched defenders across open ground. Packenham relied on the courage and experience of the British infantry to win the day, but they marched into a killing ground. Two main thrusts were made against American positions, but the advance was slowed by a series of small irrigation ditches and the attackers were shot down. On the British left, the momentum was lost before it reached the Rodriguez Canal, but on the right troops reached the line of American defenses before being hurled back.

When the smoke cleared, some 2,100 British casualties littered the ground in front of the American line. American casualties were just seven men killed and six wounded. The British dead included Packenham himself, and the campaign was abandoned. A week later the British returned to Jamaica.

Unknown to the battle's participants, the Treaty of Ghent had been signed on December 24, 1814 guaranteeing the territorial boundaries of Canada and the U.S.A. and ending an otherwise futile war. As for Jackson, his victory helped him secure the presidency in 1828.

Because of the extended communications between Washington and the Mississippi, when the Battle of New Orleans was fought in January of 1815 it was two weeks after the War of 1812 had officially ended. Major-General Andrew Jackson's leadership in the battle brought him national fame, which later helped him attain the U.S. presidency.

One Hundred Days

The Waterloo Campaign, 1815

After his abdication, "the ogre was caged," and Napoleon went into exile on the Mediterranean island of Elba. France became a monarchy again and tried to forget a quarter-century of terror, bloodshed, victory and defeat. To many, this was turning back the clock, since in the train of King Louis XVIII (r.1814–24) came a host of exiled aristocrats demanding a return to the pre-Revolution society they remembered. But France had moved on and—although the "revolutionary" tricolor was abandoned in favor of the Bourbon *fleur de lys*—Napoleon's old government apparatus was left intact.

The most significant social change was in the reduction of the army, as tens of thousands of Napoleonic veterans were demobilized. Numerous officers sat around in cafés discussing the changing times, and soon the days of empire came to assume a grandeur hardly deserved. The carnage forgotten, memories of former glories remained.

Above all, it was the peasantry who had most to lose from a return to the *ancien régime*, and who viewed the king with the greatest suspicion. Most government posts and key army commands were filled by former Napoleonic appointees, and they were equally suspicious of a king who seemed little more than a puppet of the former allied powers.

From his island state of Elba, Napoleon was well informed of developments in France. Many of his old marshals now served the new regime and some kept in touch with Napoleon, providing him with insights they probably denied Louis. While he devoted some energy to reforming Elba and the training of its thousand-strong army of French veterans and volunteers, Napoleon mostly plotted a return to political life.

By early 1815, he decided that the situation in France had shifted sufficiently in his favor. By posing as an ally of those who felt disenfranchised and portraying himself as the embodiment of revolutionary progress, he had a chance to regain control of France. On February 26, he left Elba with his small army and landed in France three days later.

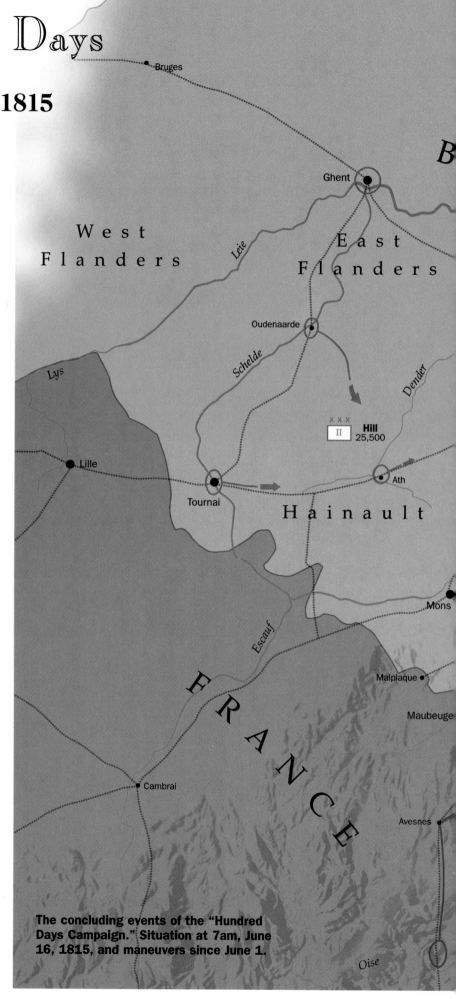

The concluding events of the "Hundred Days Campaign." Situation at 7am, June 16, 1815, and maneuvers since June 1.

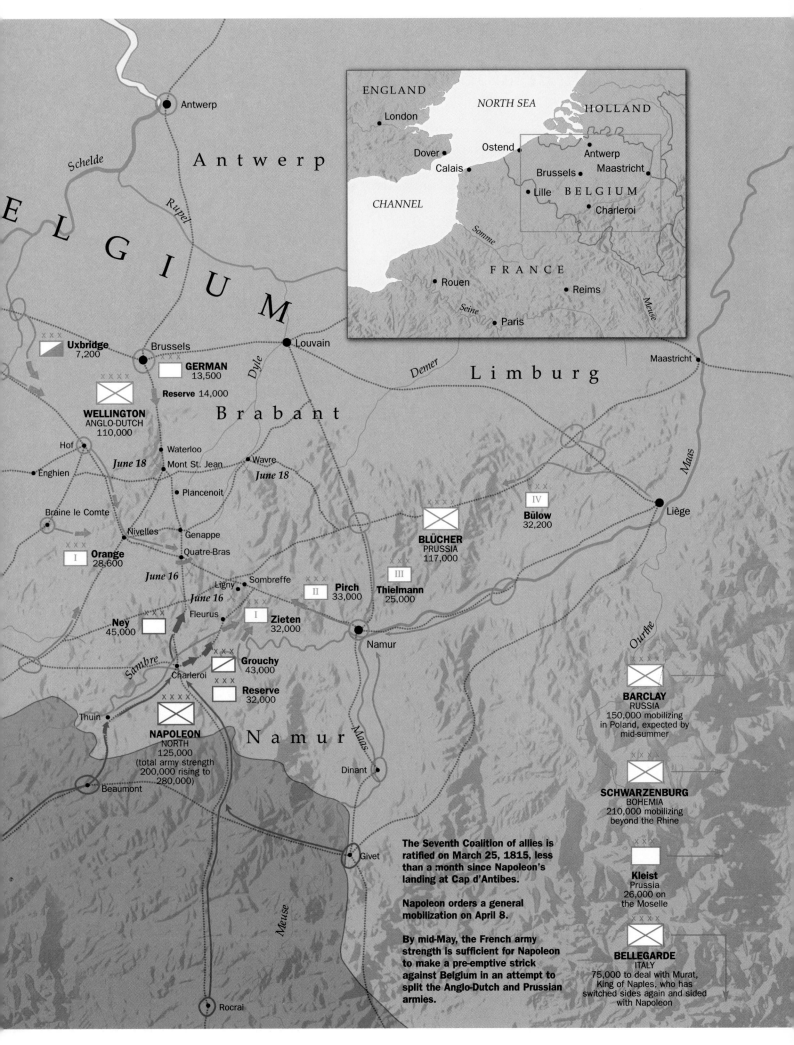

ENGLAND

NORTH SEA

HOLLAND

London

Dover

Ostend

Antwerp

Calais

Brussels

Maastricht

CHANNEL

Lille

BELGIUM

Charleroi

Somme

FRANCE

Rouen

Reims

Seine

Meuse

Paris

Antwerp

Schelde

Rupel

B E L G I U M

Antwerp

A n t w e r p

Louvain

Demer

L i m b u r g

Maastricht

Uxbridge
7,200

Brussels

GERMAN
13,500

Dyle

Reserve 14,000

WELLINGTON
ANGLO-DUTCH
110,000

B r a b a n t

Maas

Hof

Waterloo

Wavre

June 18

Mont St. Jean

June 18

Liège

Enghien

Plancenoit

IV

Bülow
32,200

Braine le Comte

Nivelles

Genappe

BLÜCHER
PRUSSIA
117,000

Orange
28,600

Quatre-Bras

III

Ourthe

June 16

Sombreffe

Ligny

II

Pirch
33,000

Thielmann
25,000

Ney
45,000

June 16

Fleurus

I

Zieten
32,000

BARCLAY
RUSSIA
150,000 mobilizing
in Poland, expected by
mid-summer

Sambre

Charleroi

Grouchy
43,000

Namur

Reserve
32,000

Maas

Thuin

NAPOLEON
NORTH
125,000
(total army strength
200,000 rising to
280,000)

N a m u r

SCHWARZENBURG
BOHEMIA
210,000 mobilizing
beyond the Rhine

Beaumont

Dinant

Kleist
Prussia
26,000 on
the Moselle

Meuse

The Seventh Coalition of allies is
ratified on March 25, 1815, less
than a month since Napoleon's
landing at Cap d'Antibes.

Napoleon orders a general
mobilization on April 8.

By mid-May, the French army
strength is sufficient for Napoleon
to make a pre-emptive strick
against Belgium in an attempt to
split the Anglo-Dutch and Prussian
armies.

Givet

BELLEGARDE
ITALY
75,000 to deal with Murat,
King of Naples, who has
switched sides again and sided
with Napoleon

Rocrai

Return from Elba

Napoleon landed near Cannes on March 1, 1815. So began the period known as The Hundred Days, when Napoleon regained his throne, rebuilt his army, then led his men into a last great campaign against the allies.

*N*apoleon was accompanied by the thousand men of his retinue and only four guns, attended by three former French generals, Henri-Gatien Bertrand (head of the royal household), Viscount Pierre Cambronne (an ex-imperial guardsman, and commander of the Elba guard), and Jean-Baptiste Drouet, Count d'Erlon (a Peninsular War commander). News of his landing reached Paris in five days and within weeks all of Europe learned of the incredible venture. As the British press put it, "the devil is unchained."

Surrounded by his small but faithful retinue, Napoleon prepares to leave Elba for the mainland of France.

regiment that now served the Royalist government.

Napoleon made an emotive plea, baring his breast to the waiting soldiers. He exclaimed, "Soldiers of the Fifth, you can shoot your emperor if you dare! Do you not recognize me as your emperor?" They did. The muskets were lowered, and amid cheers of "Vive l'empereur" the soldiers joined his army. It was a decisive moment, since it showed how willing the military was to resume its old allegiances. The following day Napoleon's small army entered Grenoble, cheered by the townsfolk and welcomed by the city authorities. As Napoleon later recalled, "Before Grenoble I was an adventurer; at Grenoble I was a ruling prince."

The scene was repeated at every major settlement along the road to Paris. The acclaimed emperor made speeches promising a return to revolutionary

Avoiding the pro-Royalist region of Provence and the city of Marseilles (where the politically suspect Marshal Massena was governor), Napoleon marched north through the mountains toward Grenoble. His first crisis came 15 miles south of Grenoble at Laffrey, on March 7. Napoleon's path was blocked by the Fifth Regiment of Line, a former Napoleonic

values and ironically guaranteed future peace and prosperity. He also promised land reform, which naturally gained him the support of the French peasantry, and the repeal of new taxation introduced by the Bourbon monarchy. He became all things to all people and, although most knew that Napoleon's return meant war, they responded favorably. The old

showman had not lost his touch, and the French countryside rose in support of their old emperor.

Unassailable support

Louis XVIII soon became alarmed by the progress of the Napoleonic army, and sent several (and increasingly substantial) detachments of troops to bar his progress. The most significant was the division commanded by Marshal Ney, which confronted Napoleon and his small but growing army outside Auxerre on March 14.

Ney had promised King Louis that he would "bring him back in an iron cage." Ney's problem was with his own men—the loyalty of almost all French troops was questionable during this crucial period. Ney found his men unwilling to fight Napoleon. Ney stated: "They will fight; I will begin the action myself, and run my sword to the hilt in the breast of the first who hesitates to follow my example."

Despite his loyalty to the king, Ney was unable to prevent a mass desertion of his troops. Envoys sent by Napoleon assured him that all the other marshals had agreed to defect, and that the allies tacitly approved of the removal of the Bourbon monarchy. Reluctantly Ney switched sides, an act of betrayal that eventually cost him his life.

This was the final nail in the Bourbon coffin. Some Parisian wit pinned a sign up in the Place Vendôme, which read, "From Napoleon to Louis XVIII. My good brother, there is no need to send any more troops. I have enough."

As the Paris mob that had so welcomed the allies on their capture of the city in 1813 rose in revolt against the monarchy and prepared to welcome Napoleon, Louis XVIII and his family fled north to exile in Holland on April 19. The following day Napoleon entered Paris. Once again, he was master of France. While he no longer aspired to mastery of Europe, he realized it would take a war to secure his hold on the French throne.

Napoleon's landing at Cap d'Antibes, on March 1, 1815. The "Emperor of Elba" was accompanied by the three generals who had gone into exile with him.

The Struggle Renewed

Napoleon was back in Tuileries Palace on March 20, 1815, once again controlling the fate of France. He hoped for a peaceful co-existence with the European powers, but planned for the likely response.

Although Napoleon became the head of state in France, he lacked the absolutist power he had enjoyed before his abdication. The government institutions were wary of a full commitment to a regime that might not last until the summer. His first task was to send emissaries to the former allied powers, expressing the disillusionment of the French with Bourbon rule, and their earnest desire to live in peace… under their old emperor. While he recognized that a calm acceptance of his *coup d'etat*

Contemporary engraving of mutinous French royal troops greeting Napoleon during his journey toward Paris in March 1815.

was unlikely, the possibility remained that political divisions might divide Austria, Prussia, Russia, and a Britain still recovering from the failure of the American campaigns.

His hopes were soon dashed. News of Napoleon's landing in France reached Vienna on March 9. Representatives of the major powers were already gathered for the Congress of Vienna—at which they were still tidying up the political structure of Europe from the effects of Napoleon's last time on the French throne. On March 14, a treaty of alliance was

drafted in response to the percieved threat that Napoleon represented. Britain earmarked £5 million ($8 million) as a war subsidy and promptly mobilized the army, as did Prussia. The other powers promised to begin operations against France as soon as possible. The Seventh Coalition was formally ratified on March 25.

This warlike attitude at least meant that Napoleon was able to cast the allies as the aggressors and he called on the people of France to repel the expected invasion. A general mobilization was ordered on April 8, and three weeks later conscription was introduced in an effort to build up the army to a level where it could match the allies.

While the French manufacturing workshops and arms factories produced the necessary uniforms, weapons, munitions, and equipment, Napoleon organized the men. Following the accession of Louis XVIII, the French army was scaled down to 200,000 men. This was to be the basis for the new army and former soldiers flocked back to the colors, their enthusiasm matched by a new generation of volunteers. This effort increased Napoleon's available force, but it was still far short of the troop quantities available to the allies.

Taking the initiative

In Belgium, Wellington was gathering an Anglo-Dutch army of 110,000 men. To the west, Field-Marshal Blücher was mobilizing a Prussian army of 117,000, earmarked to operate in conjunction with Wellington's force. An Austrian army of up to 210,000 men was being gathered beyond the Rhine under the command of Prince Karl Philipp Schwarzenberg (1771–1820). An additional 75,000 Austrians and their Italian allies were available for operations in Italy, where Murat—opportunistically switching sides again—had declared the Kingdom of Naples' support for Napoleon. Finally, a Russian army of 150,000 men under Barclay de Tolly was ready to march west from Poland and expected to reach the Rhine by mid-summer. When all these armies were ready, allied strategists planned to launch a simultaneous advance toward Paris from the north and east. Sheer weight of numbers would guarantee the defeat of France.

By May 1815, Napoleon had about 280,000 soldiers under arms. He had two strategic options.

Unfinished business: Napoleon's first task was to secure a peace between himself and the European powers that had evicted him. Portrait of Napoleon by Anne-Louis Girodet-Trioson.

He could stand and defend Paris, using his central position to keep the allies at bay, or he could try to destroy the Prussian and British armies in Belgium before the Austrians and Russians were in a position to intervene. Always preferring to maintain the initiative, Napoleon marched north at the head of 125,000 men, leaving the rest to protect the eastern and southeastern frontiers.

Although the allies in Belgium outnumbered him and their forces were commanded by two of the best allied generals, their armies were constrained by logistics. Wellington's lines of communication stretched back to the Channel coast, while Blücher's army traced its supply east into Germany. As his army marched north, Napoleon formulated a typical plan to split the enemy armies, then destroy each in turn.

Skirmish at Quatre Bras

In mid-June 1815, the French army made a pre-emptive strike into Belgium. While Napoleon concentrated his army against the Prussians, Marshal Ney attacked an isolated formation of British troops occupying a strategically important crossroads.

When the French arrived in Belgium, the allies' forces were widely scattered. Blücher's 105,000 infantry, 12,000 cavalry, and 296 guns in the korps of generals Zieten, Thielmann, and Bülow were deployed along the Maas (Meuse) and Sambre rivers from Charleroi to Liege. A fourth Prussian korps of 26,000 men commanded by General Kleist was stationed on the Moselle. Wellington had 79,000 infantry, 14,000 cavalry, and 196 guns around Brussels, with another 17,000 men deployed in garrisons guarding the lines of supply. Scattered British and allied divisions extended as far south and west as Grammont and Nivelles. The term British is somewhat misleading, since over half of Wellington's army in 1815 was composed of allies—Dutch-Belgians, Hanovarians, and Brunswickers, among others. This polyglot force contained a significant portion of untried units and regiments who had

served Napoleon only a year before.

Napoleon was well aware of the location and composition of all the allied formations in Belgium. He calculated that it would take three days for the two armies to concentrate into one force, giving him time to move his army between them. The main road from Paris to Brussels passed through Quatre Bras, where it crossed the road linking Liège to the east and Ath to the west. By seizing the crossroads, Napoleon could prevent an early link-up between the two allied armies.

The assembly of 100,000 infantry, 22,000 cavalry, and 366 guns on the Belgian frontier was achieved in great secrecy, and before dawn on June 15 the army crossed the Sambre in three columns. The Prussians had only learned of the French concentration the previous day, and while Blücher gave orders for his army to concentrate north of Ligny, no attempt was made to link up with Wellington. Wellington only learned of the French advance on the evening of June 14, but he misread his intelligence reports and assumed that Napoleon planned to move west to cut the British off from the Channel ports. His redeployment to cover his western flank played into Napoleon's hands by increasing the gap between the two allied armies.

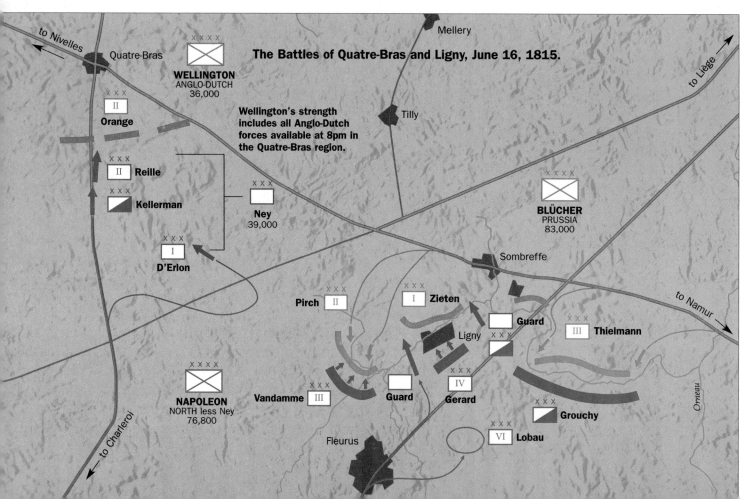

Crossroads struggle

On the afternoon of June 15 Napoleon sent Marshal Ney with II Corps (General Reille) and the Third Cavalry Corps (General Kellerman) to seize the crossroads of Quatre Bras, while he led the rest of the army to engage the western flank of the Prussian army around Ligny. Ney failed to appreciate the urgency of his mission, and his force halted to the south of Quatre Bras for the night, after his cavalry made contact with a brigade of allied infantry.

By dawn the infantry had been reinforced by the rest of their Dutch-Belgian division and other British and Hanovarian troops were on their way after Wellington understood that the French were heading toward Ligny. At about 11am General Reille's corps advanced toward Quatre Bras and fighting continued in the vicinity of the crossroads into the afternoon, with both sides feeding reinforcements into the battle.

The allies formed themselves into a good defensive position around the hamlet and crossroads, their right flank anchored on a thick wood. The French attack was overly cautious but the allies were outnumbered, and by mid-afternoon their line began to crack. At that point Wellington arrived with a division of British troops, bringing allied strength up to 20,000 men, a total that increased to 36,000 by nightfall.

Ney repeatedly sent Kellerman's cavalry against the allied line and himself led infantry attacks against enemy positions, but the allied line remained intact and the crossroads remained in Wellington's hands. Reinforcements would have tipped the balance in Ney's favor, but incompetent staffwork meant that despite being ordered to join the fight, General Drouet's corps failed to arrive before nightfall.

Both sides had lost over 4,000 men during the day, but Wellington's army had held its ground and could be considered the victors. Only the defeat of Blücher at Ligny (*see following page*) and the collapse of the allied flank forced Wellington to abandon his position and withdraw up the Brussels road to a ridge he considered a good defensive site, just south of the village of Waterloo.

French engraving of the Battle of Quatre Bras, June 16, 1815.

"The Duke of Wellington on the Road to Quatre Bras" by Robert Alexander Hillingford.

Battles of Ligny and Wavre

While Marshal Ney fought the Anglo-Dutch army at Quatre Bras, Napoleon moved against Blücher's army at Ligny. The hard-won victory over the Prussians allowed Napoleon to concentrate his army against Wellington.

Originally, Napoleon planned to concentrate his army against the isolated Dutch-Belgian position around Quatre Bras, but reports of Blücher's concentration at Ligny forced him to change his plans. Leaving Drouet, Comte d'Erlon,

reserve, to crush the Prussian center.

Blücher drew up his 84,000 men along a series of ridges on the northern side of the Ligny stream, with large detachments posted in the villages of Ligny, St. Amand, and Sombreffe. General Thielmann's III Korps held the Prussian left, General Zieten's I Korps held the right, and General Pirch's II Korps was held in reserve behind Zieten.

At 2.30pm on June 16, 1815, Napoleon launched Vandamme and Gérard against the villages of St. Amand and Ligny, while French artillery

During a final desperate cavalry charge against the French at Ligny, Blücher was unhorsed and left for dead. He was rescued unharmed some minutes later.

and his I Corps to support Ney, Napoleon directed the Imperial Guard, two army corps, and four cavalry corps toward Ligny with a speed that took the Prussians by surprise.

The plan was to pin Blücher with III and IV Korps (generals Vandamme and Gérard), then recall Comte D'Erlon to outflank the Prussian right wing. At the crucial moment, the Imperial Guard would be sent in, supported by the massed cavalry of the

pounded the Prussians on the slopes behind the stream. Marshal Grouchy pinned Thielmann with I and II Cavalry Corps (generals Pajo and Exelmans), allowing the attacks on Zieten's forward positions to continue without interruption.

At this stage, Napoleon was unaware that Ney faced more than a small force of allied troops at Quatre Bras, so he ordered Drouet to move north into position to hit the Prussians in the flank and

Ney to send a detachment to support Drouet's flanking attack. Drouet prevaricated, torn between conflicting orders from Ney and Napoleon, but eventually he marched toward Ligny, arriving on Vandamme's left flank at about 5.30pm.

Trapped at Wavre

Meanwhile, the French had cleared the Prussians from St. Amand, but both sides committed troops to the western portion of the battlefield, and Vandamme became bogged down in a fight against the Prussian II Korps and part of I Korps. While losses were high on both sides, the last Prussian reserves had been committed to the battle, while Napoleon still held his Imperial Guard in reserve.

To the east, Gérard finally captured Ligny just before 6pm, but a counterattack led to a renewed fight for the village that continued for another two hours. Just when Blücher managed to roll back Vandamme's troops, Drouet appeared and provided an anchor for the French left wing. With the Prussian line stretched to breaking point, Napoleon sent in the Imperial Guard, who smashed through the Ligny defenses and opened a gap for the IV Cavalry Corps (General Milhaud) to exploit.

Grouchy also launched a cavalry charge on the Prussian left wing, and by 9pm the entire Prussian line was in retreat.

The battle was costly: the French lost 12,000 men but inflicted 16,000 dead on the Prussians, who were spared further losses by the onset of darkness. Napoleon ordered Grouchy to pursue the Prussians with Vandamme and Gérard's corps, while the rest of the French army marched to fight Wellington. The defeated Prussians halted their retreat at Wavre on the River Dyle, 15 miles north of Ligny and 10 miles east of Waterloo.

On June 18 Grouchy discovered that the Prussians were sending troops westward to reinforce Wellington, so he launched an immediate attack against General Thielmann's Prussian rearguard of 17,000 men. The Prussians held their positions throughout the day, pinning two French corps in a futile battle, while the fate of Europe was being decided a short distance to the west. This meant that some 33,000 French troops were within a half-day's march of Waterloo, but failed to intervene. In contrast, Blücher and 70,000 Prussians marched to the sound of the guns, arriving at Waterloo in time to tip the scales in the allies' favor.

Blücher and his exhausted Prussian army marched to join Wellington at Waterloo, leaving only a portion of the army behind to face the French at Wavre. A Victorian engraving.

Waterloo

The climactic battle of the Napoleonic Wars, Waterloo was a clash between the two great commanders of the age. Napoleon had to crush the allies quickly, before the Prussians could intervene and turn the tide of battle.

The Duke of Wellington ranged his army on the rear slope of a long, low ridge that bisected the Paris–Brussels road near a farm called La Haie Sainte. A lane ran along the ridge from east to west, leading from the Braine l'Alleud on the allied right wing to Papellotte on the left. In between La Haie Sainte and Braine l'Alleud was the walled Château de Hougoumont, which Wellington turned into a redoubt. At his disposal were 50,000 infantry, 12,500 cavalry, and 156 guns, of which around a third were British, the remainder troops from Holland, Belgium, Brunswick, and Hanover.

Napoleon's army consisted of 49,000 infantry, 15,750 cavalry, and 246 guns; barely enough to attack a similar-sized army in a good defensive position.

Marshal Soult recommended caution, but Napoleon ignored him, boasting that "The whole affair will not be more serious than swallowing one's breakfast." Napoleon was in no doubt who was the better general.

The battle began with a brief but largely

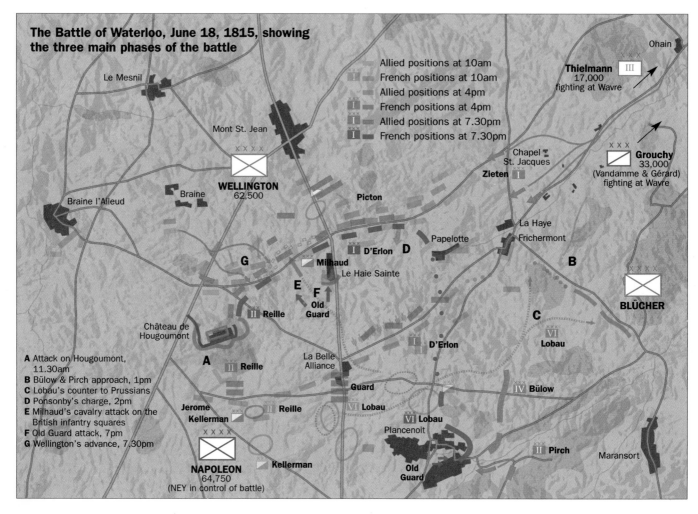

The Battle of Waterloo, June 18, 1815, showing the three main phases of the battle

Allied positions at 10am
French positions at 10am
Allied positions at 4pm
French positions at 4pm
Allied positions at 7.30pm
French positions at 7.30pm

Ohain

Le Mesnil

Mont St. Jean

Thielmann 17,000 fighting at Wavre

Chapel St. Jacques

Zieten

Grouchy 33,000 (Vandamme & Gérard) fighting at Wavre

WELLINGTON 62,500

Picton

Braine
Braine l'Alleud

La Haye
Papelotte Frichermont

D'Erlon D

G Milhaud
Le Haie Sainte

B

Château de Hougoumont

E
F
Old Guard

Reille

BLÜCHER

D'Erlon

Lobau

C

La Belle Alliance

A Reille

Guard

Lobau

Jerome
Kellerman

Reille

Lobau

IV Bülow

VI Lobau
Plancenoit

Pirch

Maransort

NAPOLEON 64,750
(NEY in control of battle)

Kellerman

Old Guard

A Attack on Hougoumont, 11.30am
B Bülow & Pirch approach, 1pm
C Lobau's counter to Prussians
D Ponsonby's charge, 2pm
E Milhaud's cavalry attack on the British infantry squares
F Old Guard attack, 7pm
G Wellington's advance, 7.30pm

ineffective artillery bombardment. Around 11.30am on June 18, Jerome Bonaparte's division of Reille's II Corps advanced toward Hougoumont. The plan was to force Wellington to commit his reserves to protect his line. Instead, the resolute defense of Hougoumont led to the involvement of most of Reille's corps in the fighting around the château.

At 1.30pm D'Erlon's I Corps advanced against the allied center, formed into large columns. Sir Thomas Picton's British division checked the French advance with musketry, and although Picton was killed, the French attack was halted. Wellington ordered a cavalry charge and the French divisions were routed. The Scots Greys cavalry regiment pursued as far as the French artillery line, to be virtually annihilated by French cavalry. Although Wellington had lost a third of his cavalry force, the French mass attack had failed.

At this crucial moment, the first Prussian reinforcements arrived on the eastern edge of the battlefield, forcing Napoleon to divert an increasing number of troops to hold them near the village of Plancenoit. Time was not on Napoleon's side, since he needed to defeat Wellington quickly before the Prussians arrived in force.

The first and final retreat

Around 3.30pm Napoleon allowed Ney to launch a massed charge of 10,000 cavalry against the allied center between La Haie Sainte and Hougoumont. The British closed up into square formations to protect themselves, but Ney failed to support his cavalry with infantry and artillery. While it was a glorious martial spectacle, it only squandered Napoleon's horsemen.

Two Prussian korps were involved in the fighting around Plancenoit by 6pm, forcing Napoleon to commit the Imperial Guard to the fight. This was his last reserve. Back to the north, Ney led another French attack on the allied center, capturing the fortified outpost of La Haie Sainte before advancing to the top of the ridge behind. This time the allied center almost broke, but reinforcements from other parts of the line helped to halt the French advance.

By 7pm, Napoleon had re-deployed the Old Guard to the west of La Haie Sainte, then sent them into the attack. As the French crested the ridge, British guardsmen rose from hiding in the cornfield beyond and poured fire into the French ranks from three sides. For the first time ever, the Old Guard broke and ran. The defeat of the Old Guard led to the collapse of French resistance and, within minutes, the army had disintegrated.

Wellington ordered a general advance, while the newly reinforced Prussians swept up from Plancenoit, threatening to cut the French line of retreat. The Old Guard reformed to cover Napoleon's retreat, only to be cut down by advancing allied troops. Over 40,000 French and 20,000 allied casualties lay on the battlefield, a mass multi-national bloodletting that saw the end of the second Napoleonic dream.

As dusk fell, Wellington met Blücher near what had been Napoleon's headquarters. The victory was complete, but as Wellington remarked, it had been "a close-run thing."

"The Battle of Waterloo" by Sir William Allan, painted c.1843.

End of the Napoleonic Era

Napoleon's reputation was in tatters. Although he continued resistance to the allies and tried to raise another army, the French—who had greeted his return with such adulation—had had enough.

*N*apoleon's world collapsed when the words "La Garde recule!" were uttered. The defeat of the Imperial Guard on the battlefield of Waterloo prompted the collapse of the French army. With no army, there was to be no Napoleon, since for the past decade-and-a-half his power had been maintained at bayonet point.

That evening, Napoleon tried to rally the remnants of his army, but it was a hopeless task. Despite this setback, he entertained hopes that the defeat would not lead to the collapse of all French resistance. Grouchy still had a force of some 32,000 men to the northeast and Davout's corps of almost 40,000 was outside Paris. Over the next few days Grouchy withdrew south, linking up with the remnants of the Army of the North at Philippeville. As Napoleon continued toward Paris, Soult was given the task of rallying what troops remained. Fortunately for him, Wellington and Blücher's armies were also in poor condition and unable to pursue Soult's army into France.

The Hundred Days campaign had cost the French some 60,000 men. With Grouchy's force, Soult had 55,000 men under his command, too small a force to oppose the inevitable allied advance south. In addition to Davout's Paris corps, Napoleon could call on national reserves (National Guardsmen and reservists) and create another force of almost 80,000

The Battle of Waterloo, after a painting by Henri George Jacques Chartier.

troops. Another 170,000 conscripts could be called to the colors within a few months. French armies on the Rhine and the Italian Alps could be recalled to defend Paris if the need arose. Napoleon therefore felt that he could recover from his defeat—all he needed was the support of the French government and people.

What followed was a battle of wills between Napoleon and his government. Davout urged his emperor to seize control of the principal government ministries in the capital and to ring the senate with troops. While Napoleon retained the support of the majority of the population in Paris, the senate was less forgiving. Their support for him during the *coup d'etat* was ultimately dependent on Napoleon's ability to defeat the allied armies in Belgium. After Waterloo and faced with the prospect of another long war, the politicians abandoned him.

No escape

Joseph Fouché, Duc d'Otranto, was Minister of Police during the Hundred Days. When news of Napoleon's defeat reached Paris, Fouché addressed the Chamber of Representatives, calling for a second abdication. When Napoleon reached Tuileries Palace early on June 21, he found the political establishment of Paris ranged against him. The members of the Chamber of Representatives declared their assembly indissoluble by imperial edict, then rallied the National Guard to protect them as the legitimate government of France. In the past, this would have been unthinkable, but under the new circumstances, the Guard could only agree to the request.

Secure from Napoleon's interference, the representatives renewed their call for his abdication. With nowhere else to turn, the emperor was forced to comply. On June 22 he renounced his imperial title in favor of his son, the King of Rome. As the effective leaders of the French government, Fouché and Talleyrand opened peace talks with the allies.

While Soult retreated toward Davout's army outside Paris, Napoleon saw a last-minute opportunity to snatch victory from defeat. Blücher's army had reached the outskirts of Paris, but Wellington was a week from the capital. Napoleon approached the government, offering to lead a counterattack. His offer was rejected.

With Paris on the verge of falling to the enemy, Napoleon left the city and headed for the port of Rochefort, where he hoped to arrange passage to America, a nation he felt would welcome him as an enemy of Britain. Within days the provisional government recognized Louis XVIII as their sovereign, and Napoleon became a political embarrassment. On July 3 he arrived in Rochefort to find the port occupied by a British naval squadron. For the next 12 days he considered several avenues of escape, but when word reached him that the government had ordered his arrest, he gave himself up to the British.

With good reason to fear Napoleon's fortitude in defeat, there was to be no attempt at leaving him with any honorary titles and a comfortable Mediterranean "retirement" in exile this time. The European powers wanted General Bonaparte firmly removed from any sphere of influence, so they sought an isolated island for a prison, and found the ideal spot in the middle of the Atlantic Ocean.

Wellington and Blücher meet at the close of the Battle of Waterloo. An aquatint from *Historic, Military, and Naval Anecdotes*.

Back in power: Louis XVIII (1755–1824), king of France.

CHAPTER TWELVE

Aftermath

The Napoleonic Legacy

Napoleon Bonaparte defies easy categorization. Certainly he was a military genius with an innate ability to predict his opponents' moves, a highly skilled politician, gifted civic reformer, and a popular national leader. Since his death, Napoleon has been condemned by many, and idolized by others. Generations of French schoolchildren have looked on him as a national hero, standing alongside Joan of Arc as a symbol of French national identity and pride. While his sometimes needless military campaigns cost the lives of hundreds of thousands, they created a French military tradition that has supported the nation through later periods of national despair.

How can we understand a man who cried seeing the casualties of Borodino but appeared callous when faced with the carnage at Leipzig? A child of the Revolution, Napoleon encouraged the abolition of feudalism across Europe; he freed peasants from bondage and instituted laws to safeguard their rights. At the same time, he developed a ruthless—though rarely murderous—police state. In his youth he approved of the Revolution's opposition to the Catholic Church, but later established a concordat with the pope; and in his will Napoleon declared he would "die in the apostolic and Roman religion."

Wellington once commented that Napoleon was worth the presence of 40,000 men on the battlefield, and remained in awe of his military reputation even after Waterloo. By contrast, on the eve of the same battle, Napoleon told Marshal Soult that he considered Wellington to be a "bad general." Bombast to raise the morale of his marshals perhaps, but it also demonstrates how, even as late as 1815, Napoleon considered himself superior to other men. Almost all his biographers describe Napoleon as egotistical, but that ego also served as a driving force that spurred him on to greatness.

Napoleon's genius lay in engineering a campaign and refining the tools he was given to create the perfect military machine. He operated on the strategic and operational level, planning a campaign long before his troops crossed a border, studying the road network, then calculating with unnerving accuracy where best to place his army to inflict maximum damage to the enemy. Napoleon could read a battlefield, knowing exactly when to send in his reserves or launch a counterattack.

He motivated men to achieve the near-impossible—from his first campaign in Italy until his catastrophic invasion of Russia. Critics suggest that by 1809 Napoleon was losing his touch, relying on grand batteries of artillery to crack the enemy, or deploying his infantry in ever-increasing massed columns—a tactical cudgel rather than a rapier. This fails to take into account the steady attrition of French veterans, leaving him no choice but to adopt these tactics to overcome his army's declining standards. Even after 1812, he could raise fresh recruits, and encourage them to outfight experienced veterans of Russia, Prussia, and Austria.

Time has only added to his martial reputation. While there are hardly any images of Wellington or Blücher in the souvenir shop beside the battlefield of Waterloo, busts and pictures of Napoleon are everywhere, almost as if the emperor had won the final battle.

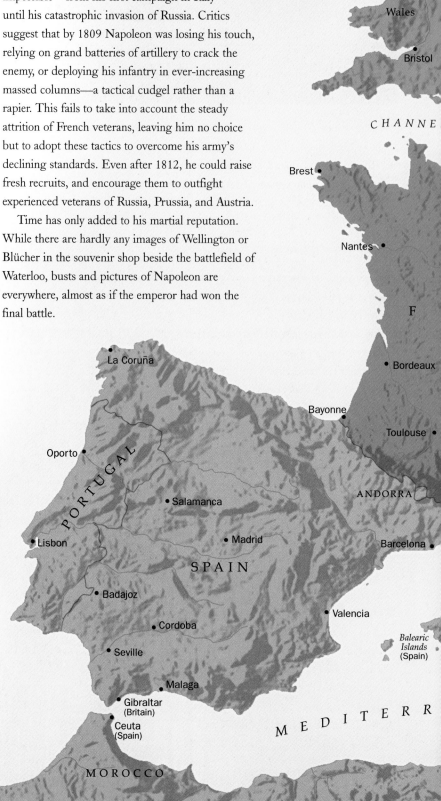

Europe after the Treaty of Vienna, 1815

NORWAY

Union from 1815

• Stockholm

SWEDEN

• Göteborg

BALTIC SEA

• Riga

DENMARK

Copenhagen

Schleswig
to Prussia 1865

NORTH SEA

MECKLENBURG-
SCHWERIN

Pomerania

• Tilsit   • Kovno

• Königsberg   • Vilna

• Danzig

East Prussia

• Hamburg

England

• Bremen

HANOVER
to Prussia 1866

• Stettin

Brandenburg

PRUSSIA

RUSSIAN
EMPIRE

Amsterdam •

NETHERLANDS

Berlin •

• London

Brussels •

Westphalia

Belgium
1830

Dresden •

Silesia

• Warsaw

Poland

to Austrian
empire 1847

• Paris

Luxembourg

HESSE

• Frankfurt

BADEN

BAVARIA

Prague •

• Krakow

Galicia and
Lodomeria

• Orléans

WÜRTEMBERG

Ratisbon
(Regensburg)

Alsace-Lorraine
to German empire 1871

N   C   E

• Basel

SWITZERLAND

Salzburg •

Tyrol

Salzburg

Vienna •

AUSTRIAN EMPIRE

• Vienna

Styria

Buda • • Pest

MOLDAVIA
autonomous 1829

Geneva •

Carinthia

• Lyon

Savoy
to France
1860

Hungary

Transylvania

Venetia
to Italy 1866

• Milan

Lombardy

Venice •

Slavonia

Turin •

to Sardinia 1815–48
to France 1848

Parma

Genoa •

Croatia

Bosnia

WALLACHIA
autonomous 1829

Dalmatia

Herzegovina

SERBIA
autonomous 1817

• Marseilles

LIGURIAN SEA

Florence •

Tuscany

Papal States

ADRIATIC SEA

OTTOMAN EMPIRE

MONTENEGRO

Corsica

Rome •

Europe in 1815

France

Austrian empire

Russian empire

Prussia

United Kingdom & Hanover

Ottoman empire

German Confederation

Naples •

SARDINIA
to Italy 1861

Sardinia

TYRRHENIAN SEA

KINGDOM OF THE TWO SICILIES

E A N   S E A

ALGIERS
occupied by France from 1830

Palermo •

Sicily

Exile to St. Helena

The "ogre" was caged again, and this time the allies were taking no chances. Rather than leaving him on European soil, the British sent Napoleon into exile on the remote Atlantic island of St. Helena.

On July 15, 1815, Napoleon Bonaparte went aboard the 74-gun ship-of-the-line HMS *Bellerophon* in Rochefort harbor and surrendered to her commander, Captain Maitland. By placing himself under the protection of Britain's "princes and laws," Napoleon hoped to win the support of the Prince Regent, writing to him as "the most generous of my enemies."

Bellerophon immediately set sail for Britain, entering Torbay on July 26. Despite Napoleon's plea for mercy, neither the Prince Regent nor Prime Minister Lord Liverpool were willing to compromise. By the time *Bellerophon* reached Plymouth on July 31, Napoleon's fate had been sealed. He was to be exiled to St. Helena, a small, windswept island in the South Atlantic.

The British dependency of St. Helena, some 1,200 miles from the African coast, measured only 47 square miles, roughly half the size of Elba. Napoleon told Captain Maitland that he would sooner die than be sent to such a place, and resented British insistence on calling him merely General Bonaparte. Admiral Sir George Cockburn, the man who burned Washington, was given the task of transporting

Admiral Sir George Cockburn and Major-General Sir Hudson Lowe, Napoleon's keepers.

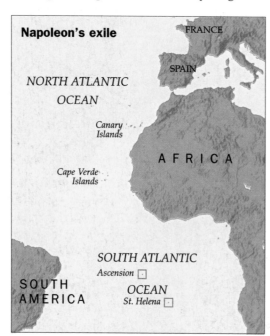

Napoleon's exile

FRANCE

NORTH ATLANTIC OCEAN

SPAIN

Canary Islands

AFRICA

Cape Verde Islands

SOUTH ATLANTIC

Ascension ·

SOUTH AMERICA

OCEAN

St. Helena ·

Napoleon to his island prison.

HMS *Northumberland* dropped anchor in St. Helena's James Bay on October 15, and Napoleon and his personal retinue of 30 staff were taken ashore two days later. The refurbishment of his intended residence at Longwood House—the summer residence of Governor John Skelton—had not been completed, so in the interim Napoleon and his party lodged with a Balcombe family for two months in their boarding house. By Christmas Napoleon was safely ensconced in his new residence, with sentries guarding its perimeter.

The British considered that a rescue attempt was a real possibility, and consequently gun emplacements covered any likely landing places. As an added precaution three frigates and two dispatch vessels were based at Jamestown (the island's only port), and six other guard ships patrolled the waters around the island. The British were clearly taking no chances.

Cruelty and jealousy

In April 1816 Admiral Cockburn was relieved by Major-General Sir Hudson Lowe, who Napoleon's entourage accused of vindictiveness, paranoia, a lack of respect, and even cruelty. Although these accusations were largely unfounded, Lowe lacked the diplomatic skills that might have prevented ill-feeling on the island. After three visits, Napoleon refused to ever meet Lowe again, his principal criticism being

Lowe's failure to accord him his imperial title.

Napoleon spent a miserable six years on St. Helena, away from his wife and child, and stripped of his most trusted lieutenants. He ate simple meals, drank sparingly, and maintained a rigid daily routine, but there was little to alleviate the monotony of his final years. Denied the right to go horse riding without a British escort, Napoleon refused to ride within sight of a British soldier. While the British government, and possibly even Napoleon, considered a rescue attempt a possibility, the rest of Europe had moved on. There was no place for the disgraced emperor in the new European order.

Napoleon was determined that his legacy should not be forgotten. Consequently he spent his final years dictating his memoirs to General Gourgaud, up until the point his military secretary was forced to return to France in 1818 after a disagreement with Count Charles Tristan de Montholon, who dominated the Longwood household. Most of the disputes and jealousies that arose in the household stemmed from Montholon; first Count Las Caces, then Gourgaud were driven away, then Napoleon's physician O'Meara departed for France. While the staff attending the emperor changed throughout the period, Marchand, Napoleon's valet, and de Montholon and his wife remained until the bitter end.

One enduring legacy of the memoirs was that they ensured that Napoleon could tell his version of the events that shaped Europe during his reign. He must have considered what might have been, had he made different decisions during his final years in power.

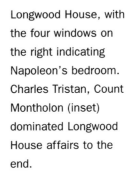

Napoleon's Civil Code granted legal rights to citizens, enhancing his image as a man of the common people. However, it is doubtful that Napoleon thought this "commonness" would extend as far as this painting of 1870 by Oliver Pichat titled "Allegory of Napoleon as a Laborer" suggests.

Longwood House, with the four windows on the right indicating Napoleon's bedroom. Charles Tristan, Count Montholon (inset) dominated Longwood House affairs to the end.

The Congress of Vienna

After Napoleon's first abdication in April 1814, the victorious allies of the Sixth Coalition held a summit in Vienna to discuss Europe's future. Napoleon's return in 1815 did little to delay proceedings, and by June that year the delegates had redrawn the political landscape.

*F*ollowing the removal of Napoleon to Elba, Louis XVIII was free to establish a lasting peace. Under the terms of the Treaty of Paris, signed on May 30, 1814, the borders of France were returned to their pre-Revolution positions, and a hereditary Bourbon monarch was reinstated. The allied powers believed they were restoring the legitimate head of the country, but to many French it was a retrograde step that denied them the civil freedoms they had fought for since 1789. This undercurrent of resentment led directly to Napoleon's *coup d'etat* in early 1815.

With France restructured to suit the tastes of the

A grateful nation awarded the Duke of Wellington the honor of his own triumphal arch to commemorate the Battle of Waterloo. A winged figure of Victory riding a chariot crowns the arch on the lawns near Apsley House, London.

allied powers, an international conference was called to discuss the fate of the rest of Europe. Summoned in late 1814, the Congress of Vienna involved the leading diplomats and representatives of the ruling houses of Austria, Prussia, Russia, and Britain. Lesser European states had little say in the major debates and simply had to live with the decisions made by the leading powers.

The Duke of Wellington and Robert Castlereagh, Marquess of Londonderry (1762–1822), led the British delegation. Czar Alexander I was head of the Russian contingent, supported by Freiherr Heinrich Stein (1757–1831), a Prussian-born diplomat who

combined German patriotism with service to the czar. The Austrian team was dominated by Prince Klemens von Metternich, who was widely regarded as the greatest statesmen in Europe, while Prince Karl von Hardenburg (1750–1822) represented the Prussian king, Frederick-Wilhelm III. Although the French were officially denied a say in the proceedings, Charles Talleyrand, Prince de Bénévent, played a crucial role behind the scenes, representing the new French political establishment.

An entertaining meeting

The first working session of the congress began on November 1, 1814, the diplomatic meetings set against a glittering backdrop of balls, concerts,

operas, theater performances, and military reviews that helped to foster goodwill between the allies. After two decades of near-constant warfare, the European establishment was determined to enjoy itself, and Vienna rose to the occasion. Prince de Ligne's comment about the proceedings, "Le congres ne marche pas, il danse" (the congress doesn't walk, it dances), was not far from the mark.

The fate of Poland was of major importance to Russia and the central European powers. After much debate the delegates decided to reduce its borders, then give it to Russia as a semi-autonomous state. Prussia and Austria gained the lost Polish territories, and parts of Saxony were also ceded to Prussia, as were parts of Westphalia and Pomerania, which effectively expanded to encompass most of its pre-1806 borders. Compensation was made to Sweden by granting her Norway.

A new German confederation replaced Napoleon's Confederation of the Rhine, comprising some 39 autonomous states. A similar solution was adopted in Italy, where the old ruling houses of Savoy-Piedmont, Tuscany, and Naples were restored, Switzerland was declared independent, and other small city-states and duchies were created.

The Hundred Days campaign delayed the formal signature of the treaty, but on June 9, 1815 the work of the congress was finally ratified. With the second defeat of Napoleon, Europe was free to live in peace within the borders defined by the politicians in Vienna. While this neat arrangement provided stability between the major European powers, it did not calm the groundswell of nationalist aspirations, most notably in Germany, France, and Italy. While the arrangement was largely successful, it carried the seeds of discontent that led to a string of minor wars and revolts in the following century.

After Napoleon's defeat in 1814, the political leaders began to redraw the map of Europe at the Congress of Vienna. The lengthy event was interrupted by Napoleon's return from Elba, although the diplomats continued discussions while their military colleagues dealt with the threat. This contemporary engraving depicts the closing moments in June 1815.

The Death of Napoleon

Napoleon's health had been deteriorating since 1812. While his death on St. Helena can be ascribed to this steady physical decline, rumors of foul-play have continued to surround his passing.

Napoleon's final resting place is a massive, simple but elegant tomb amid the grandeur of Les Invalides, Paris.

*I*n 1804 Napoleon wrote to his aid General de Brigade Jacques Lauriston: "Death is nothing, but to live defeated is to die every day." The man who was responsible for the death of thousands in battle spent his final six years living this daily death.

Napoleon's health had been in question for years. Formerly a robust and healthy man who ran his staff

into the ground from exhaustion, he began to suffer from minor medical problems. During the Austerlitz campaign (1805) he suffered from conjunctivitis and after the Battle of Aspern-Essling he suffered an uncharacteristic bout of acute depression. These maladies were relatively minor compared with what was to follow.

In the Battle of Borodino (1812) Napoleon's ability to command the Grande Armée was impaired by acute bladder problems (dysuria) and swelling of the legs. The following year at Dresden (1813) he was taken sick again, probably from food poisoning. While rumors of real poisoning persist, this bout, followed by the melancholia and stomach cramps he experienced during the Battle of Leipzig, were probably the result of a growing intestinal problem, most likely a duodenal ulcer. He was 43 years old, an age when most healthy men would find it difficult to maintain the rugged military lifestyle expected of a general on campaign.

Much has been made of his medical condition during the Hundred Days campaign (1815), particularly on the battlefield of Waterloo. He suffered from an ailment which is often said to have been acute piles, but may have been a recurrence of his intestinal problems, and this clearly affected his ability to control the flow of the battle.

When he arrived on St. Helena, Napoleon's health was generally sound, given his known bladder and intestinal problems, and his tendency for melancholia. Exile on the barren island would have depressed anyone, and it may well be that depression encouraged the onset of more serious medical problems.

Murder or suicide?

By 1819 Napoleon's health was clearly deteriorating, and the attendance of a new physician (Dr. Antomacchi) did little to help. Modern medical experts consider that he suffered from a carcinoma of the stomach, which was untreatable in the early 19th century. By February 1821 Napoleon was bedridden and his health deteriorated rapidly, despite his staff's best efforts. He died around 5.30pm on May 5, his final words being "Josephine" and "head of the army."

While the post-mortem revealed the presence of a gastric lesion and inflammation of the liver (hepatitis), no other medical problems were discovered. Inevitably, the allegation that Napoleon was poisoned was made, and the cry of murder has been repeated ever since. Traces of arsenic were detected in his hair, but the poison was widely administered in minor forms during this period so its

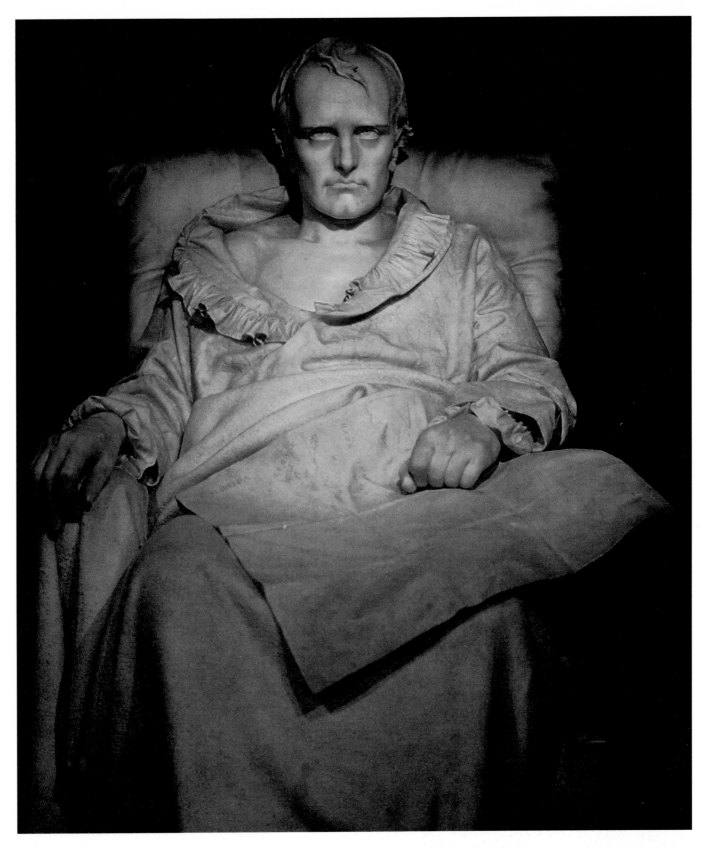

presence is far from conclusive. Another rumor suggests self-administration of arsenic, as a result of Napoleon's depression.

Medical historian Dr. Ben Weider argued the case for arsenic poisoning, but his modern findings have been both supported and refuted by eminent historians. Apart from the medical evidence, theorists have named Sir Hudson Lowe as the man responsible, possibly aided by Count Charles Tristan de Montholon, who ran the emperor's household. Recent evidence suggests that the British authorities were not involved in any poison attempt, but rather, if an assassin existed, he was a Frenchman on Napoleon's own staff. Montholon remains the chief suspect.

Napoleon Bonaparte was buried in a simple grave on St. Helena, where his body remained until 1840, when it was exhumed and returned to Paris. Today his remains lie in a great casket in Les Invalides, a grandiose final resting place for France's greatest military hero.

Napoleon I, Emperor of France, by Antoine Denis Chaudet.

French Napoleonic Heritage

A myth built up around the Napoleonic image that encouraged a national obsession with the French empire that still endures. More importantly, it sowed the seeds of a notion of European unity that is at the center of today's political agenda.

Charles X

Louis-Philippe I

The Treaty of Paris (1814) established the modern French frontier, and through the efforts of Talleyrand and others, France emerged from the Napoleonic Wars as an accepted power. Louis XVIII drew on his newfound allies to ensure stability in his country, but he also understood the need for peace. Many fears expressed on his return to power proved unfounded, and Louis left many of Napoleon's civic and governmental institutions untouched.

He retained the *Code Napoléon* as the basis of the French legal system, and refused to return to the pre-Revolution social structure. He even retained many of Napoleon's marshals, ensuring a continuity of tradition that guaranteed stability within the military. Unlike pre-Revolution sovereigns, Louis was in favor of a constitutional monarchy, working with parliament to heal the wounds left by the events of the French Revolution.

Unfortunately, after Louis XVIII's death in 1824 the new king was ultra-conservative Charles X (1757–1836), whose absolutist tendencies led to another revolution. The progressive Duc d'Orleans was placed on the throne in Charles's stead, becoming Louis-Philippe I (1773–1850). He was forced to abdicate in 1848, when Europe was torn apart by revolution, fueled by social injustice and national aspirations.

Control evolved into the hands of the Revolutionary Provisional Government, who declared the foundation of the Second Republic (1848) and held elections for its head of state. Candidates included Louis-Napoleon Bonaparte (1808–1873), the third son of Napoleon's brother Louis, former king of Holland. Louis-Napoleon made full use of his name to recall memories of past glories, which he pledged to recapture, but through peace, not war. He was elected as French president in a landslide victory. After some three decades, the Napoleonic legacy was still emotive.

Louis Napoleon won a second mandate from the people in 1852, this time with the offer of a crown. On December 1 he became Napoleon III, Emperor

Napoleon III

of the French (the king of Rome had been styled Napoleon II, but had died of tuberculosis in 1832). While Napoleon III tried to restore France to political and military greatness, he lacked his uncle's flair.

New vision of an old system

France was at a war with Russia in 1854–5, Austria in 1859, and Prussia in 1870–1. Defeat in the Franco-Prussian war led to the national humiliation of France (during which Paris suffered its third allied occupation in six decades), the collapse of Napoleon III's French empire, and the foundation of the Third Republic. Ironically Napoleon III used the same "la patrie en danger" propaganda in 1870 as Napoleon had used to galvanize national resistance in 1814. Despite his pretensions and name, Napoleon III was no military genius.

France has moved on since 1815, or even 1871. As a founding member of the European Union, it is part of an alliance that includes most of the old national adversaries of 1792–1815. Only Russia remains on the fringe of the new Europe, waiting to become a participatory member but lacking the financial muscle to make her presence felt. Ironically, it was the Russians who played a leading part in the collapse of the European Union's forerunner, the Napoleonic Continental System.

Nearly two centuries before the introduction of the single European currency, Napoleon wrote, "I wished to found a European system, a European Code of Laws, a European judiciary: there would be but one people in Europe." Having replaced the old Holy Roman Empire with his own realm, he watched this unity dissolve under the weight of warfare and the rise of national identity in Germany. Today, Napoleon Bonaparte's vision of a powerful European super-state is close to becoming reality. European union may be Napoleon's final legacy.

Napoleon still inspired French artists at the end of the century he made his own, as this 1895 drawing by Henri de Toulouse-Lautrec suggests.

At the heart of the French capital stands the magnificent Arc de Triomphe. Begun in 1806, Napoleon intended to march his armies through the arch to celebrate his victories in a manner similar to ancient Roman emperors. Wellington put paid to that. The monument was completed in 1836, and remains a centerpiece of modern-day French military parades.

Napoleon's Art of War

The Battle of Hanau (1813), where Napoleon brushed aside his former Bavarian allies during the retreat from Leipzig. Painting by Horace Vernet, 1824.

Although Napoleon did not revolutionize warfare, he took full advantage of a military system created by the French Revolution and made it his own. Soldiers were organized into a strict hierarchy of groups, allowing easier command and movement of forces. During the French Revolution, the old term "regiment" was abandoned in favor of the demi-brigade. They were similar sized formations, a unit of three battalions, each of about 700 men. French commanders used a pre-revolution infantry battalion as the core of the demi-brigade, then added two newly raised units of conscripts to form the unit. Each of the three battalions consisted of seven companies of one hundred men. Five of these were regular line infantry companies, the sixth was a *voltigeur* (light infantry) company, and the seventh a company of veteran grenadiers.

While the old soldiers were trained to fight in a linear formation, the poorly trained revolutionary infantry was often sent into the attack in dense columns, preceded by clouds of skirmishers. This developed into the standard French formation known as *l'ordre mixte*; a line of infantry providing firepower, flanked by columns of infantry that could bring an overwhelming force into close combat against an enemy line. Eventually, the differences disappeared, and by the end of the Revolutionary Wars the French infantry was consistently trained and equipped.

Not all demi-brigades consisted of line infantry. Approximately a third of the army was formed into light infantry demi-brigades, capable of fighting either as regular infantry or as skirmishers. This preponderance of infantry trained in light infantry tactics gave the French a significant advantage in combat. By 1802 the term "regiment" had been reintroduced.

Cavalry was traditionally divided into heavy cavalry and light cavalry. The former, which included cuirassiers and dragoons, was kept as a reserve to launch a decisive attack during a battle. Light cavalry was more versatile, used for scouting or patrolling, as well as battlefield combat. If cavalry caught infantry in the open, the soldiers on foot would be ridden down. The best form of protection for infantry was to form square, a box-like formation that presented a solid wall of muskets and bayonets to the approaching horsemen.

The secret to success on the battlefield was to balance the use of all military arms. For instance, although infantry in square was safe against cavalry attack, the square was particularly vulnerable to artillery fire, or even an assault by another infantry column. A good commander would know how to support his troops and could place them in the best position to ensure victory.

Artillery could bombard enemy formations at long range, and when an enemy approached a gun battery the artillerymen would switch from firing roundshot to cannister, a lethal projectile that scattered musket balls from the gun like a large shotgun. If an attacker survived this, the guns could be overrun before they were reloaded.

Regiments rarely fought alone, but formed part of a larger unit. During the Napoleonic Wars, regiments of two, three, or four battalions were grouped together into brigades, with an average of two regiments in each infantry brigade, or three cavalry regiments (each of about 500 men) in a cavalry brigade.

A division consisted of two or more brigades, usually supported by one or more artillery batteries. A corps was formed from two or more divisions and, in the French army, these miniature armies were usually commanded by a marshal. In addition to their infantry divisions, most corps had their own artillery train of heavy gun batteries and a brigade of light cavalry.

The idea behind the corps system was a force that could march and fight independently; a building block that simplified the task of army commanders, since they had to order the movement of several corps, not dozens of smaller units. The real genius of commanders like Napoleon or Wellington is that they could visualize a map of an area and know where each corps was and how fast it could march. Once the troops reached the battlefield, they also knew exactly how to fight with them.

APPENDIX 2

The Rating System of Ships-of-War

*D*uring the Napoleonic era, sailing warships were rated according to the number of guns they carried. These were the ships-of-the-line, warships large and powerful enough to form part of the main battle fleet. Smaller vessels such as frigates were classified as fifth- and sixth-rates, while even smaller vessels were "un-rated."

Rate	No. of Guns	Tonnage	Crew	Length (ft.)
First	100 guns plus	2,100–2,750	750–900	175–220
Second	98 guns	1,900–2,100	750–800	175–190
	80 guns	1,900–2,000	650–700	180–185
Third	74 guns	1,400–1,900	500–600	165–180
	64 guns	1,350–1,400	500	160–165
Fourth	50 guns	1,200–1,400	450	155–160

Example of a fleet

British fleet at the Battle of the Nile

Alexander	74-gun third rate
Audacious	74-gun third rate
Bellerophon	74-gun third rate
Culloden	74-gun third rate
Defence	74-gun third rate
Goliath	74-gun third rate
Leander	50-gun fourth rate
Majestic	74-gun third rate
Minotaur	74-gun third rate
Orion	74-gun third rate
Swiftsure	74-gun third rate
Theseus	74-gun third rate
Vanguard	74-gun third rate
Zealous	74-gun third rate
plus one brig	18 guns

French fleet at the Battle of the Nile

Aquelon	74-gun third rate
Conquérant	74-gun third rate
Franklin	80-gun second rate
Généreux	74-gun third rate
Guerrier	74-gun third rate
Guillaume Tell	74-gun third rate
Heureux	74-gun third rate
L'Orient	120-gun first rate
Mercure	80-gun second rate
Peuple Souverain	74-gun third rate
Spartiate	74-gun third rate
Timoléon	74-gun third rate
Tonnant	80-gun third rate
plus four frigates	36–48 guns

Other ships of the Napoleonic era

French

Bucentaure	80-gun second rate
Ça Ira	80-gun second rate
Fougueux	74-gun third rate
Redoutable	74-gun third rate
Sans Culotte	74-gun third rate

British

Agamemnon	64-gun third rate
Albermarle	28-gun frigate
Belleisle	74-gun third rate
Britannia	100-gun first rate
Captain	74-gun third rate
Frolic	18-gun sloop
*Guerrière**	32-gun frigate
Hinchinbrook	36-gun frigate
Java	38-gun frigate
Macedonian	38-gun frigate
Mars	74-gun third rate
Peacock	24-gun sloop
Pelican	18-gun brig
Phoebe	36-gun frigate
Royal Sovereign	100-gun first rate
Shannon	38-gun frigate
Téméraire	98-gun second rate
Victory	100-gun first rate

Spanish

Principe de Asturias	112-gun first rate
San Josef	112-gun first rate
San Nicolas	80-gun second rate
Santa Ana	112-gun first rate
Santissima Trinidad	130-gun first rate

American

Argus	18-gun sloop
Chesapeake	36-gun frigate
Congress	36-gun frigate
Constellation	36-gun frigate
Constitution	44-gun heavy frigate
Essex	32-gun frigate
Hornet	18-gun sloop
President	44-gun heavy frigate
United States	44-gun heavy frigate
Wasp	18-gun brig

* Captured from the French at the Faeroe Islands, July 18, 1806

The Marshals of France

On May 19, 1804, Napoleon created the rank of Marshal de France to fill the commands of his newly formed Corps' d'Armée. While many proved unequal to the responsibility, others were among the best commanders of the Napoleonic era. His original 18 appointments included former heroes of the Revolutionary Wars and companions from his campaigns in Italy and Egypt. While not all saw active military service, all were experienced soldiers. A further eight marshals were added between 1807 and 1815.

Augereau, Pierre François Charles, Duc de Castiglione (1757–1816)

A Parisian of humble birth, Augereau served Bonaparte in 1796, but later clashed with his mentor and saw little active service after Jena (1806) and Eylau (1807).

Bernadotte, Jean-Baptiste Jules, Prince de Ponte-Corvo (1763–1844)

Bernadotte married into Bonaparte's family, but his failures at Auerstadt (1806) and Wagram (1809) led to his removal from active service. Made Crown Prince of Sweden (1810), he became King Charles XIV of Sweden and Norway in 1818.

Berthier, Louis Alexandre, Prince de Neuchâtel, Prince de Wagram (1753–1815)

Berthier was Napoleon's invaluable Chief-of-Staff.

Bessières, Jean Baptiste, Duc d'Istrie (1763–1813)

He commanded the Guard Cavalry, but acted as a corps commander in Spain (1808) and at Wagram (1809). He was killed at the Battle of Rippach.

Brune, Guillaume Marie Anne (1763–1815)

Brune served as a diplomat until his republicanism led to disfavor. He was killed by a pro-Royalist mob at Avignon after Waterloo.

Davout, Louis Nicolas, Duc d'Auerstadt, Prince d'Eckmühl (1770–1823)

One of the most capable of Napoleon's marshals, Davout was a stern disciplinarian, nicknamed the Iron Marshal.

Jourdan, Lean Baptiste, Count Jourdan (1762–1833)

An ardent republican, Jourdan was distrusted by Napoleon and denied the opportunity for active service.

Kellerman, François Etienne Christophe, Duc de Valmy (1735–1820)

A French Revolution general, Kellerman served as an administrator during the Napoleonic era.

Lannes, Jean, Duc de Montebello (1769–1809)

A close friend of Napoleon, Lannes fought with bravery in most Napoleonic battles until mortally wounded at the Battle of Aspern-Essling .

Lefebvre, François Joseph, Duc de Danzig (1755–1820)

A French Revolution general, Lefebvre commanded a corps at Danzig (1807), then in Spain (1808), Austria (1809), and Russia (1812).

Massena, André, Duc de Rivoli, Prince d'Essling (1758–1817)

A gifted commander, Massena fought in almost every campaign from 1796 onward. He developed a reputation as an inveterate plunderer of art while on campaign.

de Moncey, Bon Adrien Jannot, Duc de Conegliano (1754–1842)

A political appointment, Moncey proved a poor field commander in Spain (1808–9).

Mortier, Eduard Adolphe-Casimir-Joseph, Duc de Trévise (1768–1835)

Fought with distinction in Prussia (1806), Poland (1807), and Spain (1808–10). In 1813 he was given command of the Imperial Guard.

Murat, Joachim, Grand Duc de Berg, King of Naples (1767–1815)

Flamboyant, and renowned as a cavalry commander, he fought alongside Napoleon from 1795 onward, and was executed after Napoleon's defeat in 1815.

Ney, Michel, Duc d'Elchingen, Prince de la Moskowa (1769–1815)

Nicknamed "the bravest of the brave," Ney commanded with more courage than distinction from 1805–15, when he fought at Waterloo. He was executed in 1815.

Perignon, Dominique Catherine, Marquis de Perignon (1754–1818)

A political appointment, Perignon saw no active service.

Sérurier, Jean Mathieu Philibert (1742–1819)

A distinguished gunner, Sérurier fought in Italy (1796), where he was nicknamed the Virgin of Italy for his exemplary moral conduct. He held no active command after 1800.

Soult, Nicolas Jean de Dieu, Duc de Dalmatie (1769-1851)

Soult was a capable corps commander in most Napoleonic campaigns, but saw most action in Spain.

Marshals appointed after 1804

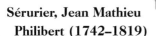

Gouvion St. Cyr, Laurent, Marquis de St. Cyr (1764–1830)

Appointed August 27, 1812

St. Cyr's republican views made Napoleon suspicious of this skilled commander, but his performance in Russia in 1812 led to the award of his baton. He fought at Dresden (1813) but was forced to surrender the city.

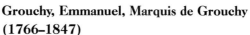

Grouchy, Emmanuel, Marquis de Grouchy (1766–1847)

Appointed June 3, 1815

A mediocre cavalry commander, Grouchy took part in the Hundred Days campaign, where he failed to prevent the Prussians from reaching Waterloo.

Macdonald, Jacques-Etienne Joseph-Alexandre, Duc de Tarente (1765–1840)

Appointed July 12, 1809

Napoleon's "Scottish" marshal was born of exiled Jacobite stock, fighting as a corps commander in Spain (1810–11), Russia (1812), Germany (1813), and France (1814).

Marmont, Duc de Raguse (1774–1852)

Appointed July 12, 1809

A long-time comrade of Napoleon, he commanded in Spain with little distinction, then participated in Napoleon's final campaigns of 1813–14, where he abandoned Napoleon and joined the allies.

Oudinot, Nicolas Charles, Duc de Reggio (1767–1847)

Appointed July 12, 1809

The most frequently wounded marshal, Oudinot fought at Aspern-Essling, then participated in the 1812–14 campaigns.

Poniatowski, Josef Anton, Prince Poniatowski (1763–1813)

Appointed October 16, 1813

A Polish prince, Poniatowski commanded a Polish corps with distinction in 1812 and 1813, but was drowned crossing the River Elster after the Battle of Leipzig.

Suchet, Louis Gabriel, Duc d' Albufera (1770–1826)

Appointed July 1, 1811

A skilled independent commander, Suchet spent most of his career in Spain (1809–14). He was one of the only marshals to emerge from the country with his reputation intact.

Victor (Perrin), Claude, Duc de Bellune (1764–1841)

Appointed July 13, 1807

Victor distinguished himself at Marengo (1800), and fought at Friedland (1807) and Talavera (1809) before participating without much distinction in Napoleon's campaigns of 1812–14.

Index

2nd/3rd Republic 184
3rd Estate 10
100 Days 164–175

A

Abensberg 89
Aboukir (Bay) 42, 45
Achmed Pasha 44–45
Acre 44–45
Agamemnon 38
Albermarle 38
Albuera 111
Alessandria 48
Alexander I 61, 63–64, 66, 80, 121–122, 124, 132, 134, 138, 180
Alexandria 40, 42
Almeida 110–111
Alvintzi, General 32–35
Ambleteuse 57
Amiens, Peace of 46, 51
Anti-French Coalition *see* Coalition
Aquelon 42
Arakcheev, Alexei 84
Arapiles, Los 114
Arcis-sur-Aube 149
Arcola 32–33
Areizaga, General 110
Argus 157
army formations 15, 26, 84, 106, 186
army organization 46, 54–55, 68–69, 84, 106–107, 122–123, 166, 186
Army of Italy 20, 22–25, 28–35, 48, 94
Army of Portugal 110–111, 115
Army of the Main 136, 140
Army of the Orient 37
Army of the Reserve 48
Army of Twenty Nations 120
Aspern 93, 182
Assaye 104
Asturias 103
Ath 168
Auerstadt 71, 73
Augereau, Pierre 25, 28, 30–33, 72, 76–77
Austerlitz 64–65, 182
Austria 12–13, 24–35, 46, 48–49, 60, 62–66, 87–96, 118, 138–144, 151, 180, 184
Austrian Empire 20, 26, 138
Austrian Netherlands 12
Auxerre 165

B

Badajoz 111, 114
Bagration, General 63–65, 78–79, 120, 124–125
Bainbridge, William 156
Baltic League 46
Baltimore 159
Barney, Joshua 158
Barras, Paul 18, 46, 96
Basel, Treaty of 100
Bastille fortress 10
Baton Rouge 160
battles: Abensberg 89, Aboukir 45, Albuera 111, Arcola 32–33, Assaye 104, Austerlitz 64–65, Auerstadt 73, Bautzen 137, Baylen 103, Borodino 124–125, Caldiero 63, Castiglione 31, Chateaugay 154, Chrysler's Farm 155, Coruña/Corunna 104, 109, Craonne 148, Dennewitz 142, Eylau 76–77, Fleurus 13, Friedland 78–79, Fuentes de Orono 111, Gross-Beeren 141, Hohenlinden 46, Hondschoote 13, Jemappes 13, Jena 72, Katsbach 141, Lake Erie 154, Lâon 148, Ligny 170–171, Lützen 137,

Marengo 48–49, Mondovi 25, Neerwinden 13, Nile 42–43, Novi 48, Ocaña 110, Quatre Bras 169, Queenston Heights 154, Raab 90, Talavera 109, Thames 155, Toulon 16–17, Trafalgar 58–59, Valmy 13, Waterloo 173, Wavre 171
Bautzen 137
Bavaria 61–62, 87–89, 96, 142
Baylen 103
Bayonne 102, 116–117
Beauharnais, Prince Eugène de, 60, 90, 120, 124–125, 128, 132, 136, 152
Beaulieu, Johann 24–25, 28–29
Belgium 12, 166–169
Bellegarde, General 89–93
Belleisle 58
Bellerophon 42, 178
Benedict 158
Bennigsen, Count 74, 76–79, 140, 143
Beresford, General 111
Berlin 71, 74
Bernadotte, Jean-Baptiste 65, 71–74, 94, 135, 138, 140, 142–143
Berthier, Louis Alexandre 22–23, 55, 97
Bertrand, Henri-Gatien 143, 164
Biktil 40
Black Forest 62–63
Bladensburg 159
Blücher, Gebhard von 70, 72, 74, 140–141, 143, 146–148, 166–168, 170–171, 173
Bohemia 88
Bonaparte, Jérôme 120
Bonaparte, Joseph 100, 102–103, 115–116, 149–151
Bonaparte, Josephine 53, 96–97, 152
Bonaparte, Louis 74, 96
Bonaparte, Louis-Napoleon 184
Bonaparte, Marie-Louise 97, 138, 151
Bonaparte, Napoleon: abdications 151, 175, death 182, emperor 53, exiles 162, 178–179, 182, First Consul 46, marriage 96–97, return from exile 164–165, youth 16
Bon, General 40
Bordeaux 117
Borisov 129
Borodino 124–125, 182
Boston 157
Boudet, General 49
Boulogne 57
Bourbon monarchs 10–11, 98, 165–166, 180
Brazil 156
Brest 58
Brienne 146
Britain 13, 16–17, 36–39, 42–43, 46, 48, 56–59, 61, 86–87, 103, 106–111, 113–118, 134–135, 138, 152–161, 166–169, 172–173, 178–180
Britannia 59
Brock, Isaac 154
Broke, Sir Philip 157
Brueys, Admiral 42
Brünn 64
Brunswick, Duke of 70–73
Brussels 13
Bucentaure 58–59
Burrard, Sir Harry 108
Busaco 110
Buxhowden, Count 74

C

Cadiz 58, 101
Ca Ira 38
Cairo 40–41
Calais 57
Caldiero 32, 63

Cambacérès, Jean-Jacques de 46, 52–53
Cambronne, Viscount Pierre 164
Campo Formio treaty 35, 152
Canada 154–155, 158, 161
Cape St Vincent 38
Captain 38
Carnot, Lazare 13, 15, 18, 24
Carteaux, Jean-Francis 16–17
Castiglione 31
Castlereagh, Viscount 149
Catherine the Great 122
Caulincourt, Armand-Augustin 151
Ceva 25
Champaubert 147
Channel, English 36, 51, 56–57
Charles IV 100
Charles X 184
Charles, Archduke 63–64, 87–91, 94–95
Charles, Hippolyte 96
Chateaugay 154
Chateau-Thierry 147
Chaumont, Treaty of 148
Chesapeake 157
Chesapeake Bay 158–159
Chile 157
Chrysler's Farm 155
Church (French) 10
Cintra, Treaty of 108
Ciudad Rodrigo fortress 110, 114
Civil Code 82–83
Coalition: First 10, 15, Second 45, 48, 52, Third 51, 61, Sixth 69, 139, 180, Seventh 166
Cockburn, Sir James 158–159, 178–179
Colli, Michael 24–25
Collingwood, Vice Admiral 58–59
Confederation of the Rhine 60–61, 80, 88, 91, 134, 136, 138–139, 142, 144, 181
Conquérant 42
Constitution 156
Consular Guard 46, 53
Continental System 118
Copenhagen 46
corps system 54–55
Corsica 8, 16, 38
Corunna/La Coruña 104, 109
Craonne 148
Cuesta, Gregorio del la 109
Culloden 42

D

Dalrymple, Sir Hew 104, 108
Danzig 75, 78, 136
Davidovitch, General 32–33
Davout, Louis 57, 65, 71–78, 89, 94, 120, 125, 128, 136, 144, 174
Decatur, Stephen 156
Declaration of Pillnitz 12
Declaration of Rights of Man and the Citizen 82
Dego 25
Delaborde, Henri 108
Dennewitz 142
Desaix, General 40, 49
Directory (of Seven) 18, 46, 52, 152
Douro 109
Dresden 136, 138, 140–141, 182
Drouet, Jean-Baptiste 164, 169, 170–171, 173
Ducos, Pierre-Roger 46, 52
Dugommier, Jacques 17
Dugua, General 40
Dumouriez, Charles 13
Dupont, General 103

E
Eckmühl 89
Egypt 36, 39–45
Elba island 151, 162
Embabeh 40
Enghien, Duke of 51, 61
England *see* Britain
English Channel 36, 51, 56–57
Essen, General 77
Essling 93, 182
Etaples 57
Etoges 147
Eylau 74, 76–78

F
Ferdinand VII 100–101
Ferdinand, Archduke 62–63, 90
Ferdinand of Brunswick, Duke 13, 69
Finland 81
Fiodoroivsky 128
Fleurus 13
Floridablanca, Count of 100
Foley, Captain 42
Fontainebleau 98, 151
Fouché, Joseph 175
Fougueux 58–59
France invasion 145–151
Francis I 60–61, 63, 65, 96
Franklin 42
Frederick the Great 68
Frederick-Wilhelm (William) II of Prussia 12
Frederick-Wilhelm III 62, 66, 71, 73–74, 80, 134
French Revolution 10–17; army 14–15
French Revolutionary Wars 12–47
French Royal Army 14
Friedland 75, 78–79
Friedrich of Hohenloe, Prince 70–72
Frolic 156
Fuentes de Orono 111

G
Genoa 48
Gérard, General 170–171
Germany 60–62, 66, 70, 80, 87–88, 118, 134, 143–144, 181
Ghent, Treaty of 161
Girona 103
Gneisenau, Augustus von 69
Godly Wood 159
Godoy, Manuel de 98, 100
Goliath 42
Gortschakov, General 79
Gravina, Admiral 58–59
Great Lakes, 154, 157
Gross-Beeren 141
Grouchy, Emmanuel 79, 147, 170–171, 174
guerilla war 112–113
Guerrier/Guerrière 42, 156
guillotine 11

H
Habsburg monarchs 98
Haie Sainte 173
Hamburg 144
Hampton, Wade 154
Hanover 60, 62, 66, 74
Harrison, William 154–155
Heilsberg 75, 78
Hiller, Johann von 89, 91
Hinchinbrook 38
Hohenlinden 46
Holland 13, 48, 80, 165, 184
Holy Roman Empire 60–61, 66
Hondschoote 13
Hood, Admiral Lord 17
Hornet 157
Hougoumont chateau 172–173
Hull, Isaac 156

Hull, William 154
Hundred Days 164–175

I
Ibrahim Bey 40
Imperial Guard (French) 46, 55, 65, 70, 171, 173
India 104
Indians *see* Native Americans
Ingolstadt 89
Ionkovo 76
Ireland 56, 104
Italy 20, 25–35, 48–49, 60–62, 66, 96, 122, 146, 166, 181

J
Jackson, Andrew 160–161
Jaffa 44
Jamaica 160
Jefferson, Thomas 152
Jemappes 13
Jena 69, 71–72
Jervis, Sir John 37–38
John, Archduke 90–91
Joubert, Barthelemy 34–35, 46
Junot, Jean 98, 108, 125

K
Kalisch, Treaty of 134
Katsbach 140
Kellerman, François 13, 22, 24
Kellerman, (Marshal) François 48–49, 168–169
Keys, Francis Scott 159
Kléber, General 44–45
Kleist, General 168
Klenau, General 94
Königsberg 75–76
Krasnoe 121, 129
Kremlin, the 126–127
Kulm 141
Kutuzov, Mikhail 62–63, 121, 124–125, 128–131

L
Laffitte, Jean 161
Laffrey 164
Lake Bourgne 161
Lake Champlain 155
Lake Erie 154
Landshut 89
Lannes, Jean 28, 49, 57, 62, 65, 70, 72, 78–79, 93
Lâon 148
law 82–83
Lawrence, James 157
Leander 42
Lebrun, Charles 46, 52
Lefebvre, François 74–75, 89, 103
Legislative Assembly 11
Leipzig 142–143, 182
Leopold II of Austria 12
Lestocq, General 76–77
Liege 168
Ligny 170–171
Lines of Torres Vedras 110
Lisbon 98, 110–111
Lisle, Claude Rouget de 15
Lobau Island 92–94
Lodi 29
Lonato 30
Longwood House 178
L'Orient 42
Los Arapiles 114
Louis XVI 10–11
Louis XVIII 165, 175, 184
Louis-Philippe I 184
Louisa, Queen 80
Louisiana Purchase 152
Lowe, Sir Hudson 178–179, 182
Lübeck 74
Lunéville, Treaty of 49, 60

Lusignan, General 35

M
Macdonald, Jacques-Etienne 94–95, 120, 132, 137, 141, 143–144, 147, 151
Macedonian 156
Mack, Karl 61–63
Madison, James 152, 154
Madrid 100, 102–103, 115
Maitland, Captain 178
Maloyaroslavets 127
Mamluks 40
Mantua 20, 30–35
Marchfeld 94
Marengo 46, 48–49
Maria Louisa of Parma, Queen 100
Marmont, Auguste de 94–95, 114–115, 137, 143, 147–149, 151
Mars 58
marshals 188–189
Martinique 152
Maryland 158
Massena, André 25, 28–29, 32–33, 35, 48, 63, 75, 89, 93–94, 110–111
Medina del Rio Seco 103
Menou, General 45
Metternich, Prince Klemens von 138–139
Milan 28–29
Minsk 129
Mollendorf, Richard 69, 73
Moncey, Bon Adrien de 103
Mondovi 25
Moñino, Don Jose 100
Montholon, Count Charles Tristan de 179, 182
Montmirail 147
Moore, Sir John 104, 108–109
Moreau, General 46, 51
Mortier, Eduard 78–79, 147, 149
Moscow 126–127
mountains/ranges: Faron 17, Ligurian Alps 24, Pyrenees 116–117, Tabor 44, Thuringerwald 70
Murad Bey 40
Murat, Joachim 19, 62, 65, 71, 74–77, 102, 127, 131, 143, 146, 166
Mustapha Pasha 45

N
Nantes 16
Napoleon III 184
National Assembly 10, 14, 18
National Guard 18, 175
Native Americans 154
navy formations 39, 57
Neerwinden 13
Nelson, Horatio 38–39, 42–43, 58–59
Netherlands 104
New Orleans 160–161
Newport 156
Ney, Michel 57, 72, 74, 76–79, 110, 125, 128–129, 131, 137, 142, 147–148, 151, 165, 168–171, 173
Northumberland 178
Nova Scotia 156
Novi 48

O
Ocaña 110
Olmütz 63
Oporto 109
O'Reilly, General 48
Orléans 151
Orsha 129
Orthez 117
Ottomans 40, 44–45, 118
Oudinot, Nicolas 94, 128, 131, 137, 140–141, 147, 149

INDEX

P
Packenham, Edward 114, 160–161
Pagerie, Marie Rose Josephine de la 53, 96–97
Pamplona 116
Paris 8, 10, 18, 96, 146, 149–151, 175, 183–184
Paris, Treaty of 152, 180
Pasha, Achmed 44–45
Pasha, Mustapha 45
Paul I 46, 122
Peacock 157
Pelican 157
Peninsular War 98–117
Perry, Oliver 154
Peuple Souverain 42
Phélipeaux, Louis 45
Phoebe 157
Piacenza 28
Picton, Sir Thomas 173
Piedmont 24
Pillnitz, Declaration of 12
Pitt, William 61, 66
plague 44
Planceloit 173
Plattsburg 155
Poland 74–76, 80, 118, 140, 166, 181
Polotsk 128
Poniatowski, Josef 124–125
Porcile 33
Portugal 98, 102–104, 109–111
Pratzen Heights 64–65
Pressberg, Treaty of 65–66
Principe de Asturias 59
Proctor, Henry 154–155
Provera, General 33–34
Prussia 12–13, 62, 66, 68–74, 76, 78, 80, 87, 120,
    132, 134–135, 140–143, 146–148, 166–168,
    170–171, 173, 180–181, 184
Puebla Heights 115
Pulutsk 74

Q
Quadrilateral 20
Quasdanovitch, Peter 30, 34–35
Quatre Bras 168–169
Queenston Heights 154

R
Raab 90
Ratisbon 89
Redoutable 59
Reichenbach, Convention of 139
Reille, General 168–169
Reims 148
Rensselaer, Stephen van 154
Revolutionary Directoire 46
Revolutionary Provisional Government 184
Revolutionary Wars 12–47
Rey, General 35
Reynier, General 40, 110
Rhode Island 156
rivers: Adda 28–29, Adige 34, Aisne 13, 148,
    Alle 75, 78, Anacostia 158, Berezina 129–131,
    Bormida 48, Coa 110, Danube 63, 88–93,
    Detroit 154, Dyle 171, Elbe 132, 137–138, 140,
    144, Main 144, Marne 146, 149, Niagara 154,
    Niemen 124, 131, Nile 40, Nive 117, Oder 74,
    Patapsco 159, Patuxent 158–159, Po 20, 28,
    Potomac 159, Rhine 48, 62, 144, Saale 72,
    136–137, Spree 137, Vistula 74
Rivoli 20, 34–35
Robespierre, Maximilien de 11, 18
Rochefort 175
Rodriguez Canal 161
Roliça 108
Ronco 32–33
Ross, Robert 158–159
Rostopchin, Fedor 127
Rothiére, La 146

Royal Army (French) 14
Royal Navy (British) 38–39, 46, 57–59, 61, 118,
    152, 156–157
Royal Sovereign 58
Rüchel, General 72
Russia 46, 48, 61–66, 74–81, 87, 96, 118–132, 134,
    138, 143, 147–149, 166–167, 180–181, 184

S
Saalfeld 70
Sackets Harbor 154
Sahagun 109
Saint Amand 170–171
Saint Cyr, Laurent 128, 141
Saint Helena 178–179, 182–183
Salamanca 114
San Ildefonso, Treaty of 100
San Josef 38
San Marcial 116
San Nicolas 38
San Sebastian 116
Santa Anna 58–59
Santa Cruz de Tenerife 38
Santissima Trinidad 59
Saragossa 103
Sardinia 12, 16, 20, 24–25
Saxony 66, 70, 136–137, 181
Scharnhorst, Gerhard von 69
Schleiz 70
Schönbrunn, Peace of 120
Schwarzenberg, General 128, 140–143,
    146–150, 166
Sebastiani, General 136, 144
Second Republic 184
Selim I, Sultan 44
Sérurier, Jean 25, 30–31
Seven Years War 68
Seville 100
Shannon 157
Shevardino 124
ships 14, 38–39, 46, 57–59, 61, 156–157, 187
Sièyes, Emmanuel 46
Sinai 44
slave revolt in Haiti 152
Smith, Sir William Sidney 45, 98
Smolensk 121, 128–129
Solferino 31
Soult, Nicolas 57, 64–65, 75–78, 109, 111, 114,
    116–117, 137, 172, 174–175
Spain 13, 38, 58–59, 88, 98–104, 108–117
Spartiante 42
Star Spangled Banner 159
Stewart, Robert 149
Studienka 130
Suchet, Louis 48
Suvarov, Alexander 48, 122
Sweden 61, 118, 134–135, 138, 140, 181
Switzerland 181
Syria 44–45

T
Talavera 104, 109
Talleyrand, Charles 98, 151, 175, 180
Tauroggen, Treaty of 134
Tchitchagov, General 129, 131
Tecumseh 154–155
Téméraire 59
Tenskwatawa 154
Terror, the 11
Thames 155
Thielmann, General 170–171
Third Estate 10
Third Republic 184
Tilsit, Treaty of 80–81, 98, 118
Tippecanoe 154
Tolly, Barclay de 84, 120–122, 124–125, 166
Tolstoi, General 77
Tormasov, General 120, 128

Toronto 154
Torres Vedras, Lines of 110
Toulon 16–17, 37–38
Toulouse 117
Toussaint l'Ouverture 152
Trachenberg Plan 140
Trafalgar 58–59
Tristan, Charles 179, 182
Trombalore Bridge 34–35
Tuileries Palace 18, 175
Turin 25
Turkey 44, 81
Tutchkov, General 77

U
Ulm 62–63
United States 156
USA 152–161

V
Valmy 13
Vandamme, Dominique 141–142, 170–171
Vaubois, General 32–33
Vauchamps 147
Verona 32–34
Vial, General 40
Viasma 127
Victor Amadeus, King 25
Victor, Claude 35, 48–49, 78–79, 109, 131, 144
Victory 58–59
Vienna 63–64, 91–92, 97, 151
Vienna, Congress of 135, 166, 180–181
Vienna, Treaty of 96
Villeneuve, Rear/Vice Admiral 43, 58–59, 152
Vilna 120, 131
Vimereux 57
Vinkovo 127
Vittoria 115

W
Wagram 94–95
Wahlstadt, Prince of *see* Blücher
War of 1812 152–161
War of Independence 38, 152
Warsaw 74, 76, 80, 90, 96, 118, 120, 140
Washington 158–159
Wasp 156
Waterloo 172–173, 182
Wavre 171
Wellesley, Sir Arthur 103–105, 108–111, 113–117,
    146, 166–169, 172–173, 180
Wellington, Duke of *see* Wellesley, Sir Arthur
Wilkinson, James 154
Winder, William 158–159
Wittgenstein, General 128, 131, 137
Wrede, General 70, 95, 144
Würmster, Dagobert 30–32

Y
Yorck, Johann 132, 134, 147
Yorktown 152

Z
Zieten, General 170
Znaim, Armistice of 96
Zurich 48